women in
Austria

Contemporary Austrian Studies

Sponsored by the University of New Orleans and Universität Innsbruck

Editors
Anton Pelinka, University of Innsbruck
Günter Bischof, University of New Orleans

Assistant Editor
Ellen Palli

Production Editor
Judy Nides

Copy Editor
Jennifer Shimek

Editorial Assistant
Günther Walder

Executive Editors
Erich Thöni, University of Innsbruck
Gordon H. Mueller, University of New Orleans

Publication of this volume has been made possible through a generous grant from the Austrian Ministry of Foreign Affairs and the Austrian Culture Institute in New York. The Bank Gutmann Nfg. AG in Vienna, the University of Innsbruck, and Metropolitan College of the University of New Orleans have also provided financial support.

Articles appearing in this volume are abstracted and indexed in HISTORICAL ABSTRACTS and AMERICA: HISTORY and LIFE.

volume 6

CONTEMPORARY AUSTRIAN STUDIES

women in *Austria*

Edited by

Günter Bischof

Anton Pelinka

Erika Thurner

Transaction Publishers
New Brunswick (U.S.A.) and London (U.K.)

Library of Congress Catalog Number: 97-24055
ISBN: 0-7658-0404-2
Printed in the United States of America

Library of Congress Cataloging-in-Publication Data

Women in Austria / edited by Günter Bischof, Anton Pelinka, and Erika Thurner.
   p. cm. — (Contemporary Austrian studies ; v. 6)
   ISBN 0-7658-0404-2 (pbk. : alk. paper)
   1. Women—Austria. 2. Women—Austria—Social conditions. 3. Feminism—Austria. 4. Women in politics—Austria. 5. Women's rights—Austria. I. Bischof, Günter, 1953– . II. Pelinka, Anton, 1941– . III. Thurner, Erika. IV. Series.
HQ1603.W66 1997
305.42'09436—dc21   97-24055
                                              CIP

Table of Contents

REVIEW ESSAYS

BOOK REVIEWS

ANNUAL REVIEW

LIST OF AUTHORS

TOPICAL ESSAYS

Introduction

Social and historical studies reflect social realities. In our male-centered society, women were and are underrepresented in academia. As a result of male domination (androcentricity) within the academic fields, gender has not sufficiently been taken into account as a category of investigation. Only within the last decade have Women's Studies and Gender Studies gained significant ground in universities and other scholarly institutions—in Austria even later than elsewhere. These gains coincided with the feminist engagement on the part of women in academia and in society as a whole.

In Austria, the number of women entering the ranks of political, historical, and social scientists is rising, but their academic publications—especially on topics relating to Women's and Gender Studies—are often ignored by the mainstream (that is, the patriarchy). This is true despite the fact that gender, as a structuring characteristic and as an important category of investigation, enriches and differentiates scientific discourses and results.

These are the reasons for assembling this volume. These articles it contains provide a glimpse into historical and political events involving and affecting women. Thus, they offer insight into the conditions of life and the terms of existence for women in Austria during the twentieth century.

The first four articles, written by historians, were originally presented at the German Studies Association Conference in September 1995 in Chicago. For this volume, the papers have been expanded. The intention was to trace several threads running through the fabric of Austrian history form the First Republic to the post-World War II era, in order to illuminate previously neglected aspects of the roles played by women.

In the first essay, *Helga Embacher* examines the problematic question of the assimilation of Jewish women in Austria during the 1920s. By looking at the categories middle class, liberal, intellectual, and Jewish, Embacher shows that the year 1938 witnessed the expulsion from Austria of not only "masculine rationality," but of the vast majority of female intellectuals and artists as well. Embacher also discusses the political involvement of these women in left-wing parties. She concludes that intellectual life in Austria came to a temporary end in 1938, and that the female role models present in the First Republic were largely absent in postwar Austria.

Doris Gödl provides an overview of "the contribution made by women to the political policies of National Socialism." Gödl begins with the debate which originated during the 1970s in the field of Women's Studies in Germany. This debate surrounded the question of whether women during the Nazi era could properly be considered solely as victims, or whether women must also be considered as collaborators, supporters, and enthusiastic advocates of this system. From a psychoanalytic perspective, Gödl discusses and analyzes "processes of seduction" which were targeted at women by National Socialist propaganda and policies.

The article by *Erika Thurner* sheds light upon "female resistance against Nazi fascism." This study discusses the reasons why women and their commitment to the fight against National Socialism have remained generally ignored or accorded scant attention in the research of resistance movements and society. The specific topic of investigation is the work of anti-fascist Austrian women and girls who were living in Belgian exile. Belgium was not a major center of Austrian emigration, but this small and unattractive land of exile represents one of the rare cases where a specifically female form of resistance existed.

Ingrid Bauer investigates another—or an opposite—group of "insurgent women," the "GI brides," who were scorned as "choco-ladies," "dollar floozies," and "Yankee tarts." As a topic for historical examination, the relationships, liaisons, and love affairs between Austrian women and girls and U.S. soldiers was taboo for a long time. In contrast, it was the leading conversational topic during the early postwar years. While analyzing the emotionally-charged, often irrational discussions of the "GI brides," Bauer reveals the state of mind and unconscious fears of postwar Austrian society.

In accordance with the traditional approach of *Contemporary Austrian Studies* to look at broad questions from an interdisciplinary perspective, three other researchers (one historian and two political scientists) were invited to examine "Women and Politics" during democratic periods in twentieth-century Austrian history. Taken together, they analyze and comment on the discrimination against and equality of women in Austria during the First and Second Republics. In addition, they discuss the efforts of female (and male) politicians to gain equality for women and to restructure lifestyles and conditions for both sexes, in order to create a more equitable society. It is hardly surprising that, during the periods of dictatorship in Austria, there was no equality between the genders. Highly remarkable indeed are the continuity of and persistent tendency toward patriarchalism which remained dominant in the aftermath of these drastic political shifts. These authors show how the refusal to grant equal political and social rights to women have persisted through the era of democratic government as well.

The historian *Gabriele Hauch* sheds light upon the first generation of female members in the Austrian Parliament. These nineteen National Councilwomen—out of a total 408 representatives—shared one important stance in common: they defined themselves according to their gender as females and regarded the link between their gender and their political function as self-evident. Following this central thesis, Hauch develops a broad theoretical discourse around the so-called prosographical approach. She calls for a gender-oriented historiography as a corrective to a type of political science which, because of its limited points of departure, has failed to focus on women's contributions as well as the nature of gender construction in research.

Once more, it becomes clear that a scholarly analysis, which acknowledges and takes into account gender as a structuring characteristic and as a category of investigation, delineates historical breaks and watersheds far differently than studies which presume to be gender-neutral. For example, in the following contributions which illuminate Austrian society (or its political culture) in the Second Republic, it becomes clear that the phase of stable democratic development proved to be resistant to a democracy of the genders. Viewed from this perspective, antiquated, "old-fashioned" laws *"Gesetze aus der Postkutschenzeit,"* such as the patriarchal marriage and family rights provisions, overshadowed the onset of economic upturn and modernization of a society emerging in the 1950s. Thus, stable democratic development, based on—or corresponding with—stable undemocratic gender discrimination, shaped modern Austria. Therefore, an historical break cannot be recognized earlier than in the 1970s.

In her survey, *Erna Appelt* reflects upon the conditions of women in Austria's economy over the past five decades. Because of the importance of the "Social Partnership" as the basis for the Austrian economy since 1945, Appelt focuses her main investigation on this topic. In describing and analyzing the strict hierarchical manner and the paternalistic fashion of the male-dominated organizations involved in the Social Partnership, Appelt examines the ways in which women have reacted to their subordinate status in the realms of economy, politics, and society as a whole. She shows current changes and women's responses to new challenges.

One reaction to current changes was the Women's Referendum in April 1997, in which independent women demanded not less than "half of the money, half of paid jobs, half of political life." This is the conclusion of *Sieglinde Rosenberger* in her contribution "Politics, Gender, and Equality." She examines the activities and strategies undertaken since the 1970s to enhance female participation in politics. She then analyzes the legislation for social equality in the private sphere, anti-discrimination legislation and policies for working women, as well as controversial legislation and political efforts to reconcile the dual roles of women as mothers and as members of the work force.

In 1918, women were finally given the right to vote in the newly proclaimed Austrian Republic; this was the logical starting point in gaining equal rights. Almost eighty years later, real equality is still a goal, although gender relations have become less patriarchal over the past decades. What becomes clear in discussions about this broad topic are the restrictive conditions and specific limitations (including self-limitations) which are applied to women in this society whose structure is still essentially patriarchal.

Last, but not least, my thanks to an anonymous American reviewer. She is an expert on women in Austria. Her thoughtful suggestions were very important and useful to all the authors.

Erika Thurner
Salzburg, April 1997

Middle Class, Liberal, Intellectual, Female, and Jewish: The Expulsion of "Female Rationality" from Austria

Helga Embacher

Historical research in Austria has only recently turned its attention to the problematical issue of emigration and exile, or, to formulate it more concretely, the deportation of its Jewish population.[1] Whereas the "overthrow of masculine rationality" has been treated and gradually worked through since the 1980s, such that regret for the losses thereby occasioned for Austria has become an increasingly common sentiment even in the speeches of politicians, the expulsion and murder of Jewish women as well as the deep cleft produced by the loss of 'female rationality' has been generally ignored up to now even by feminist scholars.[2] One explanation for this phenomenon can be found in the fact that feminist scholars have desired to write a history of women during the time of National Socialism with which they themselves could identify. For far too long, they have proceeded from the assumption of woman as the eternal victim, so that not only the history of Jewish women, thus the history of the "true" victims, but also the problematical subject of complicity by women or the phenomenon female anti-Semitism had to be left out of consideration.[3]

The following article traces the path of intellectual Jewish women from bourgeois backgrounds to the Socialist or Communist parties. This may essentially be regarded as the effort to achieve assimilation within non-Jewish society by means of culture and politics.[4] The term intellectual as used here is understood to include scientists, artists, physicians, and attorneys, as well as women active in politics. The source material is autobiographies, biographies, and life history interviews of women born between 1900 and 1925.[5]

German *Kultur* and Faith in Progress
as a New Religion

In 1910, 46 percent of the female students at Viennese *Lyzeum* and 30 percent of those enrolled in *Gymnasien* in Vienna came from Jewish families. At the University of Vienna, which first began accepting women in 1900, the proportion of Jewish women quickly rose to 68.3 percent, a figure which does not include those with no denominational affiliation who came predominantly from the liberal Jewish bourgeoisie. In 1919, with the opening of the university's School of Law to women, Jews made up 50 percent of the female students. During the course of the Austrian First Republic, with the dissolution of the Habsburg Monarchy and the ensuing economic crisis whose impact was felt most acutely by the bourgeoisie, a gradual retrograde trend can be noted.[6]

Studies which have examined female contributions in the spheres of art and science have clearly shown that Viennese Modernism was by no means created and fostered by Jewish men alone, rather, Jewish women contributed a disproportionately high share as co-creators of this culture.[7] By 1938, at the latest, they were forced to flee Austria or were murdered in concentration camps. Only a handful came back after 1945—women were called upon to return to Austria even more infrequently than their celebrated male counterparts. Reconstruction took place in the absence of this "female rationality." Women who had spent their adolescence in the *Bund Deutscher Mädel* served as role models for the postwar generation.[8]

What accounts for the extraordinarily high degree of participation by Jewish women in Austrian cultural and intellectual life? Why did the Jewish bourgeoisie place such high value upon educating their daughters? Answers to these imposing questions must undoubtedly be sought in the relationship of the Austrian, Jewish bourgeoisie to German *Kultur*. The path out of the *shtetl* in a world characterized by both Catholicism and anti-Semitism led to an identity crisis demanding a new definition of Jewish identity. The gradual renunciation of traditional Judaism through the acceptance and cultivation of German *Kultur* represented one possibility of acquiring a new Jewish consciousness and thereby gaining assimilation into non-Jewish society. Striving to immerse oneself in German *Kultur* was frequently coupled with the abnegation of traditional Judaism and the rejection of the

Yiddish language and culture.[9] It was only after her return from emigration that Stella Klein-Löw became aware that she had a "false conception of the difference between Yiddish and cultivated High German."[10]

It is very frequently brought out in biographical material that the exaltation of German *Kultur* displaced Jewish tradition and that the belief in progress became an ersatz religion. Simon Wiesenthal's grandmother reached first and foremost for her volume of Goethe rather than for her prayer book to rebuke and admonish her grandson.[11] As Stella Klein-Löw wrote, she was already being weaned on poetry by the time she was two years old and at the age of three she was familiar with names like Goethe, Schiller, Heine, and Grillparzer. The future representative in the Austrian national legislature read Karl Kraus' *Die Fakel* as religiously as her pious ancestors had read the Bible.[12]

Women were inculcated with these liberal values, but participation in public life was still denied to educated women in the nineteenth century. They had been raised for the salon and had to struggle slowly for the right to take part in the public forum of the cultural and political discourse of the day. Jewish women played leading roles in the bourgeois as well as the proletarian women's movement of the nineteenth century, which centered on the issues of the right to higher education, access to the universities, and women's suffrage.[13] A conspicuously high number of Jewish women were active in social work which, connecting with the Jewish tradition of charitable works, enabled them to break out of the narrow confines of the household to a more fulfilling existence. For example, Anne Fried described how her extremely highly-educated mother revolted against the decrees which prohibited her from practicing her profession: she and several female friends founded a charitable association to care for orphans.[14]

With the opening of the Viennese universities at the outset of the twentieth century, the daughters of these were the first to be accorded the opportunity to pursue the complete path of female intellectual emancipation. Biographical sources show that at least a segment of the liberal Jewish bourgeoisie had quite progressive attitudes toward higher education for women. In interviews, women who attended college during the 1920s—thus, the female pioneers in their respective fields—describe their studies as something taken for granted,

encouraged and promoted by their parents. However, it is also necessary to dispel the long-accepted myth that the overwhelming majority
of the Jewish population provided the same opportunities to their
daughters as they did to their sons. Numerous women report that they
had to fight for their right to study. As girls, they obtained the best
possible education; however, study at the university level was regarded
as superfluous, even by intellectual fathers. "In those days, when the
father said no, it meant no," reported Anna Weiss, born in 1911, the
daughter of Nobel Prize winner Otto Löwy. She wanted to follow in
her father's footsteps and study medicine. Her father, however, was of
the opinion that women would get married anyway and their education
would turn out to have been a wasted effort.[15] By the time she finally
prevailed upon him to concede, it was too late—the seizure of power
by the National Socialists forced her to break off her studies prior to
completion.

The Way to the Party

The sudden end of Austrian liberalism at the end of the nineteenth
century left many Jews politically homeless. As early as the 1890s, the
German Nationalist bourgeoisie had been progressively excluding Jews
from their social spheres by means of *Arierparagraphen*; in Vienna, the
Christian Social Party, under Karl Lueger, gained control of the
municipal government by espousing a Christian petit bourgeois-tinged
anti-Semitism.[16] The majority of Viennese Jews, often contrary to their
own economic and religious interests, were therefore closely aligned
with the Social Democrats. During the First Republic, communism or
socialism exerted a strong attraction, above all upon many young,
intellectual Jews, even those from bourgeois backgrounds. They regarded this political involvement as an opportunity to "lose themselves"
in a mass movement and thus to complete the process of emancipation
which had been begun by their parents.

Numerous Jewish women were actively involved in the Communist
party and the Socialist party in Austria—if not as leading party
officials, at least as functionaries, journalists, social workers, physicians, and as representative in city councils and in the Austrian national
legislature. Virtually all artists and scholars were associated with the
political left. In biographies as well as interviews, the path from the
Jewish bourgeoisie to the party can be clearly traced. Despite all

assimilative efforts on the part of their parents, their relationship to Judaism was highly contradictory. While, on one hand, Judaism retained hardly any significance within the family, and the place of Jewish tradition had been occupied by German *Kultur* and rationality, these Jews nevertheless perceived themselves as outsiders in the non-Jewish society, due, above all, to the pervasive anti-Semitism. This topic, however, was not permitted to be discussed in order to avoid calling into question the subject of assimilation itself; religious questions as well were frequently regarded as "hot potatoes" that were better left untouched. Women frequently emphasize that they experienced their Judaism as a flaw that they were glad to be rid of.[17] "As for the religion, I didn't want to belong. But my resignation was rather childish. That's just the way we all were—we believed we were going to bring about a revolution and introduce Socialism," was Hilde Koplenik's analysis of her resignation from the Viennese Jewish community.[18]

The identification with communism or socialism, promising a future of greater justice and rejecting all religions equally, finally enabled them to resign from the Jewish community and to join the party. Women saw in these ideologies, moreover, the hope for an end to sexist discrimination. The Social Democratic municipal government which held power in Vienna until 1934 had made women's liberation a central element of its platform. They fought for reform in the areas of divorce and family law, sex education, and abortion, they also sought innovations to ease the burden of housework. The "comrade" replaced the housewife as the new role model for women.

However, in retrospect, many women have raised the issue of the numerous contradictions which they had to be prepared to accept in exchange for membership in a putative community. While they professed to see the future embodied in the proletariat, whom they regarded as "new and better" human beings, the anti-Semitism which was extremely widespread among men and women of the working class also had to be overlooked or reinterpreted as anti-intellectualism or anti-bourgeois prejudice. "We were so convinced that our cause was the only right way, that we would triumph, that we had to triumph. We didn't see what was going on all around us, and everything that disturbed our concept was sloughed off and repressed," wrote Hilde Koplenik after the war.[19]

Despite the fact that Jewish men and women, through their emotional relationship to the party, believed that they had at last found acceptance and a sense of belonging, in the final analysis, they generally remained among themselves. As Jewish intellectuals within the party, they formed—even if unconsciously—a closed group. Thus, in certain municipal districts in Vienna, the socialist high school students' organization was composed almost entirely of Jews, mostly from bourgeois backgrounds; a similar tendency can be noted in the socialist and communist organizations for college students. Even their intimate circle of friends was made up predominantly of Jews.

The attitudes toward and treatment of women within the party is seldom the subject of criticism in the biographies and interviews studied. In this regard, however, it must certainly be kept in mind that women in the 1920s and 1930s proceeded from a much different model of emancipation than did women in the 1970s. While modern feminism has called into question, above all, ascriptive role assignment with respect to women, this was widely accepted by earlier feminists. These women sought to emancipate themselves by, on one hand, appropriating so-called "male rights," while on the other, they strove to improve the situation of women by means of technical innovations and through progressive education. Despite the fact than women were increasingly able to break into formerly exclusively male domains, raising children and managing the household were still considered women's work.

1934: The End of All Illusions

Politically left-wing Jewish men and women frequently describe the year 1934 as the major turning point in their lives. With the establishment of the Austro-Fascist dictatorship and the outlawing of their parties, they felt politically homeless. Their hopes for a better future had proven to be illusory. Left-wing intellectuals, especially the Jews among them, were excluded from many professions and careers even before 1938. Women, moreover, were effected by the *Doppelverdienergesetz* which meant that the wife of a two-income couple lost her job.[20] Thus, many pioneering female students could no longer apply their learning in practice. Following the Nazi's seizure of power in Germany, Jewish actors and actresses could no longer pursue their careers in Austria, since the Austrian film industry also produced for the German market. "There was no future in acting or film and theaters as well and I left in 1937 to New York," wrote Fini Littlejohn.[21] The well-known author Hilde Spiel wrote that she had already left Austria in 1936 out of disgust for the system by which she did not want to be affected.[22] Intellectual Jewish women also left Austria to fight against Francisco Franco in Spain or to seek a better future in the Soviet Union. Several of them fell victim to the Stalinist purges.[23] As a result of insensitivity or bureaucratic heavy-handedness, all those who had left Austria before 1938, usually due to the anti-Semitic climate or the unpromising outlook for the future, continue to be denied "indemnification payments."[24]

Intellectual life in Austria came to a temporary end in 1938. This era of emancipation and participation in public life had lasted less than twenty years. Of these 130,000 Jews, only a few thousand returned to Austria after the war. They included a relatively high proportion of Communists and Socialists. It was precisely these Socialists and Communists who displayed so much enthusiasm in helping to construct a new Austria, a process which would later prove to be such a disappointment to so many of them.[25]

Women—often counter to their own interests and needs—also followed their husbands who desired to return or had been recalled by their parties. As one returning woman put it, "I didn't want to come back under any circumstances…I am also the victim of my husband."[26] Female returning emigrants also longed for "normality," for a family and children, and among the things they overlooked in the course of this were their own interests. "We both wished to study and to then have children. My husband ultimately earned two doctoral degrees, and I raised two children," Gundl Herrnstadt remarked rather cynically.

To live as a Jew in Austria after the *Shoah* meant looking away, repressing, and constructing one's own illusions which, nevertheless, continually threatened to collapse. Even those returning emigrants who actively participated in building a new Austria had to maintain a cleavage between themselves who had been expelled and those who had remained. For many Austrian Jews, *There's No Going Home*, as was so clearly illustrated by the title art historian Hilde Zaloscer gave to her autobiography.

NOTES

1. Werner Bergmann, Rainer Erb, and Albert Lichtblau, eds., *Schwieriges Erbe, Der Umgang mit Nationalsozialismus und Antisemitismus in Österreich, der DDR und der Bundesrepublik Deutschland* (Frankfurt, New York: Campus, 1995).

2. Meike Bader, "Unschuldsrituale in der Frauenforschung zum Nationalsozialismus," *Babylon, Beiträge zur jüdischen Gegenwart* 9 (1991): 140-45.

3. Lerke Gravenhorst and Carmen Tatschmurat, eds., *Töchter-Fragen. NS-Frauen-Geschichte* (Freiburg: Kore, 1990).

4. Another way—Zionism—was less attractive in comparison to Socialism and will not be treated in this article.

5. Edith Foster, *Maturatreffen, 50 Jahre danach* (Vienna: Verlag für Gesellschaftskritik, 1989); Helene Deutsch, *Confrontations with Myself* (New York: Norton, 1973); Marie Langer, *Von Wien bis Managua. Wege einer Psychoanalytikerin* (Freiburg: Kore, 1986); Minna Lachs, *Warum schaust du zurück. Erinnerungen 1907-1941* (Vienna: Löcker, 1986); idem, *Zwischen zwei Welten. Erinnerungen 1941-46* (Vienna: Löcker, 1992); Hilde Zaloscer, *Eine Heimkehr gibt es nicht. Ein österreichisches curriculum vitae* (Vienna: Löcker, 1988); Hilde Spiel, *Rückkehr nach Wien. Ein Tagebuch* (Frankfurt, Main, Berlin:Ullstein, 1989); idem, *Welche Welt ist meine Welt?* (Hamburg: Reinbek, 1990); Elisabeth Freundlich, *Die fahrenden Jahre. Erinnerungen* (Salzburg: Otto Müller, 1992); Ruth Klüger, *weiter leben. Eine Jugend.* (Göttingen: Wallstein, 1992); Stella Klein-Löw, *Erinnerungen* (Vienna: Jugend und Volk, 1980); Henriette Mandl, *Cabarett und Courage. Stella Kadmon - eine Biographie* (Vienna: WUV-Universitätsverlag, 1993); Gertrude Trincher-Rutgers, *Das Haus im Mias. Odyssee einer Kinderärztin.*(Vienna: Verlag für Gesellschaftskritik, 1993); Jola Zalud, *Einem Arbeiter gibt man nicht die Hand. Erinnerungen einer unfreiwilligen Kommunistin* (Vienna: Löcker, 1995); Gina Kaus, *Von Wien nach Hollywood* (Baden-Baden: Suhrkamp Taschenbuch, 1990; Anne Fried, *Farben des Lebens. Erinnerungen* (Leipzig, Weimar: Kiepneuer, 1991); Robert Streibel, ed., *Eugenie Schwarzwald und ihr Kreis* (Vienna: Picus, 1996).
Additional sources were unpublished manuscripts and approximately forty biographical interviews conducted by the author in Austria, Israel, France, England, and the United States.

6. Marsha L. Rozenblit, *Die Juden Wiens, 1987-1914. Assimilation und Identität* (Vienna-Cologne-Graz: Böhlau, 1988), especially the chapter, "Erziehung der Mädchen"; Waltraud Heindl and Marina Tichy, eds., *"Durch Erkenntnis zu Freiheit und Glück..." Frauen an der Universität Wien, ab 1897* (Vienna: Schriftenreihe des Universitätsarchivs, 1990), 151 f.

7. Helga Embacher, "Außenseiterinnen: bürgerlich, jüdisch, intellektuell - links," *L'Homme, Zeitschrift für feministische Geschichtswissenschaft* 2 (1989): 57-76.

8. Helga Embacher, "Unwillkommen? Zur Rückkehr von Emigrantinnen und Überlebenden aus den Konzentrations- und Vernichtungslagern." in: *Frauenleben 1945 - Kriegsende in Wien*. Katalog zur 105. Sonderausstellung des Historischen Museums der Stadt Wien, September-October 1995.

9. See, e.g., Steven Beller, *Vienna and the Jews, 1867-1938: A Cultural History* (Cambridge: Cambridge University Press, 1989); Harriet P. Freidenreich, *Jewish Politics in Vienna 1918-1938* (Bloomington: Indiana University Press, 1991); Bruce Pauley, *Eine Geschichte des österreichischen Antisemitismus. Von der Ausgrenzung zur Auslöschung* (Vienna: Kremayr und Scheriau, 1993); Rozenblit, *Die Juden Wiens*.

10. Klein-Löw, *Erinnerungen*, 199; Siehe auch George Clare, *Letzter Walzer in Wien. Spuren einer Familie* (Frankfurt a. Main-Berlin-Vienna: Ullstein, 1984), 109 f.

11. Interview with Simon Wiesenthal, Vienna 1992.

12. Klein-Löw, *Erinnerungen*, 26.

13. Naomi Shepherd, *Jewish Women as Rebels and Radicals* (London: Harvard University Press, 1993); Andreas Lixl-Purcell, ed., *Erinnerungen deutsch-jüdischer Frauen 1900-1990* (Leipzig: Reclam, 1992); Marion A. Kaplan, *Die jüdische Frauenbewegung in Deutschland. Organisation und Ziele des jüdischen Frauenbundes 1904-1938* (Hamburg: Hans Christians, 1981); Meike Sophia Baader, "Grenzgängerinnen zwischen den Welten. Jüdische Frauen in Geschichte und Gegenwart," *Babylon, Beiträge zur jüdischen Gegenwart 13/14 (1991)*: 140-45.

14. Fried, *Farben des Lebens*, 49 f.

15. Interview with Anna Weiss, Menschenbilder, ORF, Ö1, 1995.

16. Peter Pulzer, *The Rise of Political Anti-Semitism in Germany and Austria* (London: Peter Halban, 1988), 121-185.

17. Embacher, "Außenseiterinnen," 71f.

18. Hilde Koplenig, unpublished manuscript, 69; also see Langer, *Von Wien bis Managua*, 85. Membership in the Jewish Community is a formal process, like church membership for Catholics or other Christians, which entails payment of a yearly tax.

19. Koplenig, manuscript, 78.

20. Irene Schöffmann, "Frauenpolitik im Austrofaschismus," in *"Austrofaschismus." Beiträge über Politik, Ökonomie und Kultur 1914-1938*, ed. Emmerich Tálos and Wolfgang Neugebauer (Vienna:Verlag für Gesellschaftskritik,1988).

21. Fini Littlejohn, letter to the author dated 25 November 1996.

22. Hilde Spiel, Im Gespräch, ORF, Ö1, 1989. See as well Video-Interview with Gundl Herrnstadt-Steinmetz, Salzburg 1995.

23. Quittner, *Weiter Weg*; Rosa Puhm, *Eine Trennung in Gorki* (Vienna: Verlag für Gesellschaftskritik, 1980); Meinhard Stark, ed., *"Wenn Du willst Deine Ruhe haben, schweige" Deutsche Frauenbiographien des Stalinismus* (Essen: Klartext, 1991).

24. Brigitte Bailer, "Der NS-Opfer-Fonds: Enttäuschte Hoffnungen der Betroffenen," *Informationen der Gesellschaft für politische Aufklärung* 45 (1995): 7-8.

25. Helga Embacher, *Neubeginn ohne Illusionen. Juden in Österreich nach 1945* (Vienna: Picus, 1995); idem, "Unwillkommen? Zur Rückkehr von Emigrantinnen und Überlebenden aus den Konzentrations- und Vernichtungslagern."

26. Embacher, "Außenseiterinnen," 73.

Women's Contributions to the Political Policies of National Socialism

Doris Gödl

The point of departure for my considerations is the debate which originated in the early 1970s in the field of women's studies in Germany. This debate surrounded the question of whether women during the era of National Socialism could properly be considered only as victims, or whether women had not also been collaborators, supporters, and enthusiastic advocates of this system. Who were the twelve million women who, both before and after 1933, supported National Socialism and worked together with it?

The initial public discussion of this issue was tantamount to the breaking of a taboo, since the majority of women had, until then, been considered victims of National Socialism and/or regarded themselves as such:

> Even as recently as a few years ago, the very idea that women collaborated in, or even bore criminal guilt for, National Socialism was virtually a taboo subject in historiography relating to both women as well as to the so-called Third Reich. Whereas one side completely closed its eyes to female collaborators and perpetrators in order to focus upon the victim's role of women in the patriarchy, the fixation of the other side upon the person of Hitler and his role in the male-dominated *Führerstaat* led to women being generally ignored as irrelevant within this framework. [1]

Nevertheless, there were women who, in a variety of ways, permitted themselves to be seduced by National Socialism into collaboration. The use of the term "seduction" in this context seems to me to be legitimate since it refers to an active decision reached by a subject performing an action—in this case, women. According to Michel

Foucault, the significance of seduction lies in the process whereby the seduced individual, at a certain moment, crosses a threshold to obtain a share of power or to come to an arrangement with it.[2] What, then, were the policies pursued by National Socialism to seduce women to support its political program, to activate their willingness to take part?

In my opinion, this process of seduction can be identified on three separate levels:

1. On the political level, "Aryan women" experienced an enhancement of their status in National Socialism as a result of the public statements and activities of the Nazi women's association and its representatives.

2. A significant factor was the individual career chances which National Socialism opened up for many women—as a political functionary in the women's association, with a position of responsibility in the system of social services, as a mother awarded the "Mother's Cross."[3]

3. On the personal level, relationships to the political *Nomenklatura* (through marriage, party membership, or "having given birth to a child on behalf of the *Führer*") were capable of forging such close ties to the movement that wives or children were prepared to denounce their own husbands or parents.[4]

The Seducer and the Seduced

In the following section, I would like to provide a few examples in order to put the relationship between the seducers and the seduced on the political and individual levels in concrete terms.

The Political Level of Seduction

The National Socialist Women's Association (NSF) was founded in 1931. It was quickly able to assert its claims to leadership within the League of German Women's Clubs, a confederation of bourgeois and liberal women's organizations and associations, so that those member groups whose policies and goals did not conform to those of the NSF were successively excluded from the league. Until 1935, the NSF could "operate relatively freely" as an independent organization. This changed after 1935, when the NSF relinquished its autonomy and became part of the Nazi party (NSDAP). Girls and young women continued to be organized within the Federation of German Girls

(BDM) up to the age of 30, at which point they could apply for membership in the NSF. Since the NSF wished to remain an elite group, only a limited number of members were accepted. Women now had to undergo an examination of their qualifications and convictions in order to gain admission. From this point on, acceptance by the NSF meant automatic membership in the NSDAP, and thus constituted a change in women's attitudes toward the party as well as their position within it: in place of an "autonomous" women's organization, there emerged "subordination" in a clear party hierarchy. Instead of being free to take independent positions, as had previously been the case, the group now had to conform to the dictates and expectations of the "top party leadership," for whom the areas of women's responsibility consisted primarily of providing unskilled labor and health care services for the party and its members, pursuing educational and cultural activities, as well as offering economic training for German housewives. The goals established within these areas of responsibility are impressively illustrated by a call to action issued by NSF leader Gertrud Scholtz-Klink:

> Our entire struggle and all of our labors in recent years have been devoted to improving the living conditions of the German people. This striving will now reach its fulfillment in the mightiest exertion of effort the world has ever seen. Our men have taken up arms, and we women will provide them with the weapons they need until final victory has been achieved. Along with the inner strength which we are naturally prepared to commit, this effort demands putting into action the full indus-triousness of the German woman, a force which can be matched by no nation in the world. Victory must be ours![5]

This example reveals the methods by which Nazi ideology had to be formulated and staged in order to gain access to the everyday life of women and led to, among other things, women's accession to power as agents of exclusion, persecution, and destruction. The activities of women in the areas of community welfare and childbearing were in-strumentalized by the movement, which publicly construed them as a means of serving "a good cause." This issue clearly reveals the political and ideological tension between autonomy (publicly participating in a cause) and subjugation (being reduced to traditional women's roles). This was a tension which had to remain unconscious so that the political/ideological centers of power would not be called into question, and the arrangement between the genders which was integral to it would not be disturbed. Furthermore, it is probable that this relationship of tension could be maintained intact only because a segment of the female population remained steadfast in their support of Nazi ideology and tolerated no deviations. This can be clearly seen by reviewing essays and texts published by the NSF. Thus, in a 1933 newspaper article, Guida Diehl proclaimed the goals of the NSF's political work:

> We are fighting to preserve the purity of the Aryan race and, therefore, to free the German *Volk* from influences which are foreign to it. ...We recognize...the necessity...[of] education of women and the integration of all the powers women possess on behalf of the greatest good of the whole nation, to the extent that they are not performing their service to the *Volk* for their immediate kin in marriage, family and motherhood. ...Therefore, the female citizen of the coming Third Reich is that German woman who commits all of her vital energies as a wife and mother or as a female worker on behalf of her *Volk* and Fatherland. To advocate these fundamental principles publicly throughout the land, to remain loyal to this struggle and to fight with unflagging energy, this we National Socialist women solemnly vow to our *Führer*, Adolf Hitler.[6]

In this way, "Aryan women" experienced an enhancement of their social status as a result of the public activities of the Nazi women's association—a form of enhancement whose significance, although highly relative, women found quite convincing. Thus, they became highly visible (staged), even if this visibility did not correspond to their actual political influence. Of prime significance was obtaining an integral share of *Führer, Volk und Vaterland*, and the submersion in the collective narcissism and megalomania which was connected with it. In this enhanced status as "Aryan woman," it is precisely those qualities which are enhanced and mystified which have been so highly characteristic of the conflict of genders which has taken place since the eighteenth century, with which women have been essentially defined, and now essentially define themselves. Simultaneously, this enhancement, as an element of racism, inherently demands the debasement of that which is foreign. In excluding others, one's own self-worth stems from one's not having been excluded. However, this type of exclusion, in the form of anti-Semitism and racism, hardly gave rise to the slightest protest. A few female historians, such as Claudia Koonz, for example, have identified an important aspect of perpetration on the part of women in this very connection. Women offered resistance when women's interests were at stake; when it was a matter of racism and anti-Semitism, however, they offered none or very little.

These highly ambivalent conditions between enhancement and debasement of women by Nazi ideology also acted to restrict the commitment of women to the cause of National Socialism and their readiness to work together with it. Although women were basically indispensable, they were denied access to Hitler and his inner circle. Thus, women indeed belonged to the so-called "master race," which endowed them with a certain enhanced status, which they were nevertheless then deprived of as members of an inferior gender. In this way, women readily accepted racial prejudices and venerated the Führer; they disavowed, however, any claim to a voice in political matters or to a share of political power. While swearing their obedience to men, they labored under the cloak of subjugation on the glorification of those spaces in which their own female life was played out: children, kitchen, church, culture, and hospital. Although women thus assumed responsibility for reproduction—the production of the "new generation"—as well as remaining available as a supplementary labor force, they were ultimately excluded from real political power:

> The National Socialist state was based just as fundamentally upon the separation of the genders as it was upon the exclusion of the Jews. A totalitarian society without its female half would not have been in the position to function. Therefore, the process of writing the history of this society cannot be finalized as long as the role and the significance of women in this society has not been thoroughly investigated.[7]

The Individual Level of Seduction

I have chosen the story of Trude Mohr-Bürkner to exemplify this level, since, in my opinion, her case makes very clear the connection between political seduction and individual benefits in the sense of personal career opportunities.

Trude Mohr was born in 1902 to parents whose political convictions were German nationalist. In the 1920s, she was actively involved in the German nationalist youth organization, the forerunner of the Hitler Youth (HJ). An NSDAP party member since 1928, she was entrusted with the assignment of establishing a BDM organization in the Brandenburg district by the HJ in 1930. In 1933, she was furloughed from her position in the national postal administration to be able to devote full-time attention to the organization and expansion of the BDM in the districts of Brandenburg and Berlin. When the HJ was outlawed for a few months in 1932, the ban of course applied to the BDM as well. This imposed illegality elevated Trude Mohr's sense of her own importance:

> *Ach*, that was a lot of fun. I had been in South Tyrol (Northern Italy) and had a stopover in Berlin on my way to Masuren (East Prussia). A woman on my staff was supposed to meet me at the train terminal to bring me a suitcase packed with clean clothes. In the meantime, the ban had be decreed, and she met me at an out-of-the-way station disguised in civilian clothing. But, of course, the BDM's work went forward, and no one paid the slightest attention to the ban.[8]

In 1934, as a result of feuding and internal intrigues in the organization, Trude Mohr was appointed national chairwoman of the BDM by *Reichsjugendführer* Baldur von Schirach, a position she held until 1937. Her most important goal was to try to bring about a change in the appearance of female youths. This had assumed importance following Hitler's horrified reaction to the "girls" who marched past him on the occasion of the 1932 national youth day celebration.[9] Heinrich Himmler had also expressed serious doubts about the attractiveness of German girls. "I regard it as a catastrophe. If we continue to masculinize women in this way, it is only a matter of time until the difference between the genders, the polarity, completely disappears."[10] Mohr then attempted to postulate a new type of German girl based upon this critique:

> Our *Volk* needs a generation of girls which is healthy in body and mind, sure and decisive, proudly and confidently going forward, one which assumes its place in everyday life with poise and discernment, one free of sentimental and rapturous emotions, and which, for precisely this reason, in sharply-

defined femininity, would be the comrade of a man, because she does not regard him as some sort of idol but rather as a companion! Such girls will then, by necessity, carry the values of National Socialism into the next generation as the mental bulwark of our people.[11]

On the personal level as well, Trude Mohr's actions met party expectations; her marriage to *SS-Obersturmführer* Bürkner was in accordance with provisions requiring BDM leaders to marry members of the SS. This wedding almost did not take place, however, as a result of a motion submitted by the Central Office for Racial and Settlement Policy (RuSHA). Mohr's "certificate of proof of Aryan origin" was indeed impeccable; her extreme shortsightedness, however, diminished her genetic-biological value in the eyes of the defenders of racial purity. It was only after heavy pressure was applied by the party's district administration upon the RuSHA that permission to marry could be obtained. Quite striking in this connection is the fact that the responsible RuSHA official seems to have been completely unimpressed by Trude Mohr's high rank as national chairwoman of the BDM. However, despite coming into conflict with the regime in this existential question, Trude Mohr-Bürkner, like many others, did not draw the obvious conclusion from this incident, and her loyalty toward the regime remained undiminished. By 1937, when she stepped down from her leadership position in the BDM as a result of her pregnancy, the combined national organization for girls had grown to nearly 2,758,000 members.[12] By fully acceding to the educational demands of the state, she participated in the regime's project of placing German youth into the service of the party and the state, or, to be more precise, the person of Adolf Hitler. The "total commitment" which she demanded would later find its concrete expression for BDM girls in the form of war.

Although she no longer appeared in public life after 1937, Trude Bürkner did not take complete leave of the political stage. She was assigned the task of setting up a system to provide social welfare services for plant workers at the Hermann Göring Works which had been opened in the summer of 1937. If, up to this point, she had seemed to have gone about her job with little regard for public recognition, this matter now took on great importance for her. At least she wanted to obtain a lower party membership number. Until then, she had not had to document to the public at large her key position within the party by means of a low membership number, but her new assignment changed that. "Is there a possibility," she inquired, "that I could assume a lower membership number that has subsequently become free? This would mean a great deal to me, since, as can well be imagined, a membership number over one million gives a completely false impression of the circumstances of my membership in the NSDAP."[13] The party bureaucracy rejected her application, and Bürkner was once again forced to capitulate. The fact that she knew that such backdating was a common practice in the case of prominent male party members must have made this even harder for her to accept. But thereafter as well, the level of her approval and her commitment was undiminished. In fact it had the opposite effect of spurring her to redouble her efforts (for example in the NSF and in the national civil defense organization) in order to make up for the lack of a low membership number. Not much is known about the job she did at the Hermann Göring plant complex, other than the fact that she performed her social service work for the so-called "foreign and Eastern European laborers" in an exemplary fashion. These "presumably exemplary social services, provided at all such plants throughout the entire *Reich*, helped to insure that, of the 1.3 million such slave laborers recruited to work in these plants, at least 523,000 did not survive their terms of employment."[14]

Trude Bürkner was imprisoned by the British in June 1945. Following her release, she neither granted interviews nor did she express herself in print. It was not until 1980 that Martin Klaus was able to convince her to go on record. In this interview, she summed up her life as follows: "It certainly makes a big difference if, from out of the abundance of experiences one has in life, one devotes one's entire self with complete commitment and total effort to a single idea, or whether one follows events from the sidelines, smiling maliciously and observing with cool irony. I belong to the first group and I'm not ashamed of it.[15]

Women as Active Subjects

Proceeding from the investigative perspective that women were active subjects in the National Socialist system, the discussion formed around two leading criteria. The first of these was the highly relevant fact that National Socialism had been possible only through having secured wide popular consent. This means that this system cannot be comprehended without taking into consideration the significance of the mass basis of support organized by the regime. The second point weaves the question of the operative effectiveness of gender relationships into the context of meaning, if one proceeds from the assumption that a totalitarian society would not have been in the position to function without the female half of the population. The history of this society, therefore, can not be definitively concluded as long as the role and importance of women in this society have not been thoroughly investigated.

From the point of view of the present, however, it does not seem to be so easy to arrive at differentiated points of view and patterns of interpretation which avoid the pitfalls both of forgiving women *en masse* or accusing them all in retrospect. It is necessary to navigate between each of these two extremes.

The emerging public discussion surrounding this issue constituted the breaking of a taboo, since the majority of women had long been regarded as victims of National Socialism and/or saw themselves as such. The subsequent discourse became a process of developing a consciousness in which the National Socialist past was expressly conceived as a part of the history and continuity of their own lives. This, however, could only take shape along highly defined lines of conflict, whereby the conflict has been and continues to be a function of the diverse approaches of scholars working on this issue. One common denominator among the numerous interpretational differences, though, seems to be the emotionally charged nature of the topic, which finds expression in moral judgments and the question of guilt. The denial or repression of guilt on the part of women in National Socialism, as well as the complete taboo placed upon the subject of anti-Semitism, was clearly demonstrated in the work carried out by Gisela Bock on the subject of forced sterilization by the Nazis. She contrasted the patriarchal policies of the National Socialists with the "historic innocence" of women.[16] Among other consequences, this had the effect of placing the sole burden of responsibility upon white German men. The "Aryan" woman, whose elevated status was a fundamental principle of Nazi ideology, did not even come into consideration as bearing a share of the guilt, neither did the category of anti-Semitism appear even once in the entire work. Early in the 1990s, a task force against anti-Semitism began to increasingly criticize the "victim thesis" within women's studies in Germany, though it must certainly be remarked that there was no accompanying inquiry into women as perpetrators.[17] That does not mean, however, that the victim question does not continue to be of importance; rather, it is a matter of criticizing the writing of history within women's studies which derives a concept of victim that is characterized by the psychoanalytic process of identification, in which all women are indiscriminately labeled as victims.

In order to escape the polarization of victim and perpetrator—as well as the question of guilt which is always implicit in it—the American historian Claudia Koonz has developed the concept of the "historical agency" of women in the preparation and formation of fascistic power relationships.[18] This concept is, in my opinion, particularly appropriate to provide a way out of the "victim-perpetrator dilemma" and to advance a realistic process of coming to terms with the responsibility of women, because as long as we remain trapped within a traditional frame of thought—a system of "above" and "below" in which politics is identified with violence and masculinity must be proven through violent acts—the question of the joint involvement and shared responsibility of women will continue to be purely an act of denunciation. However, by differentiating between the concepts of power and violence—as was put forward by Hannah Arendt, for example—a line of reasoning emerges in which the concept of collaboration finally attains practical significance.[19]

Violence and Gender Difference

Let's return to the question of the extent to which women, both historically and in the present, have been involved in the commission of violent crimes. How do we deal with the fact that women may no longer be seen as peaceable and nice, and thereby as being free from guilt and absolved of responsibility? Which conceptual models do we have at our disposal in addressing this question? The central core of this topic seems to be the question of violence. It continues to be the dominant conceptual and perceptual pattern that women suffer from, rather than commit, acts of violence and it continues to be seen as the breaking of a taboo to reflect openly upon the possibility of breaking out from this cliché. It is, thereby, clear that a simple reversal of this construction—that is, to imagine women in positions of violence—does not constitute a way out of this dilemma. Therefore, the question of co-responsibility on the part of women remains a matter of denunciation as long as we pose it within a traditional framework, in a system in which there is always an "above" and a "below," in which politics is identified with violence and masculinity must be proven through violent acts. A possible way out of this dilemma is, in my opinion, differentiating between the concepts of power and violence, whereby a line of reasoning emerges in which the concept of collaboration finally attains practical significance. The decisive point in this differentiation lies in the gain of a rational conception of power in contrast to one which admits only an "above" and a "below." Reciprocities of action and the consent of the involved parties are relevant for this rational conception of power. This differentiation, which can be traced back to the work of Hannah Arendt, constitutes an important argument against the prevailing tradition of political thought. She juxtaposes the conception of "the demand to exercise power over others" with its diametrically antithetical construction "the refusal to allow the exercise of power over oneself," whereby Arendt assesses the manifestation of submissive acquiescence as politically relevant.

In my opinion, it is only by means of this differentiation between power and violence as undertaken by Hannah Arendt that a scope of potential action opens up as a precondition to an investigation of the subject of complicity. If the refusal to make use of one's power also becomes visible as implicit acquiescence, then the motives that stand behind this tacit approval also become relevant. For Arendt, this use of power means, in the final analysis, the assumption of responsibility. In this respect, complicity can exist in a case of delegating responsibility and thus not making use of one's own power.

It is, of course, no simple matter to measure in retrospect the scope of potential action which women had in the National Socialist system. Nevertheless, it was obviously much larger than has been previously assumed, which has also been shown by contemporary historical investigations.

NOTES

1. Andrea Böltken, *Führerinnen im Führerstaat* (Pfaffenweiler: Centaurus, 1995).

2. See Michel Foucault, *Diskurs und Wahrheit* (Berlin: Merve, 1996), 37-39.

3. See Angelika Ebbinghaus, ed., *Opfer und Täterinnen* (Hamburg: 1987).

4. See Helga Schubert, *Judasfrauen: Zehn Fallgeschichten weiblicher Denunziation im Dritten Reich* (Frankfurt: Luchterhand, 1990).

5. Gertrud Scholtz-Klink, quoted in Claudia Koonz, "Frauen schaffen ihren 'Lebensraum' im Dritten Reich," *Frauen und Macht: Der alltägliche Beitrag der Frauen zur Politik des Patriarchats*, ed. Barbara Schaeffer-Hegel (Berlin: 1984), 52.

6. Fundamental Principles of the NSF.

7. Koonz, *"Frauen schaffen ihren 'Lebensraum,'"* 49.

8. Trude Mahr-Bürkner, quoted in Böltken, *Führerinnen im Führerstaat*, 68.

9. See Claudia Koonz, *Mütter im Vaterland*, (Freiburg: 1991), 72.

10. Heinrich Himmler, quoted in Böltken, *Führerinnen im Führerstaat*, 73.

11. Trude Mohr, quoted in *Völkischer Beobachter* 6 September 1934.

12. See Martin Klaus, *Mädchenerziehung zur Zeit der Faschistischen Herrschaft in Deutschland: Der Bund Deutscher Mädel*, (2 vols.), vol. 2 (Frankfurt: 1983).

13. Letter dated 17 July 1938 from Trude Bürkner to party member Görlitzer, quoted in Böltken, *Führerinnen im Führerstaat* , 81.

14. Böltken, *Führerinnen im Führerstaat*, 82.

15. Trude Bürkner, quoted by Klaus, *Mädchenerziehung*, vol. 2, 32.

16. See Gisela Bock, "Nationalsozialistische Geschlechterpolitik und die Geschichte der Frauen," *Geschichte der Frauen*, (5 vols.), vol. 5, ed. Georges Duby and Michelle Perrat (Frankfurt: 1995), 173-205.

17. Arbeitsgemeinschat Frauen gegen Antisemitismus, "Der National-sozialismus als Extremform des Patriarchats. Zur Leugnung der Täterschaft von Frauen und zur Tabuisierung des Antisemitismus in der Auseinandersetzung mit dem NS," In *Beiträge zur feministischen Theorie und Praxis*. (Cologne: 1993), 77-89.

18. See Koonz, *Mütter im Vaterland*, 1991.

19. See Hannah Arendt, *Elemente und Urspünge totaler Herrschaft* (Munich: 1986); and idem, *Macht und Gewalt* (Munich:1970).

FURTHER LITERATURE

Theodor W. Adorno, Minima Moralia (Frankfurt: 1985).

Gisela Bock, *Zwangssterilisation im Nationalsozialismus* (Opladen: 1986).

Lerke Gravenhorst and Carmen Tatschmurat, eds., *TöchterFragen: NS-Frauen Geschichte* (Freiburg: 1990).

Isle Korotin, *Am Muttergeist soll die Welt genesen* (Vienna: 1992).

Anette Kuhn, *Frauenleben im NS-Alltag* (Pfaffenweiler: 1994).

Ina Paul-Horn, *Faszination Nationalsozialismus?* (Pfaffenweiler: 1993).

Austrian Women in the Anti-Nazi Resistance Movement in Belgian Exile[1]

Erika Thurner

Preliminary Remarks: Resistance and Scholarly Research on Resistance

Immediately following the war, anti-fascist resistance assumed enormous importance. The resistance fighters were needed to solidly establish Austria's position as a "victim of German Nazi fascism" and to thereby receive more favorable treatment from the Allies (the Antifascist Declaration of Principles of the "founding fathers" of the Second Republic). Nevertheless, by 1947-48—with the onset of the Cold War at the very latest—resistance was almost completely excluded from public discourse. Those who had been active in the struggle against fascism or former concentration camp inmates received little recognition in postwar society. Quite the contrary. The resistance fighters were shunned and socially ostracized; they were regarded as a provocation and evoked deep resentments on the part of most of the population of Austria. The majority of Austrians—men and women alike—had belonged to the Nazi *Volksgemeinschaft*, voluntarily or involuntarily, actively or passively. As a result of their enthusiasm or conviction, tacit approval, indifference, or mere toleration, National Socialist rule had received their affirmation and/or complicity. Only a tiny minority was engaged in active resistance. Only a small, although somewhat larger, minority had supported this resistance.[2]

It was not until much later that the historical study and evaluation of these events was taken up by universities and other scholarly institutions. The *Dokumentationsarchiv des österreichischen Widerstandes*, founded in 1963, led the way. Interest initially remained focused upon the fates of high-profile, often heroically stylized individuals.[3] One of the reasons for this was the effort to bestow belated recognition upon these resistance fighters; on the other hand, this was also due to the state of available archive material as well as a methodology oriented toward biographical research.

Thus, historical scholarship bears a share of the responsibility for the long-term blockage of the process of taking a comprehensive and multi-faceted approach to this issue. Furthermore, as a result of male domination (androcentricity) within the field of historical studies, "gender" has not been taken sufficiently into account as a category of social investigation. For this reason, women and their commitment to the fight against National Socialism have remained generally ignored or accorded scant attention in the research of resistance movements. To this can be added the fact that numerous scholars have had difficulties with these "insurgent" women who deviated so clearly from the traditional image of femininity.[4]

Moreover, the concept of resistance itself has long been too narrowly defined. A much wider conception of resistance, on the other hand, makes possible a much more highly differentiated research approach, which permits the entire spectrum of oppositional behavior patterns employed against the Nazi regime to be taken into consideration and enables the resistance activities of women to be more clearly perceived.[5] Furthermore, it was precisely the combined effort encompassing the most diverse covert actions that made possible large-scale political resistance against the Nazis. The maintenance of an active, large-scale resistance struggle such as partisan warfare only became possible through the wide variety of essential support operations carried out behind the scenes—above all by women.

Thus, the process of coming to terms with "female resistance"—as a separate topic within the field of resistance studies—began very late. It coincided with the feminist engagement on the part of women in academia and in society as a whole. Writers and social scientists began to investigate the subject of women's resistance early in the 1980s.[6] Doing so required newer methods (oral history) and investigative approaches to gradually uncover the traces of female resistance and commitment to the anti-fascist cause.

After all, politics—and thus political resistance against the Nazi regime as well—was a male domain. Women were clearly underrepresented. The citation of figures and relative proportions posed problems.

Just as an overall quantitative picture of the entire resistance movement is barely feasible, precise numbers regarding the percentage of women involved are also virtually impossible to provide. Radomir Luza's early quantitative analyses which cited a female component of 11.65 percent were based on an extremely narrowly-defined concept of resistance.[7] An estimate of female participation in the range of 20-30 percent is certainly much closer to reality.[8]

Thus, anti-fascist resistance as well reflects social realities. The traditional hierarchy of genders—the assignment of roles and spaces on a gender-specific basis—remained valid to a great extent. The "absolute rule of men" predominated, according to the summation of one female veteran.[9] Only in exceptional cases did a specifically female form of resistance develop. One of these rare instances of covert activities performed by women was the so-called *Mädelarbeit* carried out in two nations occupied by Nazi Germany: France and Belgium.

Staging Area: Belgium

The choice of Belgium as an area of investigation for this inquiry into women in resistance presents us with a small land of exile that has received little notice. Belgium was neither politically nor culturally a major center of Austrian emigration—surely another reason for its neglect by Austrian historians. A single exception is constituted by the impressive literary essays written by Jean Améry, the most famous Austrian *èmigre* in Belgium.[10] In 1987, this gap in the historical record was closed with the appearance of *Österreicher im Exil in Belgien*. The extensive and informative introduction to this publication was written by Gundl Herrnstadt-Steinmetz, one of the activists in the Belgian *Mädelgruppe*.[11]

Belgium became a land of exile for those whose means of escape, both in the form of financial resources and human relationships, were either quite limited or nonexistent. For those who fled to it, Belgium meant an insecure, provisional existence. It was impossible for most exiles to legalize their refugee status, and their ability to start a new life there suffered a further setback with the advance of Hitler's troops early in the war. Belgium was occupied by the Nazis on 10 May 1940. In this context and in the face of this background situation, a relatively strong female resistance group was formed.

Austrian Women in Belgian Exile

The group chosen for investigation was composed of women and young girls who had already gone through a process of "political enlightenment" prior to the rise of National Socialism and the passage of the Nürnberg Racial Laws. The majority of this group of women came out of the labor movement or sympathized with it. They had been socialized in "Red Vienna" and had experienced first hand the highly charged political atmosphere of everyday life in the Austrian First Republic and the events of the Austrian Civil War in February 1934. Many had been members of the Social Democratic Party or the Communist Party and had engaged in illegal underground activities after these political groups had been outlawed. Some of these women and girls were assimilated Jews. For these women, Judaism was either no factor in their personal identities or played a subsidiary role. Due to their "Jewish heritage," however, they were doubly endangered following the seizure of power by the National Socialists in Austria.

It was no mere coincidence that Belgium became the exile land for these "leftists" (Revolutionary Socialists/Communists). Belgium became the country of asylum for emigrants possessing meager financial means and no personal contacts, which made the journey to a more distant and more secure land of exile an impossibility.

Exile in Belgium

Belgium was a traditional land of labor migration. However, following the beginning of the economic crisis in the 1930s—even before the influx of political and Jewish refugees had begun—the Belgian right-wing parties had been successful in enacting restrictive asylum and immigration legislation, though these laws had been made less harsh through the efforts of leftist and liberal politicians. Thus, in August 1938, Vanderveken, the secretary of the Matteotti Fund, was one of many who expressed their indignation and sharply criticized the barter trade in exit visas being conducted with political and Jewish refugees:

Everyone who has taken up the question of foreign immigrants knows from personal experience that numerous Austrians whose departure is desired by Hitler have truly had to buy their way out of their homeland, and this has gone on with the blessings of the (Nazi) *Reichsleiter* and probably with the help of a few Belgian policemen as well. We certainly cannot condone illegal emigration of this kind...but it must also be taken for granted that political refugees who have been qualified as such will continue to be granted the right of residency here.[12]

Entry into Belgium thus remained possible only through illegal channels.[13] The chances of success were extremely difficult to reckon, and many of those fleeing the Nazis needed several attempts. Rarely did a border crossing succeed without paid assistance from border guards and policemen, though the amount demanded "per head" varied greatly. The freedom that they attained upon reaching Belgium was strictly limited; despite the facts, most exiles had to refrain from attempting to legalize their refugee status, since the risk of deportation back to the land from which they had escaped was considerable. For those caught in this double bind, that meant a life without identity papers, no possibility of regular employment, and no food ration cards.

Nevertheless, Belgium was for a short time a relatively pleasant country of exile. There were good possibilities to get in contact with a network of like-minded individuals and a large number of aid organizations. For those with no political affiliation and/or for Jews who had dissolved their links to an orthodox religious community, though, the process of adjustment to life in the land of exile was indeed difficult.[14]

The Jewish refugees by no means constituted a unified community with shared religious beliefs or a common political orientation, and the Jewish population of Belgium was equally heterogeneous. Up to the early 1930s, approximately 10,000 Jews lived in Belgium, some of them extremely well-to-do members of the bourgeois establishment residing primarily in Brussels. These assimilated Jews indeed provided refugee organizations with profuse financial aid but refused direct involvement with them. The orthodox Jews of Antwerp took a very different approach, making an effort to absorb refugees into their community. This met with rejection on the part of assimilated exiles. The "non-Jewish Jews" (Isaac Deutscher) who had been made into such by the National Socialists neither had ties to the Jewish faith and traditions nor were they fluent in the Yiddish spoken within the Antwerp Jewish community.[15]

In contrast to these groups, political refugees had better chances to achieve integration. Through a process of taking root in familiar political terrain, whereby Socialists, Monarchists, and Communists were able to establish contact with ideological compatriots, it became easier to cope with the loss of one's geographic as well as linguistic homeland.

All in all, the populace was for the most part not anti-Semitic and only a small segment collaborated with the Nazis. There was relatively strong mutual support and assistance.[16]

Emancipation through Flight and Exile?

Only a very few women arrived in Belgium alone. Once there, though, they quickly made contact with others whom they knew from their respective milieux in their home country. As one *èmigre* put it, "There were a great many Austrian *émigres* in Brussels in 1938— political exiles as well as Jewish refugees. There was a group of Austrian comrades with whom I immediately made contact."[17] Indeed, several of the women had already proven themselves in their commitment to the struggle against fascism, some through their involvement in the Spanish Civil War. As a result, their route of escape had been stipulated by the Communist Party. These women played an especially significant role in the resistance groups.

The flight into exile constituted a break with their former lifestyle and traditional forms of existence. Girls from the ranks of the labor movement, like their bourgeois "sisters," had also been raised in preparation for a "typically female" way of life, primarily as mothers and housewives. Nevertheless, the atmosphere in such families was to a certain extent more permissive than in bourgeois homes. Male-female partnership relationships were not unusual. Through participation in sports and other recreational organizations, young people developed and cultivated more natural forms of association with members of the opposite sex. The lives of these working class girls were not as isolated and protected as was the case for many of their female contemporaries from (petit) bourgeois backgrounds. This factor, along with the network of relationships with sympathetic colleagues and comrades, eased the way for these women and girls to gain a foothold in exile. Despite their illegal status, women (and girls) usually had a much easier time earning their living in exile than did their male counterparts. Women and girls were able to keep their heads above water by doing typical "women's jobs." Some found positions as household help in (Jewish) homes.

While emigrants to Palestine or to other countries such as the United States could immediately get about the business of establishing themselves in a new, and at least provisional, existence, life in Belgian exile for members of racially and/or politically persecuted groups meant assuming the identity of a stranger in a strange land and struggling daily to survive.[18] It represented, at most, a place of temporary safety; for these women, establishing a "normal" life was out of the question. And it was not long before Belgium was occupied as well, so that those who had fled were again confronted by their persecutors—the National Socialists and their Nürnberg Racial Laws.

The Initiation and Intensification of (Female) Resistance: *"Soldaten- und Mädelarbeit"*

Belgium was under German military administration from May 1940 until the fall of 1944. The male Austrian immigrants were immediately arrested as suspicious aliens and shipped to internment camps in the south of France. Women, who were not regarded as politically suspect by the Nazis, were permitted to remain in Belgium. The "blessing of female birth" and the traditional view which regarded politics, and thus political resistance as well, as a man's business acted to protect women, particularly in the initial phase.

Then, resistance to the Nazi regime not only did not diminish, it was even intensified. Among these activities were the production of fliers and a newspaper for soldiers, as well as their circulation using methods which had already proved successful. However, the changed circumstances in the land of exile—above all, the deportation of the majority of the male *émigres* to France—had necessitated a change of orientation of both content and organization:[19]

> Around the fall of 1940, we began to put out placards (referred to as *Pickerln* by the Austrians) displaying slogans, which we posted on walls and fences in the immediate vicinity of army bases and other *Wehrmacht* facilities. So-called "amorous couples" did the job—a man and a woman seeming to be tenderly embracing one another while he was affixing the placards behind the back of his partner.[20]

Beginning in 1941, a new, specifically female form of resistance was begun—the so-called *Soldaten-und Mädelarbeit*. Between fifteen and twenty Austrian girls and younger women, the so-called *Mädelgruppe*, went about trying to make the acquaintance of members of the *Wehrmacht* in the attempt to win them over to the cause. With the help of these soldiers, anti-fascist propaganda (handbills and newspapers) was smuggled onto army bases and distributed. Indeed, the concept for this form of resistance was the brainchild of men. The care and provisioning of the girls was also organized by men, members of the resistance organization who had either been able to remain in Belgium or had fled back to Belgium from France.

The *Mädelarbeit* was a form of resistance which could only have been carried out by women. In other resistance activities, women stood generally in the background, performing in supporting roles such as cooks, nurses, etc. In the case of the *Mädelarbeit*, however, women bore the entire burden of the resistance operation. The selection of the soldiers and execution of the operation were entirely in their hands, and they were constantly exposed to the greatest danger. They had to carefully sound out the soldiers whom they met, probing their attitudes to assess their potential readiness to cooperate, simultaneously challenging their courage and allaying their fears. The very fact of having met a girl—along with the hope for more intimate contact connected with it—encouraged some of the soldiers to collaborate. The women, though, were persistently admonished to confine their contacts, following the first "inviting" conversation, to the political assignment at hand. It can well be imagined, however, that these activities also held a latent and tempting fascination for these women and girls, that is, they desired to prove their ability to stimulate the interest of men.

Arrest and What Followed

Along with the *"Soldaten-und Mädelarbeit,"* women's inventiveness and creativity (displayed, for example, by the ideas they contributed concerning transport methods and hide-out possibilities) made a rich and essential contribution to the resistance effort. Due to the role they played at "center stage" of the operations, they were exposed to the most extreme danger. For almost all women and girls who were active in the resistance movement in Belgium, these activities ended with betrayal and arrest:

It was on July 22, 1944, a Saturday, and I still had three more *rendezvous* planned for the day. ...I had a date with a soldier who had intimated in a letter that he wished to join our organization. ...No sooner had I offered him my hand in greeting than two civilians suddenly converged upon us, their appearance leaving no doubt that they could be anything but German policemen. ...I immediately seized the only possible means of escape...throwing my bicycle at the policemen's feet, I ran as fast as I could ...As my pursuers confronted me again, their revolvers in their hands, ready to fire, I made one final attempt, ...The first shot rang out, immediately followed by the second and the third. I felt a stabbing pain in my leg, it collapsed and I fell...."[21]

For eight of these women, what followed was torture, imprisonment and sentencing to a concentration camp. One member of the group did not survive this torment.[22] Several of them, following their deportation to Auschwitz, joined the resistance organization there, carrying out daring acts of sabotage despite the deadly sanctions.[23]

Continuities and Breaks

These women and girls, integrated as they were into a tightly-knit group, experienced exile and persecution not only as their own individual "fate" but also as a collective one. Nor did it constitute a total break with their previous life. Indeed, the long duration of the Nazi domination and the war, along with the additional threat their Jewish descent posed to their existence, forced them to lay aside any hopes for a "normal woman's life." Only a very few gave birth to children during this period. Plans for the future, including the realization of a portion of their female identity, had to be postponed. Relationships and marriages were torn apart. Arrest, torture, internment in concentration camps, the loss of spouses, friends, and family members—all of these were traumatic experiences that had to be worked through first.

For Jewish victims of persecution, following the experience of the Holocaust, the wish to raise a family was given the highest priority.[24] As for those women who survived their persecution, the joy they felt at the downfall of the Nazi reign of terror was, however, overshadowed by postwar social developments in Austria. The reluctant and slack denazification efforts, as well as the jubilant revival of anticommunism during the Cold War, were particularly painful to left-wing former resistance fighters. Many anti-fascist women joined the ranks of the Communist Party. These "private" and social disappointments strengthened the inner need to withdraw, already present as a result of poor health and disease. Most women resigned themselves thereby to their traditional role, in society as a whole as well as in their personal relationships.

In the 1980s, female anti-fascist resistance fighters were discovered as role models and figures of identification, both by the feminist movement and by historians working in women's studies. These new "idols," however, were also confronted with the question—or even the charge—that they had relinquished during the postwar era the emancipated position and the lifestyle characterized by self-determination which they had previously attained. Dealing with this question calls for multi-faceted analyses and answers which take into account all aspects of this issue.

Public affairs and political life in Austria has remained an arena of men's interests and male decision-makers. Experiences with socialization, cultural patterns, and updated forms of established rights—along with concrete social, economic and specifically regional circumstances—constitute ordering principles and limiting patterns. For example, the severe labor scarcity during the immediate postwar period was quickly followed by a shortage of jobs. Many women were let go, forced to give up their jobs to returning war veterans.[25]

Certainly, the response should take into consideration the entire complex of cultural and political patterns understood as "Western integration" with its associated concepts of the re-establishment of traditional gender and class hierarchies. The development of postwar society was a product of this, whereby, in a contradictory historical continuum of reconstruction and new beginning, the strong imposed themselves upon the weak—on the international and national levels, in politics and public life, in matters of career and employment as well as in the private sphere. Attitudes and internalized role conceptions eased this process and contributed to the establishment and consolidation of the restorative climate.

NOTES

1. A shorter version of this article was prepared as a paper for the German Studies Association's Nineteenth Annual Conference, held on 21-24 September 1995, in Chicago. It has been expanded for this publication.

2. See Wolfgang Neugebauer, "Widerstand und Opposition," in *NS-Herrschaft in Österreich 1938-1945*, ed. Emmerich Tálos et al. (Vienna: Verlag für Gesellschaftskritik, 1988), 537-552.

3. An early researcher on female antifascists was Tilly Spiegel, *Frauen und Mädchen im österreichischen Widerstand. Monographien zur Zeitgeschichte* (Vienna: Europa-Verlag, 1967).

4. See Brigitte Bailer-Galanda, " Zur Rolle der Frauen im Widerstand oder Die im Dunkeln sieht man nicht," in *Jahrbuch 1990*, ed. Dokumentationsarchiv des österreichischen Widerstandes (Vienna: Österreichischer Bundesverlag, 1990), 13-22. On pages 14-15, there are further investigations on this topic by Inge Brauneis, Elisabeth Reichart, and Erika Weinzierl.

5. See Wolfgang Neugebauer, "Was ist Widerstand? Referat. Internationales Colloquium: Widerstand gegen das Dritte Reich. Forschungsstand und Forschungsmöglichkeiten, Berlin 1983," in *DöW-Jahrbuch 1986* (Vienna: Dokumentationsarchiv des österreichischen Widerstandes, 1986), 61-71.

6. In Austria, a particularly strong commitment was displayed by a team of four women: Karin Berger, Elisabeth Holzinger, Lotte Podgornik, and Lisbeth N. Trallori. See Karin Berger et al., *Der Himmel ist blau. Kann sein. Frauen im Widerstand. Österreich 1938-1945* (Vienna: edition-spuren, promedia, 1985); Karin Berger et al., "Ich geb dir einen Mantel, daß Du ihn noch in Freiheit tragen kannst," *Widerstehen im KZ. Österreichische Frauen erzählen* (Vienna: Picus, 1987).

7. Neugebauer, "Widerstand und Opposition," 549-50.

8. Bailer-Galanda, "Zur Rolle der Frauen im Widerstand," 17.

9. See Berger et al., *Der Himmel ist blau*, 250.

10. Jean Améry, *Örtlichkeiten. Mit einem Nachwort von Manfred Frank* (Stuttgart: Klett-Cotta, 1980); idem, *Jenseits von Schuld und Sühne. Bewältigungsversuche eines Überwältigten* (Stuttgart: Klett-Cotta, 1977).

11. Gundl Herrnstadt-Steinmetz, "Introduction," *Österreicher im Exil in Belgien. Belgien 1938-1945. Eine Dokumentation*, ed. Dokumentationsarchiv des österreichischen Widerstandes (Vienna: Österreichischer Bundesverlag, 1987), 15-54.

12. Herrnstadt-Steinmetz, "Introduction," 19. See also Betty Garfinkels, *Belgique, terre d'accueil. Problème du réfugié 1933-1940* (Brussels: 1974), 126.

13. Friedrich Adler, secretary of 2nd Socialist International in Brussels, said to a fellow party member in August 1938, "It's completely impossible for persons of Jewish descent to obtain an entry permit for Belgium. For non-Jews, if they're Austrians, it's extraordinarily difficult." Quoted in Neugebauer, *Österreicher im Exil in Belgiem*, 61.

14. See the autobiographical report by Susanne Kriss, *Wien - Belgien - retour? Materialien zur Zeitgeschichte*, vol. 7 of *Erinnerungen aus Verfolgung und Widerstand*, ed. Erika Thurner (Vienna: O. J.,1989), 37-52.

15. See Jean Améry, *Mein Judentum*, ed. Hans Jürgen Schultz (Stuttgart: Kreuz-Verlag, 1978), 85.

16. See *Österreicher im Exil in Belgien*. In eyewitness reports, there are numerous passages mentioning helpful officials and private citizens. See, for example, those on page 121.

17. Ibid., report of Hertha Stuberg-Wiesinger, Doc. No. 79, 119.

18. See Gabriele Kreis (Darmstadt: Luchterhand, 1984). See also Anna Rattner - Lola Blonder, *1938 - Zuflucht Palästina. Zwei Frauen berichten*, ed. Helga Embacher with an introduction by the editor. Materialien zur Zeitgeschichte, vol. 6 (Vienna-Salzburg: Geyer, 1989).

19. See *Österreicher im Exil in Belgien*, 52.

20. Ibid., 121.

21. Ibid., 117-19. An account of the betrayal of Gundl Herrnstadt-Steinmetz can be found in *Wien - Belgien - retour?* 203-229. Her gunshot wound and the approaching end of the war kept Gundl Herrnstadt-Steinmetz from being shipped to a concentration camp. She was not spared interrogation and mistreatment, and chronic pain in her leg has accompanied her ever since. See 117ff.

22. Marianne Brandt, the German girlfriend of author Jean Améry, did not survive the tortures of arrest and imprisonment. See *Österreicher im Exil in Belgien*, 52.

23. Hertha Fuchs-Ligeti and Lotte Genauer-Brainin, members of the *Mädelgruppe* in Belgium, later became active members of the *Kampfgruppe Auschwitz* in the *Union-Kommando*. See her autobiographical report in *Wien - Belgien - retour?* 149-50.

24. See Helga Embacher, *Neubeginn ohne Illusionen. Juden in Österreich nach 1945* (Vienna: Picus, 1995), 71-72.

25. Erika Thurner, "Die stabile Innenseite der Politik. Geschlechterbeziehungen und Rollenverhalten" in *Österreich in den Fünfzigern*, ed. Thomas Albrich et al., *Innsbrucker Forschungen zur Zeitgeschichte*, Band 11 (Innsbruck: Österreichischer Studien Verlag, 1995), 53-66.

"Austria's Prestige Dragged into the Dirt"? The "GI-Brides" and Postwar Austrian Society (1945-1955)[1]

Ingrid Bauer

Preliminary Remarks

The point of departure of this paper is the postwar period, the decade following the liberation and occupation of Austria by the Allies. The year 1945, however, constituted a historical break only in a partial sense—National Socialist patterns of thought and basic attitudes continued to provide the undertone. It was only with great emotional difficulty that many Austrians were able to grasp the fact that their defeat in World War II could have been, simultaneously, an act of liberation. Thus, in view of the long-term psychological consequences, National Socialism and war were far from being over.[2] An additional consequence included the precarious state of the basic infrastructure in a country in which systems for providing foodstuffs, consumer goods, and energy had almost completely collapsed. In this scenario of prolonged privation and *weltanschaulicher* disorientation, there grew a sentimental need for harmony and order. Restorative social strategies were employed to cope with this crisis, and Austrian society grasped hold of conservative traditions and models going back to the bourgeois philosophy of gender relationships of the nineteenth century.[3]

From this postwar period, I have selected a seemingly marginal phenomenon, that of the so-called *Besatzungsbräute* and particularly the "GI brides" for examination. Why? The various types of relationships which Austrian women shared with occupation soldiers who were stationed on Austrian territory between 1945 and 1955 were the leading conversational topic during the early postwar years. Although there were contacts and acquaintanceships in the French, English, or Soviet occupation zones as well, the occurance of "occupation relationships" was most common in the U.S. zone. However, women who did take up contact with GIs often encountered the hostility of the local populace. They were labeled "dollar floozies," "gold diggers," "choco-ladies," "Yankee tarts," "Salzach geishas," or "girls and women of a certain sort," regardless of the actual nature of their relationships.[4]

The emotionally charged nature of those contemporary discussions, made blatantly clear in numerous newspaper articles and letters to the editor, position papers issued by Catholic bishops, police reports, Department of Health files and other sources,[5] has not subsided up to the present day. Many oral history interviews I conducted made it obvious that even in the reminiscences of many postwar Austrians— male as well as female—the actual event is tightly interwoven with social interpretation.[6] The *Besatzungsbräute,* particularly the "GI brides" we are examining here, were quite obviously a multifaceted object on whom the projections of others were ascribed. Thus, by ana- lyzing the highly charged, often irrational discussions and discourses that raged about these women, we can get an idea of the mental structures and unconscious fears of postwar Austrian society.

At the same time, by examining this concrete historical scenario, the "rules of the game" of the culturally imagined system of gender roles are once again displayed for us. These are roles in which "the wo- man" is conceived as "the other" and is thereby made into a receptive field for the social processes of cleavage and projection. The "GI brides" were, in an extraordinary way, predestined to be receptors of such collective distortions of perception. In the following remarks, I will present hypotheses and considerations to make it clear why that was so.

The Specific Nexus of Woman and Nation

Feminist scholars have long discussed the complex interrelationship of Woman and Nation in the specific context of bourgeois societies— an interrelationship which does not involve actual women as social individuals, but rather one produced by means of categories of femininity and masculinity as constructs of a descriptive system.[7] The American historian George L. Mosse has perceptively shown that of greatest significance in this connection is the fact that nationalism, in all its various shadings, has constantly entered into an "alliance with bourgeois morality." Nationalism, and thus the "most powerful and potent ideology of modernity," employs the image of the "chaste woman" in order "to demonstrate its own virtuous goals,"[8] and subsequently stylizes her into the "protectress of the continuity and the immutability of the nation" and into the "embodiment of its morality."[9]

In this context of nation, women also demarcate the boundaries of the community.[10] It was precisely this symbolic barrier, based upon the elements discussed above and established in the political context of the postwar era in Austria, which was obviously regarded as jeopardized by the trespasses of the "GI brides." On one hand, contacts between Austrian women and GIs were interpreted as a threat, a "dropping out" of the hastily erected collective national identity during the difficult time of postwar reconstruction. The slogan "We Austrians," serving the formation of national identification, was propagated primarily from above by the new political elites.[11] From below—in the perception of the general population—the lifestyle of the "GI brides" was widely regarded rather as a betrayal of the so-called *Volksgemeinschaft*, whose feelings of solidarity and fellowship had been formed in and by National Socialism and which, as an emotional model, had by no means been completely eliminated.[12] In this overall context, the U.S. occupation troops were only very seldom regarded as "liberators." Much more frequently, they were looked upon as "the former enemies," as "the victorious foreign soldiers" or as "the new occupation force"—a reference to the annexation of Austria by Germany and to the denial of their own shared guilt through the portrayal of Austria as Hitler's first victim.[13]

These are patterns of thought which promoted the transformation of the GI bride into "the other": a negative myth, an evil woman. The underlying principle of this process of splitting is not new. It runs through the traditional construction of femininity. However, to the well-known and, so to speak, timeless juxtapositions of "Madonna and witch," "virgin and whore" and "wife and seductress" can now be added a concrete historical example from the year 1945: the antithetical pairing of "loyal wife of returning war veteran and perfidious *Besatzungsbraut.*" Simultaneously, after 1945, the faithlessness or honor of women was repeatedly linked to the still fragile Austrian identity, and conversely, the honor of Austria with that of its women. A good example of this is provided by a letter to the editor published

in 1946 by *Pinzgauer und Pongauer Zeitung*, a regional weekly
newspaper in the U.S. occupation zone:

> Concerning the chocolate girls: We have nothing against the
> occupation powers. But no one can blame us for publicly
> showing our contempt for those women and girls who have
> dragged our honor into the dirt, and to an extent going far
> beyond everything that our returning veterans could witness in
> any other country. This problem should not be left up to the
> men alone. It is those very women and girls who, thanks to
> their good sense, have upheld their honor until now who
> should be a bastion of strength and openly vent the disgust felt
> for these others. Boycott all those who besmirch your honor
> and that of your family and drag Austria's good name into the
> dirt.[14]

A similar nexus of proper sexual national behavior applied to Man
and Nation does not exist. The relationships of *Wehrmacht* soldiers
with women in countries that had been occupied by the Third Reich
were never discussed in this context. Another letter to the editor of the
above-mentioned Salzburg weekly is one of the few exceptions. It is
significant to note that it is an U.S. soldier fluent in German who
breaks through the one-dimensional emotional outburst by the
Austrians and at the same time succinctly names one of those sources
from which it is fed:

> The ex-soldier who condemns girls because they go out with
> Americans knows as well as I do what took place in the lands
> that were overrun by Hitler. Is he trying to shift the respon-
> sibility for this from his gender to the other? Figures prove that
> more children were born out of wedlock to French girls and
> German fathers (to say nothing of other countries occupied by
> Germany) than was the case with all the other occupation
> armies put together.[15]

What is referred to here is a type of "guilt transference" away from
the (male) front and back to the (female) home front, with a personal,
though perhaps also ideological, exoneration as its background. After
all, World War II was also a campaign conducted under the banner of
"racial purity" based upon the *Weltanschauung* of National Socialism.
Helke Sander and Barbara Johr dealt with the facts of "rape,
prostitution and intimate relationships to women in 'enemy territory,'"[16]

which had previously been well-kept secrets with respect to the German Army, and made them for the first time the subject of scholarly research which included quantitative results.

Stigmatizing Non-conformist Women as a Nationalistic Tradition

The fact that the common, everyday behavior of women may be construed as a transgression of fundamental national ideological principles has as long a tradition as does the public stigmatization of this behavior. That applies as well for the pattern which the proscriptions of these infractions takes. This can be shown through two Austrian examples.

First, the so-called "Russian lovers" of the First World War, who carried on relationships with Russian prisoners of war despite the threatened repressive measures, are once again proof of the fact that, in day-to-day life, loyalty to a *vaterländischen* policy of aggressive warfare is by no means without exception. The stigmatization, often in addition to several months imprisonment, was always aimed at the core of female honor and integrity—the prosecuting political authorities posted public notices in the convicted woman's community, naming her as one who had "engaged in intercourse with a prisoner of war."[17]

Second, during the Second World War, the National Socialist regime went one step further: the maximum penalty which threatened women who carried on love affairs which "did not conform to national standards" was a concentration camp sentence.[18] Thus, the National Socialists had further tightened the restrictive corset of "proper" femininity in keeping with women's responsibility for "racial purity." Here as well, the central element of discrimination was public denunciation, which was, however, no longer merely dictated from above, but was carried out with the energetic support of the populace. Thus, for example, a Nazi party bulletin published by the Salzburg district headquarters in January 1940 reported that:

The *Volksgenossin...*, a resident of Markt Pongau, entered into a sexual relationship with a Pole. She has thereby committed an offense against the purity of German blood and the German people. The *Volksgemeinschaft* has punished her accordingly: her hair was cut off and she was placed in the public pillory."[19]

During the time after 1945, there continue to be reports of kangaroo courts dispensing people's justice although this was a rather isolated phenomenon and generally occurred spontaneously. Their targets then were "GI brides." In several cases, these women had their hair cut off, an age-old sign of disgrace that had been revived by the National Socialists when it came to punishing a girl who had gotten involved with prisoners of war or so-called foreign workers.[20] The treatment accorded "GI brides," though, was by no means total discrimination and took place, above all, through the use of verbal attacks and social exclusion.

The "GI Bride" as an Object of Projection: The Social-Psychological and Ideological Underpinnings of an Aggressive Critique

Traditional patterns of thinking as discussed above obviously made it difficult for many postwar Austrians to accept the "GI brides'" lifestyle and to understand it for what it actually was: one of many individual attempts to make a fresh start—psychically, materially, *weltanschaulich*—in the aftermath of the deficits, privation, losses, and overwork of wartime. Naturally, the hierarchical nature of the relationship between "occupier" and "occupied" as well as the obvious material differences between the U.S. troops and the Austrian population made the establishment of contact with an U.S. GI a dangerous matter. The Austrian woman was balancing on the razor's edge between the hoped-for autonomy and sexual subjugation. But that's another story. My subject in this paper is the "GI bride" as a figure of projections, that is to say, as a stereotype. As such, she performed—beyond the concrete reality of her own life—a socially stabilizing function: as a projection screen for postwar anxieties and scapegoat for emotional cleavage (*Platzhalterin für das Abgespaltene/Verdrängte*).

In what forms of discourse, with what images and phantasms, was the "GI bride" then construed? Which fears and conflicts were socially embodied by this construct? The central metaphor surrounding the "GI brides" was that of the whore who sold her honor—and, thereby, Austria's as well—for a piece of chocolate.

To provide just one example, the bishop of the city of Linz made this issue one of the topics of his New Year's sermon in 1945. In doing so, he opened up a sad chapter in the chronicle of recent Austrian history, he said, and one which he had already addressed on many other occasions. He then posed the question of what sort of stories the men of the U.S. Occupation Forces would tell about Austria once they had returned home. The bishop voiced high praise for Austria's culture, its beautiful scenery and many other good qualities. But he was ashamed "that the number of those who would exchange their female honor and integrity as widows in return for a bottle of champagne, that the number of those who would sell their maidenly virtue for an American chocolate bar is disgracefully high."[21] In the postwar period, liaisons involving Austrian women and U.S. soldiers were stigmatized in this way regardless of whether the true nature of the relationship was a love affair, a flirt, courtship prior to matrimony, so-called prostitution as a means of survival, or actual prostitution itself. Let's now take a look behind this polemical facade.

The discussions surrounding the "GI brides" were driven forward most intently by returning World War II veterans. In the raging debates that were carried on over the course of months in the letters-to-the-editor columns of various postwar media, they expressed their infuriated, shocked, and bewildered opinions. As social-historical scholarship and biographical research on the subject of postwar Austria has convincingly shown, the military defeat had directly impacted the feelings of self-worth and sense of male identity of many former *Wehrmacht* soldiers, and left a deep and lasting impression on their patterns of perception.[22] This induced them to interpret the existence of "GI brides" as a destruction of their last remaining position of power—as the loss of their hereditary property rights to "their women." In this interpretational horizon, the occupation had not only a military-political dimension, but a threatening sexual one as well.

"The Yanks had an easy time of it," recalled one veteran in an oral history interview. Josef W. had survived Stalingrad, although he had been severely wounded. "Even as men, they were far superior to our soldiers returning hungry and emaciated from POW camps," he remembered.[23] His recourse to a Darwinian explanatory pattern—"Of course, that's the way it is in nature too. When the bucks fight it out, the doe goes to the winner"—permitted him to remain pragmatic in this competitive struggle. Embedding one's own traumatic experiences within a scenario seemingly governed by natural laws imbued them—despite the associated shock and distress—with some sort of sense. In many letters to the editor, though, raw aggression and threats of physical violence were repeatedly articulated, such as the demand for "corporal punishment for these good-for-nothing broads" or for "forced labor camps" for "GI brides."[24] "Such women of the streets should not be permitted to run around loose and drag the good name of our women into the dirt," noted the *Pinzgauer und Pongauer Zeitung* from 1 June 1946. The disparagement of the woman as a whore made bearable the personal threat which they felt as men confronted by the overpowering sexual competition from U.S. occupation soldiers.

The following excerpt from the novel *Marsch zwischen Hölle und Himmel* (*March between Hell and Heaven*), which was serialized in a weekly newspaper in the Province of Upper Austria, reflects an additional facet of the distraught mental processes of many men. The protagonist—an "Austrian" soldier captured by the Americans—observes in the POW camp the following scene involving an American guard and an Austrian woman:

> Could that girl possibly be from here? She just keeps panting "Johnny," and again "Johnny." ...After all is said and done, ya know, we were out there fighting for you too, laying in the mud somewhere between Rostov and the Crimea, between Volchov and Lake Ilmen, between the Dnestr and the Danube. For you too! And nobody can take that away from us.[25]

This almost imploring statement "And nobody can take that away from us," suggests that contacts between Austrian women and occupation soldiers also touched upon a model of repression toward which the psychic balance of many returned veterans was oriented and upon which it relied. The actions of the "GI brides"—and this, of course, is equally applicable to "occupation brides" in the other zones—threatened to relativize the immunizing effects of that "morass of Austrian phraseology"[26] in which participation in the Nazi's aggressive warfare had been mystified as a manly deed, as the defense of the homeland and of women and children. The threatened collapse of this rationalization for an individual's own wartime military service inexorably confronted that man with the true dimensions of that action, with the horrors of World War II, and thus with the "question of meaning" as well. As the explanatory potential of psychoanalytic understanding suggests,[27] one may, however, avoid the potentially explosive confrontation with one's self as long as one projects one's own abyss outward.[28] After 1945, such projections seem to have also been directed at the "GI brides."

The constantly repeated refrain of the day was that the "Americans' whores" were dragging Austria's "honor" into the dirt. Attributions of this kind were not only functional in connection with injured national-patriarchal property rights in the competitive relations between returning veterans and occupation troops. Whoever sought in this way to delegate responsibility for "Austria's honor"—and thus the honor of Austrian men and women—to women alone, sought to rid himself of his entire share of dishonor. This potentially had an enormous exonerative function, in light of the massive entanglement in the violence which had not only been suffered but had also been abetted by active complicity in the Nazi's reign of terror and war—though the loss of Austrian honor in this respect was rarely discussed then. The linguistic invention "peace criminal," as an accusatory label for those "who passively look on at the carryings-on of these sunken women,"[29] is just one additional detail in this process of playing down and eliminating the dark side of the war and *its* crimes.

Thus, subconscious coping mechanisms of the postwar period are exposed by the irrational controversies surrounding the "GI brides." Within this broadly outlined patriarchal discourse, however, there existed several ideological nuances.

As previously mentioned, along routine National Socialist lines of reasoning, the "GI bride" and the *Besatzungsbräute* phenomenon was indirectly denounced as a renunciation of membership in the *Volksgemeinschaft*. The accompanying racist undertones—as the following excerpt from a 1945 pamphlet from the French occupation zone shows—were unmistakable:

> They took five years to achieve victory over German soldiers,
> but he (i.e. the foreign soldier) only needs five minutes for the
> conquest of some Austrian women! ...But just wait, there'll
> come a day when even the Negroes tell you to get lost.[30]

Within the communist discourse, criticism of the "GI brides" was employed as a means of indirectly attacking the United States. In this context, even prostitution became an arena of anti-U.S. propaganda in the emerging Cold War. Around 1947, both the *Österreichische Zeitung* published by the Red Army and the Austrian Communist Party's *Österreichische Volksstimme* intentionally spread the canard that the

U.S. military police were conducting nightly raids to "hunt down women." They wrote that female passers-by were being arrested and forced to undergo examination by U.S. Army doctors; those found to be carriers of venereal disease were immediately tattooed.[31]

On the other hand, Catholic circles, in which female sexuality and autonomy had long occupied an established place within a matrix of beliefs equating them with "filth and shame," were driven into a state of moral panic by the "GI brides." This climaxed in the phantasm that the war had completely demolished "the mighty bulwark of purity" and the slightest sense of modesty on the part of many women and girls. The interpretational standard is a model of gender relationships going back to the nineteenth century which postulates feminine morality as an enobling countervailing pole to masculine action. In light of the extraordinarily fatal historical actualities engendered by National Socialist men consumed by the lust for power and conquest, the appropriate female corrective for the world after World War II was femininity unstained by moral disgrace. This sentimental need for harmony and order in postwar Austria was discussed earlier in this paper.

Last but not least, the fear of change in the social position of women lurked—as, so to speak, an additional patriarchal reflex— behind the wholesale defamatory attacks aimed at "GI brides." The war and the necessity it created to organize a means of survival had influenced the expectations of many women in the direction of greater independence. The "GI bride" as a social type openly occupied the position of an individual of independent judgment who made up her own mind in the selection of a partner, even going so far as to choose one from the ranks of the former enemies. The wished-for postwar arrangement between the genders, one in which a selfless Penelope waited patiently to care for the wounds of her battle-scarred hero, was thus shattered. In the traditional conception of the woman's role to which restorative postwar Austrian society had taken recourse, there was no place for independent action, self-determination, female eroticism, or the right to the realization of one's own desires and interests.

Certainly, the irrational criticism of "GI brides" must also be regarded in the context of the process of postwar normalization toward which Austria was striving. Among other strategies, calling upon women to sacrifice their professional, social and erotic emancipation contributed to the attainment of this goal. The "GI brides," for reasons of their provocative symbolic impact, were sand in the gears of postwar reconstruction.[32]

NOTES

1. This paper was prepared for and presented at the German Studies Association - Nineteenth Annual Conference, 21-24 September 1995, held in Chicago, Illinois. For further considerations on the subject, see my article, "Die 'Ami-Braut:' Platzhalterin für das Abgespaltene? Zur (De-)Konstruktion eines Stereotyps der österreichischen Nachkriegszeit. 1945-1955," *L'Homme, Zeitschrift für feministische Geschichtswissenschaft* 7 (1996): 107-121.

2. See, for example, Ernst Hanisch, *Der lange Schatten des Staates. Österreichische Gesellschaftsgeschichte im 20. Jahrhundert* (Vienna: Ueberreuter, 1994), 395-398; Siegfried Mattl and Karl Stuhlpfarrer, "Abwehr und Inszenierung im Labyrinth der Zweiten Republik," in *NS-Herrschaft in Österreich 1938-1945*, ed. Emmerich Tálos et. al. (Vienna: Verlag für Gesellschaftskritik, 1988), 601-624.

3. See, for example, Ingrid Bauer, "Frauen, Männer, Beziehungen. Sozialgeschichte der Geschlechterverhältnisse in der Zweiten Republik," in *1945-1995. Entwicklungslinien der Zweiten Republik*, ed. Johann Burger and Elisabeth Morawek, Sonderband der Halbjahresschrift *Informationen zur Politischen Bildung*, ed. Bundesministerium für Unterricht und kulturelle Angelegenheiten (Vienna: Jugend und Volk, 1995), 104-107; Reinhard Sieder, *Sozialgeschichte der Familie* (Frankfurt: Edition Suhrkamp, 1987), 236-242; Siegfried Mattl, "Die Rückkehr der Liebe. Wissensproduktion zur 'Frauenfrage' im Österreich der 40er und 50er Jahre," in *Österreichische Zeitschrift für Politikwissenschaft* 16 (1987): 363-377; Irene Bandhauer-Schöffmann, Ela Hornung, "Trümmerfrauen - ein kurzes Heldinnenleben," in *Zur Politik des Weiblichen. Frauenmacht und -ohnmacht. Beiträge zur Innenwelt und Außenwelt*, ed. Andrea Graf (Vienna: Verlag für Gesellschaftskritik, 1990), 93-120.

4. See Ingrid Bauer and Monika Pelz, "Die verhaßten 'Ami-Huren'," in *Profil*, 9 January 1995, 34-35; Franz Severin Berger and Christine Holler, *Trümmerfrauen—Alltag zwischen Hamstern und Hoffen* (Vienna: Bundesverlag, 1994), 190-194; Johannes Putz, "Zwischen Liebe und Business." Österreicherinnen und Amerikanische GIs in der Besatzungszeit, (M.A. thesis, University of Salzburg, 1995), 61-66.

5. The empirical basis of my considerations was produced during the course of the project "Leben mit den BeFreiern. Geschlechtergeschichte der Besatzungszeit in Österreich" on which I have been working at the *Boltzmann-Institut für Gesellschafts- und Kulturgeschichte/Salzburg* since 1994. Until now, my research efforts have primarily concentrated upon the U.S. and, as a point of comparison, the French occupation zone. Along with biographical interviews of Austrians who lived through the postwar era, my sources include municipial, police, and parish records, daily newspapers, letters to the editor, postwar novels, registry office records, newspapers published for occupation troops by the U.S. Army, etc. In addition, I had available to me documents from the oral history project *Befreit und Besetzt. Salzburg 1945/1955* (commissioned by the Province of Salzburg and headed by Ingrid Bauer and Reinhold Wagnleitner), for which approximately sixty biographical interviews were conducted in 1995.

6. See Ingrid Bauer, "Die 'Ami-Braut:' Platzhalterin für das Abgespaltene?"; Ingrid Bauer, "'Ami-Bräute' - und die österreichische Nachkriegsseele," in *Frauenleben 1945. Kriegsende in Wien: Katalog zur 205. Sonderausstellung des Historischen Museums der Stadt Wien*, ed. Historisches Museum der Stadt Wien (Vienna: published privately, 1995), 73-83; Ingrid Bauer, "'USA-Bräute': Österreichisch-Amerikanische Eheschließungen auf dem Salzburger Standesamt," in *Befreit und Besetzt. Chronik der Stadt Salzburg 1945-1955*, ed. Erich Marx (Salzburg: Pustet, 1996).

7. Thus, it has repeatedly been this "woman as construct" which symbolizes the nation and its ideals , as evidenced by such symbolic figures as the American Statue of Liberty, the French "Marianne" or the German "Germania." However, the concepts of "woman" and national identity display a particularly close mental connection within nationalistic-chauvinistic discourse. In present day Croatia, for example, linguistic images such as "Mother Croatia" are conspicuous in their frequency. Nationalist circles within Croatia, in their criticism of their land's withdrawal from the war in the early 1990's, couched their words in images of "Croatia as a fallen girl." See Ruth Seifert, "Weiblichkeit, kriegerische Gewalt und männliche Macht: Zur Funktion von sexueller Gewalt im Krieg und im Frieden," in *Gewalt gegen FRAUEN gegen Gewalt 2: Tagungsdokumentation*, ed. Johanna Dohnal (Vienna: Bundesministerium für Frauenangelegenheiten, 1994), 182.

8. See George L. Mosse, *Nationalismus und Sexualität: Bürgerliche Moral und sexuelle Normen* (Reinbeck bei Hamburg: Rowohlt, 1987), 111.

9. George L. Mosse, *Nationalismus und Sexualität*, 28.

10. See Ruth Seifert, "Der weibliche Körper als Symbol und Zeichen. Geschlechtsspezifische Gewalt und die kulturelle Konstruktion des Krieges," in *Gewalt im Krieg. Ausübung, Erfahrung und Verweigerung von Gewalt in Kriegen des 20. Jahrhunderts,* ed. Andreas Gestrich (Münster: Lit, 1996), 21-24.

11. See Hanisch, *Der lange Schatten des Staates,* 395-398.

12. See Siegfried Mattl and Karl Stuhlpfarrer, "Abwehr und Inszenierung im Labyrinth der Zweiten Republik," 619-622; Meinrad Ziegler and Waltraud Kannonier-Finster, *Österreichisches Gedächtnis: Über Erinnern und Vergessen der NS-Vergangenheit* (Vienna, Köln, Weimar: Böhlau, 1993).

13. Hans Petschar and Georg Schmid, *Erinnerung & Vision. Die Legitimation Österreichs in Bildern. Eine semiohistorische Analyse der Austria Wochenschau 1949-1960* (Graz: Akademische Druck- und Verlagsanstalt, 1990), 50.

14. The original letter to the editor—in German—can be found in *Pinzgauer und Pongauer Zeitung,* 6 July 1946, 7.

15. *Pinzgauer und Pongauer Zeitung,* 29 June 1946, 8.

16. Helke Sander and Barbara Johr, *Befreier und Befreite: Krieg, Vergewaltigung, Kinder* (München: Kunstmann, 1992), 65.

17. See Ingrid Bauer, "Patriotismus, Hunger, Protest. Weibliche Lebenszusammenhänge im 'Vaterländischen Krieg' - 1914 bis 1918," in *Die andere Geschichte. Eine Salzburger Frauengeschichte von der ersten Mädchenschule (1695) bis zum Frauenwahlrecht (1918),* ed. Brigitte Mazohl-Wallnig (Salzburg: Pustet, 1995), 300.

18. See Rudolf Ardelt, "Individueller Widerstand," in *Widerstand und Verfolgung in Salzburg 1934-1945,* vol. 2, ed. Dokumentationsarchiv des österreichischen Widerstandes (Salzburg, Vienna: Österreichischer Bundesverlag, 1991), 359.

19. This quotation, translated from the original German, was taken from *Widerstand und Verfolgung in Salzburg 1934-1945,* vol. 2, 410.

20. Such "hair-cut-off kangaroo courts" were a historical fact documented by numerous oral history interviews which I conducted within the scope of the previously mentioned projects (see Note 5) on the postwar and occupation era. Also see Michael John, "Das Haarabschneiderkommando" von Linz: Männlicher Chauvinismus oder nationalsozialistische Wiederbetätigung? Ein Fallbeispiel aus den Jahren 1945-1948," in *Historisches Jahrbuch der Stadt Linz 1995,* ed. Archiv der Stadt Linz (Linz: published privately, 1996), 335-359.

21. See *Linzer Diözesanblatt,* December 1945.

22. Siegfried Mattl, "'Aufbau' - eine männliche Chiffre der Nachkriegszeit," in *Wiederaufbau Weiblich: Dokumentation der Tagung "Frauen in der österreichischen und deutschen Nachkriegszeit,"* ed. Irene Bandhauer-Schöffmann, and Ela Hornung (Vienna, Salzburg: Geyer-Edition, 1992), 15-23; Siegfried Mattl, "Frauen in Österreich nach 1945," in *Unterdrückung und Emanzipation. Festschrift für Erika Weinzierl zum 60. Geburtstag,* ed. Rudolf G. Ardelt et. al. (Vienna, Salzburg: Geyer-Edition, 1985), 106-107; Irene Bandhauer-Schöffmann and Ela Hornung, "Trümmerfrauen - ein kurzes Heldinnenleben," 111.

23. The interview with Josef W. is among the oral history source materials collected by the project *Leben mit den BeFreiern* (see Note 5). The original audio tapes are in the possession of the author.

24. See *Pinzgauer und Pongauer Zeitung,* 2 February 1946, 5.

25. In *Welser Zeitung,* 1950/6, 11. See as well Johann Schoiswohl, "Der US-Amerikanische Einfluß im Alltag der Nachkriegszeit. Spuren eines Akkulturationsprozesses. Eine soziokulturelle Analyse im Raum Wels - Oberösterreich," (M.A. thesis, University of Salzburg, 1990), 89-95.

26. Ernst Hanisch, *Der lange Schatten des Staates,* 437.

27. I wish to express my thanks to Doris Gödl, a psychoanalyst in Salzburg/Austria, for a number of enlightening conversations.

28. Jean Laplanche and Jean-Bertrand Pontalis, *Das Vokabular der Psychoanalyse II* (Frankfurt am Main: Suhrkamp, 1980), 309.

29. *Pinzgauer und Pongauer Zeitung,* 5 January 1946, 2.

30. The original document—in German—can be found in Klaus Eisterer, "Fraternisierung 1945," in *Dornbirner Schriften. Beiträge zur Stadtkunde*, vol. XIV (Dornbirn: 1993), 29-30.

31. See Monika Pelz, "'Österreich bedauert, einige seiner schönsten Frauen als Kriegsbräute an Angehörige fremder Militärmächte verloren zu haben...' Heiratsmigrantinnen 1945-1955," in *Auswanderungen aus Österreich: von der Mitte des 19. Jahrhunderts bis zur Gegenwart*, ed. Traude Horvath and Gerda Neyer (Vienna: Böhlau, 1996), 387.

32. Ingrid Bauer, "Die 'Ami-Braut'- Platzhalterin für das Abgespaltene?" 119-121.

Rights At Last? The First Generation of Female Members of Parliament in Austria[*]

Gabriella Hauch

> *Get the men out of the Reichstag!*
> *Get the men out of Parliament!*
> *Get the men out of the Upper Chamber!*
> *We'll turn it into a house of women.*[1]

In June 1926, Claire Waldoff, who was well-known in Berlin's cabaret scene as *Kodderschnauze* ("Saucy Tramp"), made a recording of this song by Friedrich Hollaender, who had made a name for himself as the composer of the music for the film *The Blue Angel*. At the time, the words seemed to take stock of seven years of women's suffrage in the Weimar Republic—even though the song may have been intended to be ironic. In Berlin in the 1920s, long before discussions of quota regulations and the strategies that women could use to claim their place in the male domain of institutionalized politics began, radical demands were being put forth in song:

Get the men out of this existence!
Get the men out of here!
Get the men out of there!
They should have been long gone!
Get men out of the whole construction, and get the women in.[2]

* This is the revised version of my habilitation lecture delivered at the University of Linz on 3 October 1996. I am grateful to Rudolf G. Ardelt, Ingrid Bauer, Karl Fallend, Ernst Hanisch, Reinhard Kannonier, Roman Sandgruber, and Anton Staudinger for their suggestions and criticisms which improved this essay. Special thanks to Aileen Derieg, who translated the article into English.

What was being propagated here was not harmonious cooperation and the justice of gender equality: the radical either/or of the idea of difference was being taken to the extreme. Only the unconditional exclusion of men from parliamentary spaces and their replacement by women would be able to guarantee sociopolitical improvements. Although this position was adopted only by a small minority, it was still good enough for the lyrics of a critical, ironic popular song at the time. It led directly into the emotionally charged field of women and politics as it had been developing over several years in countries in which universal women's suffrage had become the issue. The elimination of political gender difference involved not only the continuing effect of the norms, the mentalities, and the associated inclusions and exclusions connotated by this difference, but this sociopolitical turning point was also accompanied by a reconstitution of differences—distinguished not only along gender lines, but also within the genders as well. The women representatives felt themselves under obligation to different world views, to different factions of their parties. They were of different ages and had been elected to Parliament from different parts of the republic; they were from different classes and belonged to different religions. Yet there was one essential stance that they had in common: they defined themselves according to their gender as females and regarded the link between their gender identity and their political function as self-evident. At the same time, however, they were aware of the differences among them. In other words, the way they maneuvered and played on the parliamentary stage was distinct from their postulated similitude.

This central thesis will be explained in the following article on three levels. The questions, through which a gender-oriented political history could be given new directions, will be illustrated on the basis of two political spheres from Austria's First Republic: education and social policy. The issue of the political domains, the sphere of activity, focuses on the protagonists in the legislative assembly, the National Council.[3] The context of the lives of the first generation of female representatives will be analyzed on the basis of prosopography to identify the political precondition specific to women. Although this generalizing view cannot replace biographies based on qualitative methods, it very clearly illustrates gender-specific facets in the careers of female and male politicians.

First of all, however, several aspects of the discussion of a reorientation in the writing of political history and its relationship to gender history and women's history should be considered.

Toward a Gender-Oriented Writing of Political History

In recent years, the hows, the whys, and the wherefores of the writing of history have been heatedly debated, not only among the protagonists of the discourse on the "end of certainties" that is subsumed under the term postmodernism.[4] The discussion of extending social history or of social history vs. historical cultural anthropology,[5] which is beginning to extend to the writing of political history, is also included in this debate. *Toward a New Understanding of Writing Political History* is not only the subtitle of Maurice Agulhon's collection of essays *Der vagabundierende Blick,*[6] but also a proclamation. Agulhon states a case for a political historiography that is open to the interplay of the spheres of everyday life, symbolic representation, mentalities, and the socioeconomic dictates of order. According to Agulhon, the political is this exchange per se, rather than the arena in which the exchange takes place. Although this fascinating approach is still a "work in progress," it seems inspiring as a leit motif for future works and particularly for discussing the political writing of history. However, Agulhon's ideas are oriented to the common understanding of politics, the Age of Enlightenment's concept of politics with respect to the Modern; this means that in terms of the conception, the constructors, and the beneficiaries, it is a masculine project.[7] The androcentrism that is expressed in both a manifest and a latent exclusion of women became the structural characteristic not only of state politics, but also of the history that recorded, interpreted, and analyzed them. In his conception, Agulhon also succumbs to what merely appears to be gender neutrality.

The field of economics should also be included in the analysis of the transformation from the pre-modern patriarchal domestic social structure to the modern social structure with its only seemingly gender-neutral institutions. The sphere of economics was separated from the household and transferred to the market of a monetarily determined exchange of services; this was simultaneously accompanied by a broad range of consequences for women and their spaces in society.[8] The construction of the asymmetrical "gender order" was intertwined with this extremely complex development. The two poles, between which the gender relations of modernity oscillate, were formed by a biologically defined gender difference on the one hand, and androcentric blindness to gender on the other.[9] Together, these poles formed a central—latent or subconscious—paradigm at the beginning of modern science, which also applied to the historical sciences.[10]

Androcentrism has often been explained and justified by the argument that the abstract notions of politics, state and institutions are supported by the gender-neutral concept of "citizenship." Since the normal and legitimate structures of power overlaid the relationships of power and impotence that may actually be experienced in everyday life, these seem to disappear. However, citizenship's "subliminal, unspoken text of gender,"[11] that is nevertheless effective in these relationships, has been decoded by feminists, especially by women philosophers, sociologists, and theorists of jurisprudence, particularly those from Anglo-Saxon countries.

The inequality between men and women that is legally and socio-culturally linked to norms is based on the prioritized position of the male individual. For the Habsburg monarchy, this meant that pre-modern patriarchal regulations were legally defined as gender differences in the *Allgemeinen Bürgerlichen Gesetzbuch* (*ABGB: The Civil Code*) from 1811 and later in the various regulations for associations:[12] the ideal type of the "citizen-man" became the head of the family and an individual able to engage in politics, and citizenship became a legal and a social category.

This is the central thesis for the discussion of a modern political history: gender and modern politics mutually construct(ed) and condition(ed) one another. Consequently, politics can no longer be thought of or historically researched without taking into consideration this gender-specific component. The endeavor to change the theory of citizenship must be included in the discussion of writing political history, in order to overcome the modern division into citizen/man and woman.[13] Reflecting on the gender-specific construction of politically empowered and non-politically empowered members of the same national society would in itself lead to new perspectives—in addition to the equally effective inclusions and exclusions based on social, ethnic, and religious criteria. This would be the case, for example, if the history of the effect of gender relations was automatically included; thus it would also be included in the writing of political history.

According to Karin Hausen, the ideological foundation for the construction of the system citizenship-politics was formed by the dichotomization of the characters of gender. Norms were extracted and essentialities were constructed from perceptible differences and from the division of labor between men and women. This means that the process of modernization brought a redefinition of gender differences with hierarchically structured access to society's spheres of activity. The result was the constructed division of society into a masculine public sphere and a feminine private sphere. Following the anthropological turning point described by Jürgen Kocka in German-language historiography, the so-called private spheres have been granted a scientific location within the framework of social history and the history of experience and everyday life. This is less predominant, however, in structural history and in political history.

A further central approach in discussing renewal in the writing of political history results from problematizing the social dichotomization into the public and the private. However, this does not mean that reassigning the private to the public—where freedom and equality are supposed to be able to develop—would cancel out the gender-specific asymmetries of power which are always combined with social and ethnic differentiations. On the contrary, in many cases the quietness of private life offers women more protection of their identity in the face of gender-specific power relationships. Leaving private life would prove perilous. For example, Helene von Druskowitz, born in 1856, one of the first Austrian women to study in Zurich, ended her days in a lunatic asylum. Although she had a doctorate in literature and wrote excellent analyses and essays on the situation of women, she literally broke down under social pressure and the material concerns with which she was confronted as an unmarried writer with no financial security from her parents.[14] Public hearings on sexual harassment, such as the case of Anita Hill in the United States, or the so-called "groping affair" in Austria, have also shown that the women involved were stigmatized as culprits for having broken the informal code that prohibits sexuality or sexual activities in the public sphere. The prominent male perpetrators, on the other hand, were little affected by the affairs.[15]

One way to set the scene for writing political history would be, for example, to pose the following questions in order to define the boundary between public and private as a permeable separation and, at the same time, to distinguish the oscillating intermediate zones.

In light of the associations of men that have formed the public sphere, the centers of power, can it be appropriate to continue to use the term public sphere as though it was gender-neutral? To what extent does the gender-specific inclusive and exclusive character of associations of men also include masculine private traits? Or, how do the links between the mutual conditioning of masculine political concepts, political structures, and the specifically male culture of social interaction, that is widely characterized by sexism with regard to female colleagues, function?[16]

These considerations of the political and historical concepts of citizenship and the public and the private sphere clarify possibilities and provide starting points for centrally integrating the category of gender/gender relations in political history, including the parliamentary system.[17]

Political Spheres from a Gender-Specific Perspective: Social Politics and Education

In Anglo-American countries, attention was focused on the question of women's role in political institutions as early as the 1960s and 70s. Women's studies in German-speaking countries, on the other hand, emerged from a political movement that radically questioned the institutionalized means of politics and legal systems. Feminist autonomy as a political agenda, therefore, meant not only being self-determined and self-responsible—in other words, defining one's own life independently of the "other" sex's power of definition—but also, at least partially, rejecting the traditional, middle class, democratic rules of the game and participation in institutions such as political parties and parliaments. For this reason, it is possible that the analyses and academic endeavors to define the genderedness of state constitutive institutions began later in German-speaking countries than in Anglo-American ones.[18]

Even though the history of women's movements is considered a "classical field" of historical women's studies in Austria, this is primarily directed to the study of women and their associations and only rarely addresses gender relations in parties or political milieus.[19] However, this deficit in the current state of research also applies to modern historical studies of political parties in Austria aside from the questions specific to gender studies and women's studies. In some cases, political scientists are venturing into the field of historiographic contemporary history.[20] As a field of study, the area of "women and politics" has been structured along the lines of the following fields of research:

* exclusion and opportunities for participation;
* opportunities and extent of women's legitimized activities in recognized associations;
* the consequences of their limitations for the process of acculturation, especially feminine culture vs. adapting to masculinity; and
* encountering, taking over, questioning, and redefining traditional definitions of politics.

Before 1918, the period that has been most thoroughly researched,[21] most women's movements were motivated by the demand for "gender equality," which rejected neither homogeneous conceptions of masculinity and femininity nor differences between the genders. Regardless of the political positions taken, all of the activities in these associations should be regarded as transgressing the boundaries of family life, stepping into the public sphere. Thus, these were eminently political actions—even though mostly charity work was concerned.[22]

Because women were conceived of as the female sex, they reacted, though members of varying social classes and representatives of diverse ideological orientations, by forming a collective identity specific to women. This happened despite considerable stumbling blocks created by legal regulations for associations: For example, when the first (Social Democratic) "Viennese Association for the Education of Female Workers" made a second attempt to constitute itself in 1889, it was required to explicitly renounce all political endeavors in a separate paragraph in order to receive permission for constitution. The "General Austrian Women's Movement," the radical wing of the bourgeois women's movement, did not receive permission to found its association until after three unsuccessful petitions in 1893.[23] At the same time, some sections of the bourgeois women's movement regarded themselves as the sex that could better and more ably manage state affairs. The collective identity of "we women" has always broken down into individual active women representing diverse interests, that—based on the attribution of being the unequal sex—joined together through demands such as those for active and passive voting rights and equal educational opportunities.

Following the constitution of the First Republic in 1918, which took place in a socially revolutionary situation, the formal legal exclusion of women from institutionalized political spaces was abolished. At that point, debates on strategies for guaranteeing the full participation of women in the formation of public opinion and in decision-making processes became concrete: as long as differences are ignored, the structures that discriminate against women can be hidden and reinforced. At the same time, however, there are also cases where emphasizing differences may obscure discrimination. In other words, equal treatment, for example in allocating resources, does not always meet the requirements of justice. Although women who were active at the beginning of the Republic had not (yet) been confronted with these experiences, several of them, such as Therese Schlesinger,[24] were certainly aware of this double constitution of gender relations.

In many cases, actually living in equality created disadvantages due to the power relationships of gender that were not only based on written rules, but which also characterized mentalities and abilities. As members of the institution that represented the political system— parliament—the women were confronted with the fact that they were dealing with a one-sided male creation, and they had to deal with the consequences of that fact. Anna Boschek, a Social Democratic union member and member of the committee for social policy throughout the First Republic, thus described how difficult it was for her, with only four years of grammar school education, to maintain her position in debates on legislative proposals against her lawyer colleagues. All through long nights, she had to "sink [her] teeth into...the cursed legalese of outmoded laws...at the same table with venerable crown lawyers."[25] Women were not permitted to study jurisprudence until 1919. Considering this mixture of equality and difference, Nancy Fraser's definition of "gender equality" as a "multivalent" term can only be affirmed. The elimination of the political gender difference signified not only a continuation of the norms (inclusion and exclusion) connotated therein, but also the beginning of a new constitution of difference(s).

The women who were politically active had to weave a network covering these structural links between politics and gender, by which the range of their possible actions was made clear. On the one hand, they aimed to achieve concrete goals specific to women's needs, and on the other hand, to work for more women per se in political functions. In this way, the first female members of Parliament intended to intervene in existing gender relations and change the asymmetrical power structures on the level of institutionalized politics through parties and parliament—in other words, to engage in "classical" women's politics. In this endeavor, they encountered the link between gender and politics within power structures, the symbolic order, and within concrete political spheres.

The area of welfare/public relief/social policy is considered one concrete political sphere, in which the theory of structural links between gender and politics has been most widely verified in feminist research to date.[26] This involves the area in which the progressive takeover of reproduction (reproductive work) on the part of the state has been repeatedly demanded by women or respectively criticized or attributed to women—as a characteristic of the modernization process. Results of research in this field have identified a three-step process: the state welfare institutions are recognized as not being entirely positive for women's lifestyles, that is, easing the burdens of everyday life and ensuring material means, but rather are analyzed additionally as instruments of control and discipline. Finally, an analysis can be made on the basis of social policy as to the way in which these institutions continue to influence the structure, maintenance, and reformation of gender roles.

Although women were disproportionately affected by poverty, self-help movements that did not start within the sphere of production, such as the Consumer Cooperatives,[27] as well as the institutions of the social state, were primarily oriented to the needs of men. Men's different position in working life, their more continuous state of employment and their legally defined primary status as "head of the family" throughout all social classes formed the basis for the social insurance systems that were developed.[28] The intention behind this development was not necessarily discriminatory. Even the criteria that were neutrally formulated encountered gender-specific differences in life situations and pushed women into the "second social net." Thus the introduction of "support for the unemployed" in 1918, which was linked to twenty weeks of employment and verification of health insurance for the period before the First World War, was not effective for many women because they were employed primarily in occupations that did not have health insurance.[29]

The new system of insurance that contributed to the social integration of previously marginal social classes also transformed the hierarchy of the bourgeois family model within gender-specific social insurance law. However, the dichotomy of the public and the private sphere must also be newly and differently discussed in the context of social security and reproduction. Support that was no longer granted by public means in times of crises was replaced by private support. Attempts were also made to compensate for the sinking standard of living, particularly among the middle classes, through an increase and diversification of women's employment. It is evident in speeches made by Pan German women members of Parliament that this was the case in Austrian cities, particularly in Vienna in the 1920s, when wives of civil servants concealed their supplementary employment from their husbands; this also essentially determined the nationalist Pan-German women's politics. These members of Parliament attempted to call public attention to this "private" sphere and thus politicize the issue.[30]

The second area in which the structural intertwining of politics and gender is to be considered is the issue of educational policies. This political sphere, which was not regarded as being gender-neutral in the First Republic, demonstrates the sociopolitical consequences that are involved. "Knowledge is power" was not merely an arbitrarily chosen motto for the early workers' movement which sought more rights within the framework of bourgeois society. Education and knowledge provide a basis for changing the status quo, for examining various opportunities. For women, learning a profession means economic independence from family and husband. Education and knowledge enable people to form their own opinions and question the opinions of others and thus form an eminently important function for the sociopolitical field.

In the Habsburg monarchy, there were no public secondary schools for girls.[31] The few existing institutions were church or private foundations, which were not granted public status until the twentieth century. The way in which schools for boys were thought of as public and schools for girls as private emerged in the First Republic. In July 1919, with a decree issued by Otto Glöckel, the Social Democratic State Secretary for Education, schools for boys were opened to girls as well.[32] This step was not motivated, however, by the aim of coeducation, but rather due to a lack of money. For budgetary reasons, it was not possible to institute public state secondary schools for girls, so in order to at least formally meet the requirements of equality, the boys' schools were opened to girls. However, a comprehensive women's alliance of women representatives from all political parties represented in Parliament continued to press for the transformation of private girls' secondary schools into public schools. This was combined with a demand that the mostly private teachers from these schools should be granted equal status with their colleagues employed by the state. The argument was based on the statement of equality set down in the Constitution, which would be violated by not subsidizing girls' secondary schools.[33] Although the term private is justifiably used here in the legal sense, the position and influence of these girls' schools should certainly be characterized as public.

The demand for equal educational opportunities for girls and women, particularly since this demand was made by the most varying factions of the women's movement in the Habsburg monarchy, made it demonstrably easier for the female members of Parliament to cross party lines, de-emphasize the considerable differences between them, and establish (women's) education explicitly as a political women's issue.[34] Though other considerations were effective in the background, even for the female politicians of the Christian Social Party, the end—enabling girls to attain a certificate of higher education (*Matura*)—justified the means: coeducation. Even the women who were protagonists of the second parliamentary faction, the nationalist Pan German People's Party (GDVP), which ascribed to the biological-cultural notion of difference and delegated women as representatives in the National Council, found a justification in this exceptional situation for agreeing to allow boys and girls to attend school together, which enabled them to placate their male colleagues in the Party. According to their argument, if public boys' schools were not made accessible to girls, then "Aryan" girls would be disadvantaged and more Jewish girls would receive the benefits of higher education.[35] Attending a private girls' school involved considerably more expense than attending a public school, and it had become part of the tradition of the assimilated, Jewish, Viennese bourgeoisie to enable their daughters to attain a higher education. However, the curricula were increasingly segregated according to gender, and especially the creation of a new type of school, the secondary school for women, and the introduction of cooking as a subject must be taken into consideration in terms of their sociopolitical effect on gender roles.

A Brief Prosopography of the First Women Members of Parliament

Life in Parliament between 1919 and 1934 was influenced by nineteen National Councilwomen of the First Republic who were a small total of the 408 representatives. Nineteen representatives form a quantity that mislead Herbert Matis and Dieter Stiefel in their otherwise excellent pilot study based on quantitative methods, *Der österreischische Abgeordnete* (*The Austrian Representative*—masculine form), to characterize them as a "parliamentary marginal group"[36] and thus not significant enough to be specified as a separate group. In this way, they blocked the way to gender-specific examinations and analytic approaches. A qualitative approach, however, may reveal interesting results about women who, from a gender-oriented perspective, are only *apparently* to be classified as a marginal group.

The percentage of women in Parliament ranged from 4.2 percent to 7.3 percent depending on the legislative period.[37] Seven women belonged to parties that had included the gender difference in their party agendas: four to the Christian Social Party (CSP) and three to the Pan-German People's Party (GDVP). Twelve of the women representatives (in other words the majority) came into the National Council on the election ticket of the Social Democratic Workers' Party (SDAP), which had at least adopted the postulate of equality in its agenda. Specific aspects from the findings of the prosopography of the women representatives are to be examined here: personal life experiences, milieu of origins, period of politicization, education and profession, and marital status. Although these aspects extend beyond the specific environment of Parliament, they had a decisive influence on this environment.[38]

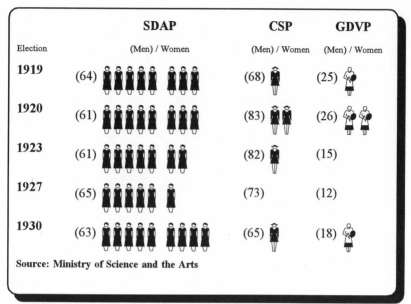

Graph 1:   Women in the National Council 1919 - 1933.

1919	*SDAP:*	Anna Boschek, Emmy Freundlich, Adelheid Popp, Gabriele Profit, Julie Rauscha, Therese Schlesinger, Irene Sponner, Marie Tusch
	CSP:	Hildegard Burjan
	GDVP:	Lotte Furreg
1920	*SDAP:*	Anna Boschek, Emmy Freundlich, Adelheid Popp, Gabriele Profit, Julie Rauscha, Therese Schlesinger, Amalie Seidel, Marie Tusch
	CSP:	Olga Rudel-Zeynek, Aloisia Schirmer
	GDVP:	Lotte Furreg, Emmy Stradal
1923	*SDAP:*	Anna Boschek, Emmy Freundlich, Adelheid Popp, Gabriele Profit, Julie Rauscha, Amalie Seidel, Marie Tusch
	CSP:	Olga Rudel-Zeynek
1927	*SDAP:*	Anna Boschek, Emmy Freundlich, Adelheid Popp, Gabriele Profit, Amalie Seidel, Marie Tusch
1930	*SDAP:*	Anna Boschek, Ferdinanda Floßmann, Emmy Freundlich, Marie Hautmann, Marie Köstler, Adelheid Popp, Gabriele Profit, Amalie Seidel, Marie Tusch
	CSP:	Emma Kapral
	GDVP:	Maria Schneider

The first approach to socialization and politicization experiences is taken by considering the ages of the representatives. A broad general pattern of experiences relating to respective generations may be described in this way. One problem that remains, however, is that there are no findings on the aspects relating to the social class, or milieu of origins, for the individuals.

The oldest representative was the Social Democrat Therese Schlesinger, born in 1863; the youngest was Marie Schneider, born in 1898, member of the German national GDVP. These two women were not only separated by age (35 years) they were also never in Parliament at the same time. Marie Schneider was thirty-two years old and the youngest National Council representative when she entered Parliament; she was also the only woman with an academic degree, and she occupied a position at the second highest level of female functionaries in the NSDAP in Vienna during the National Socialist era.[39] Therese Schlesinger had fought as a feminist activist for the admission of women to universities—and thus also for Marie Schneider—during the last decade of the nineteenth century. She barely managed to emigrate in 1939—for she was a leading socialist from a Jewish background, who was seventy-six years old at that time and seriously ill. Eleven representatives were in their early to mid-forties when they entered Parliament, two were in their thirties, which places them, according to Matis and Stiefel, in the category of "young representatives" in their comparative framework for the First Republic.[40] Six of the female representatives were over fifty. Only one of the women turned sixty during her career in Parliament and is thus considered an "old representative"—although a glance at their male colleagues in Parliament shows that, on the average, women representatives were considerably younger than their male colleagues. Although Matis and Stiefel note the "aging" of the Social Democrats, this does not apply to women.[41] On the contrary, three younger representatives were candidates for the National Council elections in 1930 to replace "older" representatives. Although the economics expert Emmy Freundlich led the debate against the Christian Social and Pan-German representatives single-handedly from 1919 to 1930, after 1930 she was assisted by the new representative Ferdinanda Floßmann.[42]

Half of the National Councilwomen of the First Republic—all of them Social Democrats—had already been politically active in the

1890s. The beginning of their political involvement was thus part of the first upswing of the organized women's movement. Unfortunately, it is not possibly to reconstruct the causes and contexts of actual politicization with the same exactitude for each one of them. For the majority of the Social Democratic women, their families, particularly male members of their families, were influential. Together with their male relatives, they were able to attend political meetings that took place in pubs in the evenings, where "reputable" women would never be seen on their own.[43] The second most important impulse in the politicization of the Social Democratic women was their place of employment. Their husbands, on the other hand, were insignificant in terms of politicization. Most of them were already involved in Social Democratic organizations before they had married. Marriages like that of Gabriele Proft, whose husband was not involved with the Social Democrats, soon ended in divorce.[44]

The politicization of the female representatives of the Christian Social Party and the Pan-German People's Party developed differently. Those belonging to these two parties, who constituted one third of the female representatives, became politicized during World War I in Catholic women's organizations, and the Pan-German network of associations assuming essential functions of state.[45] Only one woman, Marie Schneider, was young enough to benefit from the initial successes of the women's rights movement (in coalition with segments of the liberal bourgeoisie). She attended the Viennese Private Secondary School for Girls (Wiener *Mädchen-Privatgymnasium*), but after receiving her diploma, she was not able to study political science as she wished, because women were not admitted to the disciplines of jurisprudence until 1919.[46] However, even she did not see the introduction of women's suffrage until she was an adult. This means that every one of the female representatives in Parliament during the First Republic had personally experienced women's disfranchisement and limitations on the rights of political assembly—even though not all of them perceived that as a deficit. The SDAP was the first to include the demand for women's suffrage in its party agenda in Brün in 1891, but the CSP and GDVP did not follow suit until 1918, one shortly before the collapse of the Habsburg monarchy, the other during the collapse.[47]

The first generation of Social Democratic representatives who entered the Constitutive National Assembly and the National Council in 1919 and 1920 included women who brought with them decades of experience in political work. These women had particularly extensive experience in public speaking, negotiating, parleying, and formulating agendas and demands, because the Social Democratic women not only had to deal with opposition on the part of public officials, but also on the part of their own comrades.[48] Among these women were the first two "professional female politicians" in Austria: Adelheid Popp and Anna Boschek. Adelheid Popp, with only four years of grammar school education, began working for the Social Democratic women's newspaper in 1893 when she was twenty-four years old. Anna Boschek became the union secretary for women in 1894 when she was twenty years old. In comparison, the women who represented the Pan-German and Christian Social Parties as elected officials from the elections of 1919 and 1920 were less experienced. However, their lack of practical experience was countered, in the first generation at least, by a higher degree of education and the self-confidence of the bourgeoisie.

Following Rainer Lepsius' model for the representatives of the Weimar Republic,[49] almost half of the National Councilwomen of the First Republic, eight out of nineteen and all of them Social Democrats, may be categorized as coming from the proletarian, lower class milieu. Four belonged to the liberal, high bourgeoisie; two of these were from assimilated Jewish families: the Social Democrat Therese Schlesinger and the Christian Social representative Hildegard Burjan. The latter's family background is particularly surprising, since militant Catholic anti-Semitism, in addition to the racist anti-Semitism of the German Nationals, had essentially characterized "Antimodernism" in Vienna since the nineteenth century. Hildegard Burjan's Jewish background was also a central factor that led to the end of her Christian Social political career. It has been reported that Carl Vaugoin, a party colleague and later Minister of the Armed Forces, expressly said before the second National Council election in 1920 that he would no longer be pushed out of his constituency by a "Prussian Jew-sow."[50] After that, Burjan withdrew from party political work, although it was not easy for her. Two of the female representatives, one from the Christian Social Party and one from the Pan-German People's Party, came from a "conservative household," a category that, according to Lepsius, included nobility and also lawyers. The last two women belonged to the category of the Catholic urban middle-class, civil servants. One opted for the CSP, the other for the GDVP. Because of the problematic source material, it was not possible to verify the background milieu of two of the female representatives, Aloisia Schirmer of the Christian Social Party and Lotte Furreg of the Pan-German People's Party. How does the background of these women correlate to their education?

For the representatives from the proletarian, lower-class milieu, the level of education rises with younger women. From the first generation, Anna Boschek, Marie Tusch, and Adelheid Popp had not even completed the entire course of grammar school education. By comparison, Therese Schlesinger would certainly have studied at the university, if she had legally had the opportunity to do so. Aside from Therese Schlesinger and three others, however, all of the representatives were employed before, during, and after their terms in Parliament.

Six Social Democratic women (Anna Boschek, Emmy Freundlich, Adelheid Popp, Gabriele Proft, Amalie Seidel, and Marie Tusch) remained in the National Council throughout the duration of the First Republic. They were all founding members of the women's movement from the 1890s. Not only does this correspond with the theory of the "principle of seniority" and the "permanence of mandates,"[51] it also indicates the character of the SDAP as a modern type of party that took the republican-democratic form of state seriously. It assigned women, or more precisely the party groups representing women, several assured positions—such as the secretary of the women's organization, the women's press, or the women's organization of the Consumer Cooperative. Despite all the resistance to women's demands on the part of large sections of the Free Unions, Anna Boschek's mandate, as the union secretary for women's affairs, was undisputed.

This was not the case in the other parties represented in Parliament during the First Republic. The principle of seniority and the permanence of mandates was not applied in the case of the women who represented the Christian Social Party or the Pan-German People's Party. Rather, a strong fluctuation is noticeable. Only the Christian Social representative Olga Rudel-Zeynek, who was a member of the National Council with a mandate from the Province of Styria, remained in the National Council for seven years and then transferred to the

Federal Council, of which she became the first female president.[52] Between 1927 and 1930, there were no women representing the Christian Social Party or the Pan-German People's Party in Parliament. The quick response of the Catholic women's organization of the Reich and also the Pan-German women's committee of the Reich to this scandalous situation before the parliamentary elections of 1930 demonstrates how well they had learned the political mechanisms of parliamentary democracy. The Catholic women's organization, which numbered about 188,000 members, was not explicitly declared a political organization, but it did indeed represent a political power factor.[53] They made the assured candidacy of a woman a pre-condition for their support in the election campaign, and consequently, Emma Kapral, a teacher from Vienna, took a seat in the National Council.[54] The Pan-Germanic women also mobilized women from the milieu of the women's movement in the First Republic. The bourgeois-liberal Alliance of Austrian Women's Associations and the "Austrian Women's Party" that emerged from it, were moved to cast their vote for the GDVP by the candidacy of the young Marie Schneider.[55]

The lives of only seven of the nineteen women representatives corresponded to what is considered a "normal female biography"[56] (marriage, children, household)—they were married during their political involvement and had, with one exception, children. Such cases illustrate that ideological positions on motherhood and non-domestic commitments do not necessarily correspond to self-chosen reality: the nine-year-old daughter of the Christian Social representative Hildegard Burjan was sent to a boarding school and the young sons of the Pan-Germanic representative Emma Stradal did not present an obstacle to her work in Parliament either.[57] The same was true for the Social Democrats Ferdinanda Floßmann and Marie Hautmann, who both had young children and even commuted to Vienna from Linz and Wiener Neustadt respectively. All of these women delegated the work of keeping house and raising children to housekeepers, or a network of female relatives, including sisters. The other children were already older when their mothers entered Parliament. Particularly for Social Democratic women, it must be noted that children never represented an obstacle to their political activity: Adelheid Popp's children were looked after by her mother and her husband; both Emmy Freundlich and Therese Schlesinger were able to afford domestic help. Only

Amalie Seidel withdrew completely from political work for five years when her three children were born.

However, the lives of the majority of female representatives deviated from the "normal female biography:" more than a quarter of them—five—were divorced. These included not only the Social Democrats Emmy Freundlich, Marie Hautmann, Gabriele Proft, and Amalie Seidel, but also the Pan-Germanic representative Olga Rudel-Zeynek. On official occasions, such as the award of the Golden Cross of Merit of the Republic of Austria on her sixtieth birthday in 1931, Olga Rudel-Zeynek was titled the "widow" of Field Marshal Lieutenant Rudel, even though he did not die until 30 August 1938 in Vienna.[58] Since the Christian Social members of Parliament were instrumental in blocking the divorce reform laws, it would not have been appropriate for them to have a divorced woman as a candidate.[59] Three parliamentary representatives, Marie Köstler, Adelheid Popp and Therese Schlesinger, were already widowed when they entered Parliament; three others, Anna Boschek, Emma Kapral and Marie Schneider, remained single throughout their lives. This means that the majority of female representatives—60 percent—did not live within the confines of marriage during the course of their political function in Parliament. This fact appears to substantiate the theory that single women, i.e., woman who do not need to be concerned with the demanding reproduction work for their husbands and have more time for themselves, gain access more easily to the male-dominated political milieu.

Conclusion

Although an overview of this sort cannot take the place of individual biographies, it suggests trends in the formation of a typical, professional, female politician. These first National Councilwomen represented a new group of political elite, the female segment of the political class. They also suggest the ways in which it should be viewed differentially. Their acceptance depended on the respective political fields in which they were involved and the respective special interest groups that elected them. The more explicit their role of gender difference was in the individual political spheres, the more easily they were able to maintain their position within their parties and take their places in Parliament as speakers, drafters, or signatories of legislative proposals. Historical scholarship oscillates between two poles, of which historians should be aware: on the one hand, through the transmission of what has been forgotten, readers are presented with something new, which leads to a renewed impression of alienation triggering projections; on the other hand, it provides those who make history with a link to today's society, by demonstrating the roots of their everyday actions. This connection between "what is happening now" and "what has happened in the past" becomes particularly apparent in thematic fields that obviously relate to gender relations, such as "women and politics." At the end of this century, achieving a truly democratic and equal share in power for women is still on the agenda. A comparison of the environment of female members of Parliament with that of their male counterparts has yet to be accomplished.[60] In a gender historical survey, however, the theory must be examined, as to whether female members of Parliament provided a male-dominated Parliament with a democratic alibi. This observation has been made again and again by nearly all the female representatives of the Second Republic that I have interviewed[61] in the course of my work on women in politics, and it is based on their concrete practical experiences in Parliament.

Friedrich Hollaender's song quoted in the beginning has not yet lost its meaning.

NOTES

1. This song lyric is by Friedrich Hollaender. In German it reads: *"Raus mit den Männern ausm Reichstag! Raus mit den Männern ausm Landtag! Raus mit den Männern ausm Herrenhaus! Wir machen draus ein Frauenhaus."* Dieter Hildebrandt, "In die Saiten, aufs Pedal. Vor hundert Jahren wurde Friedrich Hollaender geboren," *Die Zeit*, 18 October 1996, 60.

2. *"Raus mit den Männern ausm Dasein! Raus mit den Männern ausm Hiersein! Raus mit den Männern ausm Dortsein! Die müßten längst schon fortsein! Raus mit den Männern ausm Bau! Und rin in die Dinger mit der Frau."* Ibid.

3. The Austrian National Council consisted of 156 representatives in 1919, 159 representatives in 1919/1920, and finally 165 representatives until it was dissolved. They were listed by their parties as candidates, and after 16 February 1919, they were elected in direct, general, equal, secret and free elections by the citizens of Austria. The National Council had legislative

powers and the federal government was answerable to it. The second chamber, the Federal Council, was constituted according to the principle of federation. It was able to object to legislative proposals and delay their passing, but was not able to veto them.

4. Herta Nagl-Docekal "Ist Geschichtspilosophie heute noch möglich," *Der Sinn des Historischen. Geschichtspilosophische Debatten*, ed. Herta Nagl-Docekal (Frankfurt: Fischer, 1996), 7-63. In German-speaking countries, these debates have led to the establishment of the *Österreichische Zeitschrift für Geschichtswissenschaften* 1 (1990), see "Geschichte neu schreiben," ibid.

5. Reinhard Sieder, "Sozialgeschichte auf dem Weg zu einer historischen Kulturwissenschaft?," *Geschichte und Gesellschaft* 20 (1994): 445-468. Hans-Ulrich Wehler, "Moderne Politikgeschichte? Oder: Willkommen im Kreis der Neorankeaner vor 1949," *Geschichte und Gesellschaft*, 22 (1996): 257-266: "Erweiterung der Sozialgeschichte." *Österreichische Zeitschrift für Geschichtswissenschaften* 2 (1991), Wende welcher Geschichte. Ibid. (1992), Kultur suchen. Ibid. 4 (1993), Revisionen.

6. Maurice Agulhon, *Der vagabundierende Blick. Für ein neues Verständnis politischer Geschichtsscheibung* (Frankfurt: Fischer Wissenschaft, 1995).

7. Within the area of feminist political science and feminist philosophy, there has been a boom in recent years in the production of literature, of which the following anthologies and overviews may be representative: Eva Kreisky and Birgit Sauer, eds., *Feministische Standpunkte in der Politikwissenschaft. Eine Einführung* (Frankfurt and New York: Campus, 1995); *Österreichische Zeitschrift für Geschichtswissenschaften* 6 (1995): "Frauen, Geschlechter, Geschichte"; Herta Nagl-Docekal and Herlinde Pauer-Studer, eds., *Politische Theorie, Differenz und Lebensqualität*, (Frankfurt: Suhrkamp, 1996); Institut für Sozialforschung Frankfurt, ed., *Geschlechterverhältnisse und Politik*, (Frankfurt: Suhrkamp, 1994). Sieglinde Rosenberger, *Geschlechter-Gleichheiten-Differenzen. Eine Denk- und Politikbeziehung* (Vienna: Verlag für Gesellschaftskritik, 1996).

8. Barbara Schaeffer-Hegel, ed., *Beiträge zur politischen Theorie* V, vol. 1 of *Vater Staat und seine Frauen* (Moos: Pfaffenweiler 1990); Barbara Schaeffer-Hegel and Heide Kopp-Degethoff, eds., *Studien zur politischen Kultur*, vol. 2 of *Vater Staat und seine Frauen* (Moos: Pfaffenweiler, 1990).

9. Claudia Honegger, *Die Ordnung der Geschlechter. Die Wissenschaft vom Menschen und das Weib 1750-1850* (Frankfurt and New York: Campus, 1991).

10. Examples of this discussion in the current state of research in Austria include Edith Saurer, "Frauengeschichte in Österreich. Eine fast kritische Bestandsaufnahme," *L'Homme. Zeitschrift für feministische Geschichtswissenschaft* 2 (1993): 37-63.

11. Nancy Fraser, "Was ist kritisch an der Kritischen Theorie? Habermas und die Geschlechterfrage" in *Widerspenstige Praktiken, Macht, Diskurs, Geschlecht* (Frankfurt: Suhrkamp, 1994), 174.

12. Gabriella Hauch, "Politische Wohltätigkeit - wohltätige Politik. Frauenvereine in der Habsburger Monarchie 1811-1866," in *Zeitgeschichte* 19 (1992): 200-215; Gabriella Hauch, *Vom Frauenstandpunkt aus. Frauen im Parlament 1919-1933* (Vienna: Verlag für Gesellschaftskritik, 1995), 34-59.

13. Iris Marion Young, "Das politische Gemeinwesen und die Gruppendifferenz. Eine Kritik am Ideal des universalen Staatsbürgerstatus," in *Jenseits der Geschlechtermoral. Beiträge zur feministischen Ethik*, ed. Herta Nagl-Docekal and Herlinde Pauer-Studer (Frankfurt: Fischer, 1993), 267-304. Erna Appelt, "Bürgerrechte - Feministische Revisionen eines politischen Projektes," in *Feministische Politikwissenschaft*, ed. Erna Appelt and Gerda Neyer (Vienna: Verlag für Gesellschaftskritik, 1994), 97-117.

14. At the University of Innsbruck, Petra Nachbaur is writing her dissertation on Helene von Druskowitz.

15. A young woman representative from the Social Democratic faction revealed that the Austrian minister for Social Welfare, also a Social Democrat, had reached into her dress. *Profil*, 6 September 1993; *Profil*, 13 September 1993.

16. In the course of the project "Women in Parliament," I conducted interviews with twelve representatives from the Second Republic on their life histories, which confirmed this. See Eva Rossmann, *Unter Männern. Frauen im Parlament* (Vienna: Folio, 1996).

17. For a discussion of the Second Republic, which takes the First Republic into consideration, see Gerda Neyer "Frauen im österreichischen Parlament: Chancen und Barrieren," in *Frauen in Österreich. Beiträge zu ihrer Situation im 20. Jahrhundert*, ed. David F. Good, Margarete Grandner and Mary Jo Maynes (Vienna: Böhlau, 1994), 77-101.

18. Eva Kreisky, "Der Staat ohne Geschlecht? Ansätze feministischer Staatskritik und feministischer Staatserklärung" in *Feministische Standpunkte*, ed. Eva Kreisky and Birgit Sauer (Frankfurt and New York: Campus, 1995), 203. Eva Kreisky, "Gegen geschlechtshalbierte Wahrheiten. Feministische Kritik an der Politikwissenschaft im deutschsprachigen Raum" in *Feministische Standpunkte*, 27-62.

19. Saurer, "Frauengeschichte," 47.

20. For example, political scientists are currently working on a history of the Christian Social Party in the First Republic. See Anton Staudinger, Wolfgang C. Müller, and Barbara Steininger, "Die Christlichsoziale Partei," in *Handbuch des politischen Systems Österreichs. Erste Republik 1918 - 1933*, ed. Emmerich Tálos et al., 160-176.

21. Saurer, "Frauengeschichte," literature listed in the references. A survey can be found in Harriet Anderson, *Vision und Leidenschaft. Die Frauenbewegung im Fin de Siècle Wiens* (Vienna: Deuticke, 1994); one of the most recent publications on this topic is Gabriella Hauch, "Arbeit, Recht und Sittlichkeit als Themen der Frauenbewegungen in der Habsburgermonarchie," in *Die Habsburgermonarchie: Parteien, Verbände, Vereine*, ed. Österreichische Akademie der Wissenschaften (Vienna: Akademieverlag, 1997). Birgitta Bader-Zaar, "Wahlrecht," in ibid. Renate Flich, "Frauen in Österreich," in ibid.

22. Hauch, "Politische Wohltätigkeit," 200f.

23. The *Vereinsgesetz* (law governing the constitution of associations) of 1867, in Paragraph 30, also prohibited women from founding or joining political associations with or without men. Women nevertheless had opportunities for organizing themselves in charity, educational and professional associations. Joint (political) events were organized as so-called §2 events, to which everyone—men and women—received an invitation. Hauch, *Frauenstandpunkt*, 44.

24. Marina Tichy, "'Ich hatte immer Angst, unwissend zu sterben'. Therese Schlesinger: Bürgerin und Sozialistin," in *"Die Partei hat mich nie enttäusch..." Österreichische Sozialdemokratinnen*, ed. Edith Prost (Vienna: Verlag für Gesellschaftskritik, 1989) 135-184. Hauch, *Frauenstandpunkt*, 311-315.

25. Julie Schneider-Hanusch interview, *Die Frau*, 15 May 1954.

26. Pat Thane, "Wohlfahrt und Geschlecht in der Geschichte: Ein partieller Überblick zu Forschung, Theorie und Methode," *L'Homme. Zeitschrift für feministische Geschichtswissenschaft* 5 (1992): 5-18. Susan Zimmermann, "Das Geschlecht der Fürsorge. Kommunale Armen- und Wohlfahrtspolitik in Budapest und Wien 1870-1914, *L'Homme Zeitschrift für feministische Geschichtswissenschaft* 5 (1992): 19-40.

27. The Austrian Consumer Cooperative, called *Konsum*, played a very important role in ensuring survival after World War I, especially for the people of Vienna. In Austromarxism, *Konsum* was considered the "3rd pillar of the workers' movement" (Karl Renner) alongside the unions and the Social Democratic Party. Gabriella Hauch, "Self-help - Combine - Bankruptcy. Consumer Cooperatives in Austria 1856-1995" in *Labour, Class and Consumption: Consumer Cooperation in Europe and the United States, 1840-1950*, ed. Ellen Furlough and Carl Strikwerda (Lanham: Roman & Littlefield, 1997).

28. Linda Gordon, "Social Insurance and Public Assistance" in *American Historical Review 97* (1992).

29. Stenographic protocol of the Constitutive National Assembly in Hauch, *Frauenstandpunkt*, 137-141.

30. Stenographic protocol of the National Council, Legislative Period I, Assembly 197 on 19 June 1923, 6085-6089, from Hauch, *Frauenstandpunkt*, 148f. On Nationalist Pan-Germanic women's policies see Gabriella Hauch, "Frauenpolitik - Frauenbewegungen in der Ersten Republik" in *Handbuch 1918-1933*, 283-286. Johanna Gehmacher, "'Volksgemeinschaft' der Frauen? Deutschnationale und nationalsozialistische Geschlechterpolitik in Österreich 1918-1938," in *Forschungsbericht des Jubiläumfonds der Österreichischen Nationalbank* Nr. 4319, (Vienna: 1996).

31. Gertrud Simon, *Höhere Mädchenbildung in Österreich. Anfänge und Entwicklungen. Ein Beitrag zur Historiographie und Systematik der Erziehungswissenschaften* (Vienna: Frauenverlag, 1993).

32. Hauch, *Frauenstandpunkt*, 210.

33. Stenographic protocol from the Constitutive National Assembly, 78th assembly, 29 April 1920, 2370-2374 (Therese Schlesinger).

34. Hauch, *Frauenstandpunkt*, 209-237.

35. Gabriella Hauch, "Käthe Leichter, geb. Pick. Spuren eines Frauenlebens," *Archiv für Geschichte der Arbeiterbewegung Wien* 8 (1992): 106f.

36. Herbert Matis and Dieter Stiefel, "Der österreichische Abgeordnete. Der österreichische Nationalrat 1919-1979 - Versuch einer historischen Kollektivbiographie" (Vienna, unpublished manuscript), 18.

37. *Biographisches Handbuch der österreichischen Parlamentarier 1918-1993*, ed. Parlamentsdirektion (Vienna: Österreichische Staatsdruckerei, 1993), 688; this is contradicted by the numbers in Gerda Neyer, "Parlament," 99. She bases her calculations not on the highest number of representatives, but also takes, for example, by-elections into account, thus coming to a different percentage.

38. The findings are based on the evaluation of biographies I compiled on the women representatives. See Hauch, *Frauenstandpunkt*, 241-350.

39. Johanna Gehmacher and Gabriella Hauch, "Eine deutsch fühlende Frau. Die großdeutsche Politikerin Marie Schneider und der Nationalsozialismus in Österreich" in *Frauenleben 1945. Kriegsende in Wien*, 205. Sonderausstellung des Historischen Museums der Stadt Wien (Vienna: Stadt Wien, 1995), 115-132. I am grateful to Johanna Gehmacher for the ongoing discussions dealing with women and politics.

40. Matis and Stiefel, "Abgeordnete," 23.

41. Ibid., 22.

42. Stenographic protocol from the National Council, Legislative Period VI, 39th assembly, 30 June 1931, 1019-1021.

43. Gabriella Hauch, "Der diskrete Charme des Nebenwiderspruchs. Zur sozialdemokratischen Frauenbewegung" in *Sozialdemokratie und Habsburgerstaat, Sozialistische Bibliothek, Abt. 1: Die Geschichte der österreichischen Sozialdemokratie* (Vienna: Löcker, 1988), 104.

44. Marie-Louise Angerer, "Gabriele Proft. 'Faust soll zwischen 1480 und 1580 gelebt haben'" in *"Die Partei, hat mich nie enttäuscht..." Österreichische Sozialdemokratinnen,* ed. Edith Prost (Vienna: Gesellschaftskritik, 1989) 187-223; Hauch, *Frauenstandpunkt*, 294-298.

45. Silvia Svoboda, "Die Soldaten des Hinterlandes," in *Die Frau im Korsett. Wiener Frauenalltag zwischen Klischee und Wirklichkeit 1848-1920* (Vienna: Museen der Stadt Wien, 1984), 50.

46. Hauch, *Frauenstandpunkt*, 316-323. However, Käthe Leichter's biography illustrates that there were also ways to get around this. Leichter, a Jew and a socialist, was born the same year as Schneider, attended the same school, and studied the subjects to which women were not admitted in Austria, or in Germany. Hauch, "Käthe Leichter," 97-123.

47. Birgitta Bader-Zaar, *Das Frauenstimmrecht. Vergleichende Aspekte seiner Geschichte in Großbritannien, den Vereinigten Staaten von Amerika, Österreich, Deutschland und Belgien, 1860-1920* (Vienna: Böhlau, 1997).

48. Hauch, "Diskreter Charme," 101-119.

49. Rainer Lepsius, "Parteiensystem und Sozialstruktur: Zum Problem der Demokratisierung der deutschen Gesellschaft," in *Wirtschaft, Geschichte und Wirtschaftsgeschichte,* ed. Wilhelm Abel et al. (Stuttgart: Klett-Cotta, 1966), 371-393; Christl Wickert, "Frauen im Parlament: Lebensläufe sozialdemokratischer Parlamentarierinnen in der Weimarer Republik," in *Lebenslauf und Gesellschaft: zum Einsatz von kollektiven Biographien in der historischen Sozialforschung,* ed. Wilhelm Heinz Schröder (Stuttgart: Klett-Cotta, 1985), 208-240.

50. Louis Bosmans, "Hildegard Burjan - Leben und Werk," M.A. thesis, University of Vienna, 1971), 77, cited in Hauch, *Frauenstandpunkt*, 251.

51. Heinz Fischer, "Die parlamentarischen Fraktionen" in *Das politisches System Österreichs*, ed. Heinz Fischer (Vienna: Europa-Verlag, 1974), 122ff.

52. Hauch, *Frauenstandpunkt*, 302-307.

53. Franziska Starhemberg, "Die katholische Frauenbewegung," in *Der Katholizismus in Österreich. Sein Wirken, Kämpfen und Hoffen,* ed. Alois Hudal (Innsbruck: Verlagsanstalt Tyrolia, 1931), 309.

54. *Katholische Frauen Organisation* 3 (1932), 1.

55. Jutta Pint, "Die österreichische Frauenpartei 1929-1934," (M.A. thesis, University of Vienna, 1988), 188f.

56. Erika Adolphy, "Einige Gedanken zu der Frage: Was ist eigentlich eine normale Frauenbiographie?" in *beiträge zur feministischen theorie und praxis* 7 (1981): 8f.

57. Hauch, *Frauenstandpunkt*, 254, 337-339.

58. Hauch, *Frauenstandpunkt*, 303.

59. Hauch, *Frauenstandpunkt*, 184-193.

60. This involves a research project financed by the Austrian Ministry for Science, Traffic and the Arts on "Parliamentarism, Political System and Political Elites," which I expect to finish in 1997/98.

61. This reference is to twelve oral histories with representatives from the principal political parties SPÖ, ÖVP, and FPÖ conducted in 1992/93.

Women in the Austrian Economy

Erna M. Appelt

The Short Twentieth Century[1]

If we consider Austrian history during the twentieth century, we can distinguish at least seven periods: (1) the end of the Habsburg Monarchy (until 1914), (2) World War I (1914-18), (3) the First Republic (1918-33/34), (4) the period of Austrian fascism (1933/34-38), (5) the era of National Socialism and World War II (1938-45), (6) the postwar decades and construction of the Austrian welfare state (1945-95), and, (7) Austria's entry into the European Union (EU).

These periods may differ fundamentally in regard to politics and economic policies, yet, in none of these periods has Austria seen a liberal movement in the full sense of the word. In the political as well as in the economic and cultural spheres, a conservative mood in tandem with patriarchal and/or paternalistic attitudes has molded the political and economic institutions of this country. It would go beyond the scope of this essay to analyze all these political and economic changes.[2] However, one of the crucial points here is that the inner-war politics (First Republic, Austrian fascism), by stressing monetary policy, resulted not only in the impoverishment of large parts of the Austrian population due to low wages and high unemployment, but also resulted in additional disadvantages for women. They were not only affected by high unemployment and low wages, but, beyond that, they were removed from certain segments of the labor market by law. The legal rights women had gained after World War I, contrasted sharply with their political and economic options; moreover, substantial rights were undone by the Austrian authoritarian government in 1934.[3]

Thus, I would characterize the first half of this century as a mix of the supremacy of nationalism, class domination, and patriarchal control: during this time, Jewish citizens were expelled and exterminated because they were not considered as "Aryans"; workers were oppressed because of their working class status, and women experienced hardship because they were women (while working class women were oppressed twice both as workers and as women).

After the end of the terror of National Socialism and World War II, there was substantial change regarding politics and economic policy as well as patriarchal control. Austrian politicians found new solutions for old conflicts, above all by the arrangement of the *Sozialpartnerschaft* (social partnership). During the "short twentieth century," the postwar decades (1945-95) were the period of parliamentary consolidation. During the Cold War, Austria had a kind of intermediate position between East and West, and stood as a prime example of a mixed economy. Against this "mixed economy background," the Second Republic—in sharp contrast to the inter-war period—has been successful in shaping economic and political life. Parliamentary governments on state and federal levels were successfully established. In these decades, Austrian politicians established a new cooperation of previously hostile political forces; the clear division in two separate social cleavages, characteristic of the inter-war period, were overcome; the Catholic church and the Social Democratic Party became reconciled, and the unions and the employer associations found ways to cooperate. Until the early 1980s, the rate of economic growth was high, the unemployment rate was low, and the general standard of living of the Austrian population had much improved. The postwar decades didn't even know of the hate and the militancy inherent to the political forces in the interwar period.

However, these changes in politics, economic policy, and patriarchal control, which had benefited many Austrians, coexist with voices stressing the other face of the social and political life in Austria: critical voices contest the interpretation of Austria as the first victim of National Socialism[4]; some voices insist in doubting the quality of the democratic culture in Austria; feminists attack the male dominance within the political parties, unions, associations and within the Catholic Church; female union officials criticize the paternalistic character within institutional arrangements like the "social partnership."

Indeed, the undeniable economic successes of the postwar decades were not paralleled with an equally successful and substantial democratization. Austria's construction of a parliamentary democracy has not been linked with a strong democratic culture. On the contrary, it was accomplished by watering down the importance of democratic self-determination. As many political observers are convinced, "social partnership" goes hand in hand with a lack of a political culture that included democratic conflict which resulted in limiting possible conflicts as well as the discussion of alternative solutions to those conflicts. Thus, we can characterize the postwar decades as a period of successful compromises between the political elites, and a successful management of class conflict, however, without a deeper democratization of society. Gradually, male politicians became more paternalistic instead of patriarchalistic. The Austrian politicians have learned to manage conflicts much better than before, but the hierarchical structures have not fundamentally changed.

What concerns the late 1980s and the 1990s, there is no doubt that many aspects of Austrian society have been "Europeanized." The coalition-government has privatized substantial parts of the state economic sector. In the plebiscite on 12 June 1994, a broad majority of Austrians (66.3 percent of all casted votes) voted to join the European Union. Since 1 January 1995, Austria enjoys full membership in the European Community. As a member of the European Union, Austria has become part of a political union which marches toward a common foreign and defense policy, and a common market of nearly 400 million people.

However, Austria's entry into the European Union and the intended participation in the common European currency (scheduled for 1999) are linked with a neoliberal rhetoric. The globalization of the European economy backs these arguments. Actually, the consequence is a gradual fading away of the Austrian "social partnership," a gradual transformation of the welfare state, and a weakening of relatively high social standards. In the face of these developments, Austria will be confronted with growing unemployment, a growing number of poor people and an increasing discrepancy between the very rich and the very poor. To say it more forcefully, we are witnessing the weakening of social solidarity in Austrian society. Social coherence will take on a new shape, and the familiar model of the welfare state will be transformed.

The following essay about women in the Austrian economy is based on the assumption that the economic and social developments and changes mentioned above have not been and will not be gender-neutral; they have affected and will continue to affect men and women in different ways. In the following discussion I intend: (1) to discuss the position of women in the Austrian economy and social partnership during the last decades, (2) to show how recent and current changes affect women, (3) to investigate the ways Austrian women are answering to those changes.

Women's Position in the Austrian Economy
and Social Partnership

In many regards, the status and the position of women within a national economy mirror their position in the society as a whole. More than other information, economic data suggest the options women and men have in a given society, and bring to light gender inequality. Only with the analysis of economic facts can we assess how dependent or independent women are. By analyzing economic facts we can judge how strong the hierarchy between men and women is.

Compared to other European countries, a patriarchal mentality seems to be widespread in Austria, where patriarchalism has different sources: first, in the traditional bourgeois family model characterized by a strong hierarchy between men and women; second, in Catholicism exhibiting a strong authoritarianism; and third, in traditional *machismo* within substantial parts of the labor movement which is characterized by male chauvinist habits and culture.

The inequality between Austrian men and women is revealed mostly in their economic relationship. This relationship can be found in all afore-mentioned historical periods as well as in all social classes: At the turn of nineteenth century, more and more women entered the labor market as employees, albeit in rather low positions[5]. After World War I, women were supposed to leave their jobs for repatriates of war and later for unemployed men.[6] During the Nazi regime, state policy stated that women were supposed to give birth to children as a gift for the Führer. However, women of the working class were forced to work also. After World War II, women were encouraged to stay at home and build stable families. Finally, compared with the Scandinavian countries, where a strongly corporatist economy has been linked with an egalitarian and women-friendly society, in Austria corporatism has been connected with a non-egalitarian and paternalistic mentality.

However, during the last decades, two groups fought tirelessly against this traditional patriarchalism in Austria: the autonomous women's movement and the women's movement within the Social Democratic Party. Both movements shared the common goal of weakening patriarchal structures within Austrian society, yet, they pursued different strategies. The autonomous movement was strictly antagonistic toward all established political institutions. In contrast, the social democratic women stayed firm to the Social Democratic Party and accepted more limitations than women of the autonomous movement did. In many respects the two movements were antagonistic, nevertheless they needed each other. Because of pressure from the two movements, substantial reforms concerning the legal and social situation of women have been achieved during the seventies and eighties.

Labor Force Participation and Unpaid Work
of Austrian Women

In western societies, paid work seems to be the key to structuring society and gaining rewards and recognition within society. However, this view conceals the economic contribution of unpaid work to our economies and societies, mostly done by women.

In 1995, Austria's working population included 3,808,000 people (or 47.3 percent of the whole population) compared with 1971, 3,133,000 (see Appendices 1 and 2). The number of people participating in the labor force rose from 41.8 percent in 1971 to 47.3 percent in 1995 (see Appendices 3 and 4). Demographic changes and a much stronger participation of women in the labor market influenced this development. Participation of women in the labor force grew from 1,203,000 in 1971 to 1,593,000 in 1991, or from 30.4 percent of the whole labor force in 1971 to 38.4 percent in 1995. More and more women in their thirties and forties have entered the work force. Whereas the participation of very young women and of women aged more than fifty years have been declining similarly to the corresponding shares of men. As a matter of fact, in 1995, 52.7 percent of the population did not participate in the labor force.[7] Despite the changes of the last decade labor force participation of Austrian women is still low compared with Britain, France and the countries (see

Graph 1). Like in other European countries, the Austrian labor market is gender segregated (see Appendix 4).

Today it is obvious to most of Austria's men and women that women must earn money to support the family. Nevertheless, most of the Austrian men do not really equally share the responsibility for housework in the family, for children, and for elderly people. Most of them do not want to change the traditional division of labor between the sexes. On average, Austrian men work one hour and 58 minutes in their own household, whereas women spend four hours and 34 minutes as homemakers.[8] The lower social classes often support a traditional family model, whereas the upper and the upper middle class are partly off-loading housework and care responsibilities on lower class women.

Paternalism within the Social Partnership
The Austrian Social Partnership comprises cooperation among the following organizations: the Austrian Federation of Trade Unions (*Österreichischer Gewerkschaftsbund*, ÖGB), the Chamber of Labor (*Kammer für Arbeiter und Angestellte*) both of them representing the work force; the Chamber of Business (Bundeswirtschaftskammer) representing the employers, and the Chamber of Agriculture representing the farmers. All these organizations are determined by a strict hierarchical manner and paternatilistic mentality. Over decades not only were the top positions of all these organizations occupied by men, but also almost all organizational units were chaired by men as well. In all these organizations there exist women's sections, which are integrated hierarchically. Male officials have maintained this paternalistic arrangement for decades through different ways:

* They have integrated women's sections in the organizations hierarchically.
* They did not abolish male chauvinism in language and behavior.
* Quite often, location and timing of meetings exclude women.

An analysis of the Austrian model of neo-corporatism shows that this institutional arrangement is a masculine and paternalistic one: men are responsible for bargaining with their male negotiating partners while women have only some marginal position within this institution and are excluded from collective bargaining. Women are merely considered as responsible for women's demands within the organizations.

Therefore, it is very difficult for women to gain higher positions in unions and associations.[9] The majority of male officials of unions as well as of employers' associations advocate the division between a male public and a female caring sphere. Women were supposed to be responsible for the families. Women's needs, demands, and interests have been considered as special and divergent within the needs and interests of the working class as a whole. As a consequence, social protection has been easier to initiate and pass than women's demands to change the power structure and their demand for equal opportunities in the economic sphere (see Appendix 5).

Women's Voices within the Trade Union (ÖGB)

The number of unionized women increased from 227,997 in 1946 to 512,077 in 1991 (or an increase of 125 percent). The percentage of female unionized workers has risen from 24.7 percent to 31.7 percent in 1995 (see Appendices 6 and 7).[10]

The women's organization in the ÖGB was established already in 1945 (Statutes and Articles §5.1). However, male officials decided that the committee members and rules of procedure should be determined by the managing committee of the union (*Bundesvorstand*).[11] Thus, women both in the past and in the present, were and are restricted in deciding democratically who will hold responsible positions in the women's organization, because all union officials are appointed by the chairmen of the ÖGB (ÖGB Statutes § 12.3). Moreover, Union's statutes and articles oblige the women's section's secretary to follow the orders given by the union leaders.[12] For decades, the discrepancy between the status of men and women has not been an issue in union discussions. Union politics concerning women have been protective and paternalistic. The official rules of procedure as well as the union statutes consider "the safeguarding, the improvement, and the consolidation of the protection of women and youth workers by legal acts" as primary goals,[13] whereas the abolition of the inequality between the sexes *within* the union is not mentioned. Thus, the key words describing the politics of the ÖGB are centralist and consensus-oriented. As a consequence, voices of dissent were silenced for decades, and we can characterize the Austrian federation of unions as a male-dominated organization with a small niche for women. The women's section has always tried to raise this fact to a political issue. For many decades they have argued against discrimination and the double standards and inequality within the union. However, for many years these protests have been ignored.

It was not before the late 1970s that pressures of the international and of the Austrian women's movements compelled a first revision of the union's statutes: in 1979, the number of the ÖGB vice-presidents was increased to six, and since then, one of these six vice-presidents must be a representative of the women's organization. However, this progress did not change the gender imbalance dramatically. To get an idea of the gender imbalance, we have to consider that, at the same time, the board of directors comprised fifty-three men and only one woman. At this time, 30 percent of all union members were women.

In 1983, union leaders decided to amend the union's statutes again. Since then, three members of the women's organization must sit on the board of directors, whose total number of directors was increased from fifty-three to fifty-nine.[14]

However, a stronger influence of women only led to a slight increase the involvement of women in the upper-echelons of the union. Indeed, only the changes in the statutes caused by external pressures opened the door for women in the top positions in the union. Moreover, male officials always linked the increase of female leadership with an increase of male unions officials, so the ratio did not really change. Ultimately, the share reserved for women reflects in no way the ratio between men and women in membership.[15]

Among the members of work councils 23.4 percent were women, and among the presidents of workers' councils, elected by membership, 15.6 percent were women (see Appendices 7 and 8).[16] We can thus see that women were more successful in gaining elected functions than in getting high positions in the union's bureaucracy. This also applies to companies which employ male and female workers. However, male union leaders avoided appointing women as secretaries at the district or province levels. Female functionaries can only be found in the women's sections.[17]

However, changes in society strengthened the position of women in the ÖGB. Since 1992, the women's section has been developing several strategies to improve the participation of women within the ÖGB.[18] Today the demands for equality and participation and the protests against discrimination are prominent issues within the ÖGB.

In 1995, this topics largely dominated the annual union meeting (ÖGB congress).[19] In 1994, for the first time in its history, the sister organization of the ÖGB, the Chamber for the Employed (*Arbeiter-kammer*), was chaired by a female official, Lore Hostasch.[20]

During the last decades, female unionists achieved many successes. For instance, in the 1970s social democratic policies helped gain substantial improvements for women, and today, there is women friendly rhetoric in the trade union. Nevertheless, male chauvinism exists at all levels of the organization, and most male union officials display paternalistic and protective attitudes toward women's problems and demands. These men are open-minded concerning the social protection of women, but they have difficulties understanding women's demand for full participation in decision-making processes. For almost fifty years the women's section of the union protested direct and indirect wage discrimination. However, the ÖGB, caught in the corset of social partnership, has refused to implement anti-discrimination strategies which would exceed the standards of EU cooperation. The growth participation of women in Austrian politics has not resulted in economic equality for women, and top management and executive offices are dominantly in the hands of men.

Despite the doubling of female unionization since 1946—today a third of unionized workers are women—women are under-represented in functionary positions at all levels. Nevertheless, they are more successful in obtaining elected positions than appointed positions. In 1997 as in 1945, we can characterize the ÖGB as a male-dominated institution which contains some niches for women.

Are Austrian Women Becoming "European"?

Changes in Economy/ Changes in Gender Relations

In Austria, the era of full employment lasted until the 1980s. During the 1980s, more and more neoclassic and monetarist paradigms dominated economic discussions. The economy stagnated (see Appendix 10) and unemployment rose.

Factors as membership in the European Economic Area (EEA) in 1994, and in the European Union in 1995, along with common currency policy (scheduled for 1999), have fundamentally changed the economic situation in Austria. The options for Austrian politicians to shape the economy have shrunken, as the European Union determines the economic policies. To meet the criteria for joining the *Monetary Union*, Austrian Social Democrats and conservatives did not hesitate to cut social benefits substantially. However, the goal of consolidating the national budget will be difficult to realize in an economic situation where substantial growth is lacking. In fact, the economic discourse has changed dramatically. In all countries of the European Union the achievement of the Maastricht criteria is the strongest argument for lowering social standards and against improvement of these standards. The key words of this new discourse are *deregulation*, especially of working hours, *wage cuts*, and *cuts in social benefits*. The framework for these changes is the so-called globalization and adaptation of Austria's economy to the world economy. As a result, the balance between the employers and the employed has substantially changed in favor of those employers who have a strong position in the national and international economy. Employers are no longer confronted with the demands of a unified working class any more, but with individual and specialized agendas.

The persistent problems of the European labor markets and the economic success of lower standards of industrial laws in other countries give the following arguments fresh impetus: high wages and social benefits are considered as the reason for economic stagnation and growing unemployment. More and more employers urge the passage of laws which will allow them to employ labor below wages settled in collective bargaining between their interest group and the unions. Employers also want ways to lower the social benefits to the unemployed, sick or disabled.

As in other European countries, the number and the share of self-employed and short-hour jobs is increasing. In all countries of the European Union working nights and weekends is more widespread than ever before. Because women were considered as responsible for family and children, many of them try to find part-time employment to earn some money while still caring for the family. However, these family responsibilities encourage continued sex segregation and discrimination within the labor market. More than one fourth (27 percent) of all employed women have part-time occupations[21], compared to only 5 percent of all employed men (see Appendix 9 and Graph 2). Part-time jobs not only bring in less money. They also reduce the chances for a professional career, and threaten benefits, social security and old age pensions. Part-time and marginal jobs usually are connected with dependence upon other financial resources. Women fill an enormous percent (90 percent) of part-time jobs and 72 percent of marginal jobs. The share of part-time workers is more than ten times higher among women than among men.

Part-time employment is only found in few sectors and, therefore, 74 percent of all female employees are employed in the following areas: cleaning, trade, health, accounting, and personal services. The share of part-time jobs is growing in both blue and white collar fields. The likelihood to be employed part-time is six times higher among married women than among single women. Whereas 34 percent of women with two children younger than 15 years are employed part-time, only 15.1 percent of women without children are.

Nevertheless, there are fewer part-time jobs than available workers. Asked for the reasons about part-time work, 75 percent of female part-time workers mention family duties. A third of them say they were engaged at a lower qualification than their previous job. More than half want to get full-time jobs when their family duties allow, two thirds say they could not earn their livelihood with a part-time job. The situation of persons employed in marginal positions is precarious. In Austria it is necessary to earn a certain minimum to be entitled to insurance coverage. Among those who are not integrated into insurance coverage, two thirds are women, and only half of them (52 percent) participate in their parents' or husbands' insurance.

In the countries of the European Union, the guidelines on atypical jobs are based on the 1957 Treaty of Rome and the further regulations based on this treaty (*Gleichbehandlungsrichtlinien*). The Treaty of Rome obliges the members of the Union to pay equal wages for equal work. The European Court extended this regulation to equal pay for *equivalent* work, including monetary and non-monetary benefits. Working conditions, however, were not addressed. The Austrian government implemented these regulations in the framework of a package of measures *(Gleichbehandlungspaket)*, which gave women some compensation for the raising of the retirement age required by the Constitutional Court. Female politicians insisted on improving the legal and social status of women, after the Constitutional Court decided men and women should retire at the same age.

However, economic tensions reanimate old role clichés about women and men in the United States as in European countries. To give an example for this revival of old role cliché: the well-known neo-classical theorist and Nobel prize winner Garry S. Becker defends wage discrimination with arguments based on biology. Moreover, he states that women are responsible for the families, and so it is a necessary consequence that women earn less when they sell their labor.

Although the sharp sexual division of labor in all societies between the market and household sectors is partly due to the gains from specialized investments, it is also partly due to intrinsic differences between the sexes. A man completes his biological contribution to the production of children when his sperm fertilizes a woman's egg, after which she controls the reproductive process: she biologically houses and feeds the fetus, delivers the baby, and often feeds the infant with her own milk. Specialized investments and time allocation together with biological differences in comparative advantage imply that married men specialize in the market sector and married women in the household sector. Therefore the market wages of married men will exceed those of married women, partly because women spend more time in the household and invest more in household human capital.[22]

Contrary to this reasoning, empirical research on wage discrimination has brought other factors to light: (1) Women have to be more qualified than men to attain the same position; (2) men have better opportunities for professional, and therefore financial, advancement; (3) getting a top-position for women is more difficult than for men; (4) compared with men, women very seldom have the status of civil servants. Feminist economists—in opposition to the neo-classic position—stress that economic reasons force women to care for their families rather than work because they would earn less than men.[23]

Women' Answers to New Challenges

Despite considerable changes in western societies, men have not been ready to equally share economic power with women. The status of women in society certainly has improved; but without economic power, these political and social improvement can be undone in times of economic recession when male politicians fall back on old ways of thinking. Thus feminists stress that social benefits cannot be considered a generous gift. They are rights, indeed human rights. Today many social rights are in jeopardy. For example, in many European countries budget cuts have been realized at the expense of care-givers to children, the elderly or the disabled. More and more, these care givers find themselves at the mercy of a society that is unwilling to recognize their contribution.

It appears as if the budget deficit is to be cut at the expense of the least powerful part of the society. Consequently these cuts will affect rather women who are responsible for small children or disabled and elderly persons than men. Of course, these groups are deeply disappointed. However, many women are no longer ready to accept the disadvantages they are confronted with exclusively because they are women and not men.

In Austria, the growing anger about deterioration of economic conditions is widespread. Women's voices demanding acknowledgment for their contributions to home and family, are getting stronger. Some Austrian women are thinking about starting a new political party, i.e., a women's party. Other activists are preparing a signature list for a parliamentary initiative (*Volksbegehren*).[24] This initiative is the first *Volksbegehren* in Austria, which is concerned primarily with women's issues. These activists of the *Frauen-Volksbegehren* are bringing together civic action groups, and this coalition is asking for higher wages, for more benefits for care-givers, for a better endowment of public institutions for needy people, among other things. Preparing and carrying out this subscription will be giving the activists a good deal of publicity. Consequently, ignoring the demands and claims of women will not be so easy any longer for the politicians.

The "*Frauen-Volksbegehren*" proves that Austrian women like women in many other countries are asking for a substantial change of their position in society. To express it in the words of Julie Nelson:

What is needed is a conception of human behavior that can encompass both autonomy and dependence, individuation and relation, reason and emotion, as they manifested in economic agents of either sex. (...) Overthrowing a model of autonomous choice only to end up with, for example, a model of pure social determinism would lead to no great improvement. (...) The feminist analysis suggests that there should not be just one model, but rather many economic models, depending on the usefulness of various modeling techniques in the various applications.[25]

Austrian women—like women in other countries—are asking for a new gender contract which would not only just distribute wealth, but also just distribute care and responsibility for children and other needy people.[26]

NOTES

1. Eric Hobsbawm, *Age of Extremes: The Short 20th Century 1914-1991* (London: Michael Joseph, 1994). Hobsbawm characterizes the twentieth century as the short century in contrast to the long nineteenth century to stress the fundamental changes this century has experienced.

2. See Ernst Hanisch. *Der lange Schatten des Staates. Österreichische Gesellschaftsgeschichte im 20. Jahrhundert* (Vienna: Ueberreuter, 1994).

3. Erna Appelt, *Von Ladenmädchen, Schreibfräulein und Gouvernanten. Die weiblichen Angestellten Wiens zwischen 1900 und 1934* (Vienna: Verlag für Gesellschaftskritik, 1985), 109-20.

4. See Heidemarie Uhl, "The Politics of Memory: Austria's Perception of the Second World War and the National Socialist Period," in *Austrian Historical Memory & National Identity. Contemporary Austrian Studies*, Vol. 5 (1997), 32-63; Anton Pelinka, "Taboos and Self-Deception: The Second Republic's Reconstruction of History," in ibid, 64-94; Brigitte Bailer, "They Were All Victims: The Selective Treatment of the Consequences of National Socialism," in ibid., 95-102.

5. Erna Appelt. "The Gendering of the Service Sector in Late Nineteenth-Century Austria," in *Austrian Women in the Nineteenth and Twentieth Centuries. Cross-Disciplinary Perspectives.* David F. Good, Margarete Grandner, and Mary Jo Maynes, eds. (Providence: Berghahn Books, 1996).

6. Appelt, *Von Ladenmädchen*, 1985.

7. This percentage includes children, students, elderly people, and home-makers. The term labor force includes the employed (full-employed, part-time employed and self-employed), the unemployed, young men in the military service and persons who lay claim to parental leave.

8. ÖSTAT, Microcensus 1994 (Vienna: 1996).

9. Erna Appelt, "Sozialpartnerschaft und Fraueninteressen," in *Sozialpartnerschaft. Kontinuität und Wandel eines Modells*, Emmerich Tálos, ed. (Vienna: Verlag für Gesellschaftskritik, 1993), 243-66.

10. In the last few years, unionization was declining among men and women.

11. Österreichischer Gewerkschaftsbund (ÖGB), Statutes and Articles, § 5.2.

12. Renate Schöpf, *Frauen im ÖGB: Frauenvertretung in den Organen sowie Aufbau und Stellung der Frauenabteilung* (M.A. Thesis: Vienna, 1985).

13. ÖGB, Rule of Procedures § 5. lit.b.

14. ÖGB: Statutes and Articles § 11. 3.

15. Erna Appelt, "Frauen und Sozialpartnerschaft: Ein Nicht-Verhältnis?" in *Bericht über die Situation der Frauen in Österreich*, ed. and published by Bundesministerin für Frauenangelegenheiten/Bundeskanzleramt (Vienna: 1995), 610-14.

16. ÖGB, Referat EDV, Statistik. In 1991, there were 3.8 percent female presidents of the member of workers' councils among 512,077 unionized women, and 8.8 percent male presidents among 1,126,102 unionized men.

17. Erna Appelt, "Draußen vor der Tür? Zur Frage der Mitbestimmung von Frauen in der Österreichischen Wirtschaftspolitik," *Austriaca* (1996): 49-62.

18. 12th Congress of the ÖGB Women's Section, June 1995.

19. 13th Congress of the ÖGB, October 1995.

20. At the end of January 1997, Lore Hostasch was appointed as federal minister for social issues.

21. The European statistical office considers part-time work as a weekly job with a working schedule time between 12 and 35 hours.

22. Gary S. Becker, *A Treatise of the Family* (Cambridge: 1993), 37-41.

23. Agnes Streissler, "Frauen im Sozialsystem. Die Rollenfalle in der sozialwissenschaftlichen Literatur," in *Vom Wohlfahrtsstaat zum Leistungsstaat,* Kurswechsel 3 (1996): 103-113.

24. In Austria a *Volksbegehren* must get 100,000 votes in order to be considered in Parliament for a bill draft.

25. Julie Nelson, "Feminism and Economics," in *Journal of Economic Perspectives* 9 (1995): 131.

26. Erna Appelt, "Staatsbürgerin und Gesellschaftsvertrag," *Das Argument* 4 (1995): 539-54.

APPENDICES AND GRAPHS

Appendix 1: Residential Population by Livelihood, 1991.

Working population		**3,684,282**
Employed		3,468,504
Part-time		281,927
Unemployed		215,778
Population out of work		**1,690,083**
Retired population		1,541,628
Others		148,455
Dependent population		**2,421,421**
Children, Students		1,684,770
Housewives/-men		718,893
Others		17,758
Population by economic sectors		
0	Agrarian Sector	351,575
1	Energy, water	78,463
2	Mining	28,094
3/4/5	Industry	1,550,392
6	Construction	513,735
7A	Trade, Storage	742,403
7B	Hotels, restaurants, accommodation	294,762
8	Traffic; information	441,615
9A	Banking, economic services	397,822
9B	Social, public, personal services	1,342,864

Source: Österreichisches Statistisches Zentralamt (ÖSTAT), 1991 census

Appendix 2: Households: 1991.

Persons in private households	**7,660,464**
Family households	2,029,637
One family	1,952,666
More than one family	76,971
No-family households	983,140
With one person younger than 40	244,389
With one person elder than 40	649,389
With more than one person	89,840

Source: ÖSTAT

Appendix 3: Labor Force Participation Per Sex (in percent), 1971 - 1995.

Year	1971	1981	1991	1995
Total	42.4	45.2	46.1	47.3
Men	55.1	57.0	56.6	56.8
Women	31.3	34.6	36.4	38.4

Source: ÖSTAT

Appendix 4: Labor Force Participation by Sex and Economic Sector (in percent), 1995.

Economic Sector	Total	Men	Women
Agrarian	6.5	5.8	7.5
Industrial sector	33.1	44.5	17.3
Services	60.4	49.7	75.2
Trade, storage	15.7	12.6	20.0
Accommodation	5.5	3.5	8.3
Banking and economic services	9.3	7.9	10.3
Public and personal services	23.6	17.1	32.7

Source: ÖSTAT, Microcensus 1995

Appendix 5: Income per Month of Employed Persons (Taxes Excluded) by Sex and Profession, 1993 (Austrian Schilling, ATS).

	Percent of Men		Percent of Women	
	Earning			
Professional Position	Less than 8,500	More than 23,800	Less than 8,500	More than 23,800
Blue collar	8.1	4.3	31.3	1.7
White collar	3.5	26.7	13.5	6.6
Civil servants	1.5	15.5	4.6	10.1
Public sector*	2.5	11.4	6.4	5.2
All employed	5.4	13.0	17.3	5.2

*without persons with status of civil servants

Source: ÖSTAT

Appendix 6: Male and Female Union Members.

Year	Men	In Percent	Women	In Percent
1946	696,277	75.3	227,997	24.7
1951	969,531	74.0	340,669	26.0
1961	1,085,418	71.5	432,586	28.5
1971	1,104,008	72.3	422,356	27.7
1981	1,171,172	69.8	506,093	30.2
1991	1,126,102	68.7	512,077	31.3
1995	1,081,721	68.3	501,635	31.7

Source: ÖGB Reports

Appendix 7: Unionization of Male and Female Employees in Relation to All Employees, 1951, 1961, 1971, 1981, & 1990.

Year	Among 100 male	Among 100 female employees
	Organized within the ÖGB	
1951	72.9	52.1
1961	73.3	51.5
1971	71.5	46.4
1981	70.0	45.0
1990	65.9	42.3

Source: Report of the women's section, ÖGB 1991

Appendix 8: Share of Women Members of Regional Work Councils, 1980 & 1991.

Provinces	1980	1991
Burgenland	31.87	26.49
Carinthia	18.24	18.96
Lower Austria	23.32	21.09
Upper Austria	20.42	21.64
Salzburg	1851	20.39
Styria	18.29	19.44
Tyrol	18.06	18.17
Vorarlberg	22.58	23.46
Vienna	34.65	31.12
Austria	24.05	23.43

Source: ÖGB, Bureau for Statistics

**Appendix 9: Percentage of All Workers, Male and Female, Employed
Part-time, 1993.**

	Between 12 and 24 hours		Between 25 and 35 hours	
	Male	**Female**	**Male**	**Female**
Total	0.7	11.6	1.2	8.9
Employed	0.6	12.0	1.1	9.0
- Blue Collar	0.6	14.4	0.8	9.7
- White Collar	0.6	10.8	1.5	8.6

Source: ÖSTAT

Appendix 10:   Economic Growth of GDP in Percent, 1988-1996.

Year	1988	1989	1990	1991	1992	1993	1994	1995	1996
Percentage of GDP	4.1	3.8	4.2	2.8	2.0	0.4	3.0	1.8	0.8

Source: Arbeiterkammer (Chamber of Labor), WIFO (Institute for Economic Analysis)

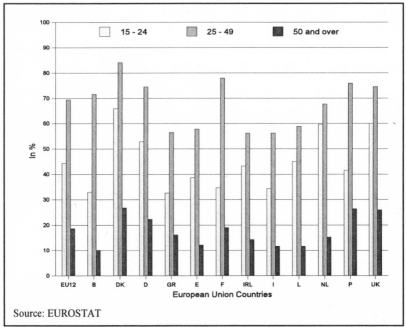

Source: EUROSTAT

Graph 1:   Labor force participation of women in Europe, 1994.

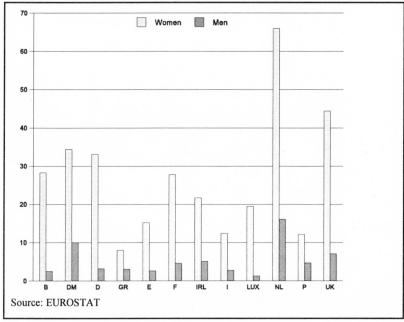

Source: EUROSTAT

Graph 2:   Part-time work in Europe, 1994.

Politics, Gender, and Equality

Sieglinde Katharina Rosenberger[*]

Introduction

In a strictly legal sense, Austrian women gained equal political rights when the First Republic was founded in 1918. The right to vote and the right to run for office or to be nominated as a candidate to governmental positions as well as the legally unrestrained access to social institutions have long been taken for granted. But legal equality itself does not necessarily lead to equal participation of women in politics and in the work force. A review of the number of women and the role they play in the public sphere clearly shows a deep rift between equality as a political principle and equality as social practice. On the one hand, equal rights and legal access to the public sphere exist on the books. On the other hand, socioeconomic differences and disproportionate participation in representative bodies continue to persist. Particularly when it comes to higher-paying jobs, both in the private sector and in the bureaucratic system, women hit a glass ceiling. Unequal opportunities and discriminatory treatment in regard to salaries and careers in traditionally male jobs are still common practices.

In spite of this ongoing discrimination, the political and social standing of Austrian women has changed for the better in the last few decades. From the 1950s into the 1970s, the dichotomy between the public and private spheres was maintained. Women's "proper" sphere was the family, whereas politics and business were viewed as the spheres of men. The institution of family, which functioned as a stable social institution in a society, was shaken by World War II. This

---

[*] I am grateful to a friend who wishes to remain anonymous. Her suggestions helped me improve the presentation of this material.

dichotomy between the public and private sphere or the caretaker/breadwinner model, preferred by homecoming soldiers, was supported by governmental policies.[1] Beginning in the 1970s, the patriarchal form of the family has been increasingly questioned. The new autonomous women's movement played a key role in criticizing the subordinate status of women. Similar to the movement in Germany, the Austrian independent women's movement and the women's movement affiliated with the Socialist Party demanded freedom of choice for women in matters related to reproductive rights and family life.[2] The political parties, especially the ruling Socialist Party, were forced to react to feminist demands arising especially from pressure outside the party structures. Since the 1970s, discrimination against women in marriage, in the family, at the work place, and in politics has been an issue of public interest.[3]

Today, more and more women are choosing a lifestyle which does not fit the traditional model. One aspect of the change in gender roles is that prescribed roles are eschewed, and a "patchwork" identity is becoming more common. State policies concerning women have directly influenced this transformation.[4]

This article addresses state policies concerning gender equality since the 1970s. It focuses on the following four topics:

1. activities and strategies which have been applied to facilitate a higher female participation in politics and to establish agencies supporting the *de facto* equality between men and women;
2. the legislation for social equality concerning private life, marriage, and family;
3. legislation and policies designed to end discrimination against working women and to achieve equal opportunities between men and women in the labor market;
4. the controversial legislation and policies implemented to reconcile the dual roles of women as mothers and members of the work force.

Empowerment of Women in Politics

One of the main goals of women's policies is to create greater opportunities for women to become full members of the polity. During the past two decades, two strategies have been adopted. One is to make the access to already established agencies of the political and administrative system easier (for example, Parliament, all branches of government and bureaucracy) through the establishment of quotas. The other strategy is to set up institutions and committees to insure the achievement of *de facto* equality.[5]

Political Participation and Quotas

Although Austrian women have possessed both the legal right to vote and the eligibility to hold all political offices since 1918, they are far from equal representation in the political and juridical system. For example, the portion of women in the National Council, which was 6 percent in the year 1919 was only exceeded in 1957, thirty-eight years later. In 1986, the percentage exceeded 10 percent. In November 1996, female representation in the National Council was 27 percent (49 out of 183 members).

Not until the mid-1960s did women play a role in the ministerial level of government (which includes ministers and state secretaries). In 1966, the Federal Chancellor appointed a women to a political cabinet position for the first time (Minister for Social Affairs). From 1971 on, at least two women served in the federal government as ministers. From 1979 to 1983, when the Socialist Party was still in power, six out of twenty-two cabinet members were female (five state secretaries and one minister). In 1983, when a coalition between the SPÖ and FPÖ was formed, the number of female cabinet members was reduced from six to three. The coalition between the SPÖ and ÖVP, which was formed after the parliamentary elections in 1986, also had three women serving on the cabinet level. During the parliamentary term 1990-95, five women were cabinet members (three ministers and two state secretaries). In 1996, four women out of sixteen members filled cabinet positions (Minister of Health and Consumer Protection, Minister of Education and Cultural Affairs, Minister of Women's Affairs, State Secretary within the Ministry of Foreign Affairs).

In the juridical system, women have also been sorely under-represented. In 1994, a woman became member of the Constitutional Court for the first time.

In male-dominated decision-making processes, the principle of a quota system is an important strategy to increase female representation in politics and public employment.[6] In Austria, quota systems have been vehemently criticized by representatives of the conservative parties. In particular, quotas for senior jobs of the bureaucracy were subject to numerous controversial debates.

In 1986, the Socialist Party (SPÖ) was first to introduce a 25 percent women's quota for candidates in national elections due to substantial pressure exerted by its women's section. Later, in 1993, the SPÖ raised the quota to 40 percent.[7] The Declaration of Principle (1990) of the Green Party (GAL) laid down the rule of a fifty-fifty split for candidates in national elections. In 1995, the Austrian People's Party (ÖVP) declared their support for a minimum of 30 percent of female representation in elected offices.[8] The Freedom Party (FPÖ) and the Liberal Forum (LIF) remain ideologically opposed to formal quotas.

The extent of the commitment to quotas which the political parties have prescribed for themselves can clearly be seen from the actual distribution of women in Parliament: the SPÖ with 31 percent (twenty-two women), the ÖVP with 18 percent (ten women), the FPÖ with 22 percent (nine women), the LIF with 30 percent (three women), and the Green Party with 55 percent (five women). Altogether, the proportion of women in the National Council comes to 27 percent and in government to 20 percent (November 1996). In comparison to the Organization for European Cooperation and Development (OECD) countries, Austria ranks relatively high and comes seventh concerning female legislators. The Scandinavian countries are in the leading positions. Compared to Austria, the United States has a lower percentage of women in the legislature: 10 percent in the House and 6 percent in the Senate (in 1994).[9]

One general characteristic of Austrian politics is the distinct loyalty of the representatives to their political parties. Given such a political culture, a transpartisan coalition of all female members of Parliament is hardly put into practice—even with issues such as equal treatment of women and men. In the history of parliamentarism, women across party lines have jointly voted in opposition to the majority of male representatives in only a few instances.

In 1989, for the first time, the political strategy to form a "Women's Caucus" in Parliament was practiced while the bill "Rape in Marriage" (1989) was being debated. As a consequence of sexist remarks made by a male representative of the ÖVP, the female legislators of all parties agreed to draft a bill without the men's assistance.

Six months later, the bill was approved by Parliament. Further examples of parliamentary co-operation among women politicians from different political parties are the "family package" concerning parental leave (1989), and the "equality package" (1992). In all of these cases, the female politicians gained greater influence and power because the women-only cooperation was not a predictable strategy at the time.

Institutions Concerned with Women's Affairs

Parallel to the gradual opening of already established institutions, there is a second model of policies intended to support gender equality. This model encourages the establishment of commissions and governmental agencies which promote an agenda of equality.

The first efforts made to support equality in the political system came as results of international developments (for example, the UNO Decade on the Status of Women, the United Nations Conventions on the Elimination of All Forms of Discrimination Against Women), as well as reaction to the new women's movement at home. In 1979, Federal Chancellor Bruno Kreisky (SPÖ) extended the government by adding two agencies for women's affairs. Johanna Dohnal headed the agency for general women's affairs which was located in the Federal Chancellory, and Franziska Fast headed the agency concerned with affairs of working women. Despite the fact that no man had to give up a position of power as the two new agencies concerning women's affairs were additions to the government rather than substitutions, the initiative was met with resistance from high ranking officials in the Socialist Party and the vehement criticism of the other political parties.[10]

These meager gains of the late 1970s were partially dismantled in the 1980s. In 1983, the Secretary for the Affairs of Working Women was eliminated as a result of the negotiations that went on between the SPÖ and FPÖ when they were building the coalition government. As already mentioned in the parliamentary term 1983-1986, the number of female cabinet members was reduced from six to three.

In 1990, the Secretary for General Women's Affairs was upgraded to a Minister for Women's Affairs. This transformation meant a minimal increase of power and better status of feminist policies (for example, the minister had the right to veto decisions at the cabinet level). But at the same time, the operating budget of the Minister for

Women's Affairs was much more restricted compared to those of the other ministers.[11]

In 1992, an ombudswoman and a Commission on Equal Treatment, consisting of members of the social partners and the government were established.[12] The task of these two bodies is the implementation of the Equal Treatment Act (1993).[13]

The Private Sphere: The Female Subject and the Family

During World War II, the traditional gender-specific division of labor could not be sustained. Most women had to work and head families. However, the year 1945 and the following decades saw a recommencement of the separation of the public and the private sphere. The gender-specific division of labor both in the family and at the work place were supported by social policies and a patriarchal Family Act. The discrimination women faced at the work place and in the exclusion from politics were results of conservative attitudes and policies which saw women's sphere as home. It was not until the 1970s that gender-egalitarian revisions to family law, tax law, the penal code, and social security law were passed.

The women's organization affiliated with the Socialist Party and the autonomous women's movement put pressure on governmental politics.[14] The new women's movement was founded by women who valued self-determination, and, for this reason, the abortion issue became a main subject of the feminist movement. The fact that abortion was illegal was seen as an affront to the right of self-determination. A second argument for woman's right to abortion referred to social hardships of those women who were not able to afford expensive illegal treatment.[15] In 1974, the SPÖ majority in Parliament passed a law allowing the termination of a pregnancy for medical and social reasons within the first three months. In practice, obtaining an abortion is still a problem for women living outside of Vienna. In many regions, especially in provinces with a strong catholic tradition, it is difficult if not impossible to find a public hospital where an abortion can be performed. There are also no private institutions for this procedure.

Until 1975, the Family Act was based on the principle of "the father as the head of the family." This discriminatory patriarchal principle, which dated from 1811, not only impacted the relationship between wife and husband, but it also influenced the situation of women in the public sphere. For example, in the case of a working wife, the husband had to give his consent for his wife to be able to work. The revision of the Family Act (1975) did away with such restrictions. "The head of the family" was replaced by a regulation emphasizing partnership and the joint rights and duties of a couple. In concrete terms, this meant that the former caretaker/breadwinner model was replaced by a family model that removed man's legal right to prevent his wife from having a career. Due to further regulations in social and family policies, marriage and the nuclear family lost some of its former exclusiveness. Other ways of life, such as families out of wedlock and single-mothers, have been given similar public treatment as married couples (that is, social protection). Nonetheless, the caretaker/breadwinner model remains favored by the state.[16]

The revision of the Family Act (1975) can be regarded as the beginning of policies supporting gender equality. However, critics rightfully claim that it is only the beginning and gender equality cannot be legislated. Some provisions of the Family Act even lessened the principle of equal rights and duties in marriage and the family. For example, the regulation that started responsibility for housekeeping depends on a person's ability supported the notion that women are best-suited for housekeeping and bringing up children. This regulation remained undisputed until the 1990s. In 1995, the Minister for Women's Affairs submitted a draft of the Family Act which assumes that women and men should be equally involved in housekeeping duties and childcare. Conservatives have opposed the draft with the argument that the state should not interfere in private matters. It remains in dispute.

The principle of partnership and equal rights and duties, which has been laid down in the Family Act, has only made limited gains in other legislation concerning marriage, social security, and protective legislation in the case of parenthood. Parental Leave and the Surname Act are good examples of gender-specific legislation.

Until 1990, women had the exclusive right to maternity leave because many efforts to introduce parental leave had been without success. The two major political parties could not agree on the conditions under which parental leave would be granted. In 1990, maternal leave was changed to parental leave. But fathers are not willing to take advantage of this regulation based on partnership (in 1994, 1,000 men and 120,000 women received parental subsidies).

The patriarchal regulation of the name used by married couples remained unchanged for a long period. Not until 1977 was the possibility to choose the birth name as part of the joint surname given. Not until 1995 was an almost equal Surname's Act passed. This last revision no longer insists that the married couple share the same surname; now each is able to keep his or her name. But the legislation could not get through on absolute equality. The wife must declare at the registry office that she would like to keep her present surname; the husband remains passive, because without a declaration he automatically keeps his name.[17]

Austrian feminist politics frequently focus on violence in the home. The issue of violence against women, especially that which is perpetrated by family members, has been brought into the public arena by the autonomous women's movement. Since the end of the 1970s, women have been active in numerous projects in which they counsel and look after victims of male violence. "Homes for Battered Women and Children" and "Hotlines for Raped Women" are run by feminist activists. Obtaining public funds for these projects is no easy task, especially in times of public cuts.

For a long period, males treated the physical violence and sexual exploitation of women within the family as taboo. It was not until 1989 that rape in marriage was criminalized. In the last few years, more positive developments have taken place. In November 1996, a law was passed stating that the police can remove violent family members from a home. Before this law was passed, the victim had to leave home and go to a shelter. Now the perpetrator can be expelled temporarily even without trial.

Since the 1970s, women's role in the family has been a controversial issue in the public arena. The two major political parties pursued different aims: the People's Party viewed women's functions as mainly related to the family; the Socialist Party emphasized their emancipation and work.

Women in the Work Force

Policies carried out by agencies concerned with women's affairs focus, to a large extent, on women and work. Earning one's own money is regarded as a key factor for personal and financial independence. The main focus of the equal treatment policy must be turned to women's entry into the work force and the establishment of equal job opportunities and salaries. As it stands, women are far from having equal access to paid jobs which are valued the same as those in which men are employed. On average, women earn 30 percent less than men. One reason is because work performed mostly by women is valued much less than work done mostly by men. Morever, the highest positions both in the private and public sector are nearly exclusively occupied by men and therefore compensated at a higher rate. In the last few years, improvements have been made as a result of the Equal Treatment Act.[18]

The presence of women in the work force has risen continuously since the 1970s. In comparison to other European countries, Austria shows an average percentage of women in the work force. About 45 percent of Austrian women over the age of fifteen are gainfully employed.[19] Explanations for this situation, which is neither good nor bad compared to other European countries, tend to be multi-causal. Disapproving attitudes of employers towards women (e.g., *Wiener Philharmoniker*), as well as distinctive protective legislation (e.g., the Mother's Protection Act) based on gender, leads to restrictions on female employees. It is worth mentioning that until 1996, women, with few exceptions (e.g., nurses) were prohibited from working at night. This prohibition was used to justify denying women access to certain job opportunities. Finally, in 1996, the law was removed because it was incompatible with European Community (EC) legislation.

A main obstacle for women has been their assumed responsibility as mothers and caregivers for the young. In contrast to women, most men are not willing to share in these traditionally female domestic responsibilities. The lack of all-day public childcare services for pre-school children leads to substantial difficulties for women employed full-time. In regard to these aspects, equal treatment policy has to incorporate activities concerning the labor market, as well as policies supporting the arranging of family and work, not only for mothers but for parents.

In Austria, public policy concerning equal opportunities and equal treatment regarding wages and promotions is addressed by the different amendments to the Equal Treatment Act (1979). Legislation concerning equal treatment at work started with a law against direct discrimination in the establishment of salaries on the basis of gender. One provision mandated equal pay for equal work (1979). However, only jobs in the private sector were subject to this regulation, and "discrimination" was seen as disadvantageous differentiation which is undertaken without "material justification." These weak points have been eliminated by the 1985 Act on Equal Treatment of Man and Woman at Work. This act enlarges the jurisdiction over voluntary social benefits and in-service training. The Act also includes concrete steps to support *de facto* equal treatment, the first of their kind. For example, enterprises are obliged to make gender-neutral job advertisements. A provision was included that stated that only companies that meet the Equal Treatment Act are eligible for state subsidies.

In 1990, a further amendment to the Equal Treatment Act extends the equal protection clause to hiring and career promotion. Furthermore, a provision obliges employers to pay a fine when violating the law. To help implement the law, a committee in the Social Ministry has been established.

In the beginning of the 1990s, the equal treatment policy was supported by a decision of the Constitutional Court in a case where a man took legal action against women's right to apply for retirement benefits five years earlier than men. The all-male Constitutional Court decided that the gender-specific age eligibility to retirement benefits (age sixty for women and age sixty-five for men) violated the principle of equality.[20] Therefore, the legislators were forced to pass a law ensuring equality under the law. But feminist politicians demanded more than equal treatment under the law, they demanded measures to support *de facto* equality. As a result of these efforts, a "package of equality" was passed by Parliament in 1992. The "package" included measures both to improve the situation of women in the work force and to reconcile the dual responsibilities of women at home and in the work force.[21] The package included the extension of an employee's right to paid leave from work from one to two weeks annually in the case of a relative's illness. A further amendment to the Equal Treatment Act (1993) incorporates the extension of pay equity to comparable worth. For the first time, sexual harassment is named as a discriminatory practice.

The last stage in the evolution of equal treatment legislation concerns employment in the public sector. The Federal Equal Treatment Act (1993) contains not only the principle "equal pay for equal work," but also an affirmative action program to promote equal opportunities. The aim of the regulation is to contribute to the promotion of a qualitative and quantitative gender balance in the public sector. The goal is that a minimum rate of 40 percent of women should represent all positions at all levels of the public sector. One provision devised to achieve this goal is an adequate representation of women on committees responsible for hiring decisions. Another is the preferential treatment provision. In cases where a female applicant is less qualified than a male applicant, she must gain preferential treatment on the basis of her sex.[22]

Combining Family and Work

Women's situation is structured by family and work. Women are responsible for housework, even when they work outside the home. The sexual division of labor within marriage and family has a lot of negative effects on women's participation in the labor force and the status of women at work.[23]

Most women are forced to arrange both family and work. The state takes measures to help women with their work in the home, enabling them to be employed. Daycare programs for children and nursing homes run by the state are opening up doors for women and improving the situation of women who go to work. As already mentioned, family leave was first introduced in 1975. The maximum period was one week a year. In 1992, it was extended to two weeks. This measure acknowledges the needs of children, the elderly, and ill people.[24] The revision of the Social Security Act (1993) also takes into consideration women's engagement in two spheres. To a certain extent, the time a mother (or father) spends child-rearing increases the retirement benefits (a maximum of four years per child are accepted). However, the regulation does not entitle one to a pension for child-rearing, but it affects the amount of the pension which is based on employment.

Feminists take a critical position towards combining policies because they often uphold a dual role for women alone. Such policies are considered a defensive strategy, because they are a far cry from transforming gender relations and the division of labor between women and men.[25] Men's roles which are based on employment and career remain nearly unchanged because the double burden of women is common practice.[26] However, the actualities of many women's lives call for measures which allow women to interrupt work temporarily or to reduce their working hours for family reasons. Therefore, many women's policies concentrate on this reality. The different political parties approach the same problem in a variety of ways. Representatives of the conservative parties demand policies enforcing gender relations on the basis of a family-orientated women's role. They claim that their policies will create more part-time jobs for mothers, and they support regulations on maternal leave instead of parental leave. Female politicians of the Socialist Party and the Greens demand measures which enable women and men to be employed and have careers. Regulations on parental leave instead of maternal leave had been a controversial issue between the ruling parties, the SPÖ and ÖVP, in the end of the 1980s. Furthermore, quality public institutions for childcare are an issue of party conflicts.

Politicians who are especially interested in creating a family-friendly environment consider part-time work as a key component in women's policies. In the mid-1980s, mothers in public employment gained the right to be employed part-time. The above mentioned "package of equal treatment" (1993) provides better legal protection of part-time jobs in the private sector. Due to demands of family life and women's continued role as major caregivers, part-time jobs are often occupied by working mothers. Statistics reveal that 19 percent of working women and 2 percent of working men are engaged in part-time employment.[27]

Conclusions

In Austria, policies affecting women generally pursues two different aims. Gender equality policies remove barriers to entry into the male-dominated public sphere (education, occupation, and politics) and strive to treat both sexes as equals under the law. Welfare state policies concerning employment and social security view working women as mothers and protect gender-specific roles (e.g., the Mother Protection Act). In contradiction to equality policies, the Austrian welfare system produces effects which preserve traditional gender roles.

As in any time of economic recession, women are most profoundly affected. The actual backlash against women is focused on cuts in social security, maternal leave, and unemployment benefits. There is a governmental trend to support equal rights policies instead of welfare benefits. An explanation for this trend is that to grant equal rights does not cause financial costs which have to be covered by the state. Typical of the trend to strengthen the "equality position" is the opening up of the military services to women on a voluntary basis.[28]

The concrete outcomes of equality policies depend on changes in the division of labor within the family. But a policy to establish partnership in personal affairs lacks measures which the government is able to enforce. For that reason gender relations have not become egalitarian, but they have become less patriarchal than they were in previous decades. This statement is supported by the following facts: nowadays, women get a higher education, more women are employed, the rate of women in white-collar jobs has increased, as has their representation in politics. Public politics give support for arranging family and work.

In the beginning of the 1990s, the Austrian women's lobby for equality was supported by EC guidelines concerning equal treatment of men and women in the work force. Though, in 1995, the European Supreme Court refused the preferential treatment proposition.[29] As a consequence of this juridical decision, the position of the Austrian opponents of equality politics and affirmative action programs has been strengthened. For that reason, alternative lobbies for feminist politics are urgently required. A chance again to exert pressure on party politics could be the general "Women's Referendum" in April 1997. Independent women who are not affiliated with political parties and the church demand not less than "Half of the money, half of paid-jobs, half of political life."

NOTES

1. Erika Thurner, "'Dann haben wir unsere Arbeit gemacht.' Frauenarbeit und Frauenleben nach dem Zweiten Weltkrieg," *Zeitgeschichte* 15 (1988): 403-19; Siegfried Mattl, "Die Rückkehr der Liebe. Wissensproduktion zur 'Frauenfrage" im Österreich der 40er und 50er Jahre," *Österreichische Zeitschrift für Politikwissenschaft* 4 (1987): 363-377.

2. In the early 1970s, the abortion question was the main political issue of the women's movements.

3. Sieglinde Rosenberger, *Frauenpolitik in Rot-Schwarz-Rot. Geschlechterverhältnisse als Gegenstand der österreichischen Politik* (Vienna: Braumüller, 1992).

4. The beginning of women's policies is regarded as the law allowing the termination of a pregnancy within the first three months (1974); they were furthered by the amendment to the Family Act (1975) based on partnership of the married couple, and policies supporting better education of all students. See Eva Cyba, "Modernisierung im Patriarchat? Zur Situation von Frauen in Arbeit, Bildung und privater Sphäre, 1945 bis 1995," in *Österreich 1945-1995. Gesellschaft, Politik, Kultur,* ed. Reinhard Sieder, Heinz Steinert, and Emmerich Tálos (Vienna: Verlag für Gesellschaftskritik, 1995), 435-457.

5. Regina Köpl, "Möglichkeiten und Grenzen frauenpolitischer Strategien: Institutionelle Frauenpolitik," in *Bericht über die Situation der Frauen in Österreich. Frauenbericht* (Vienna: Bundesministerium für Frauenangelegenheiten, 1995), 592-609; Gerda Neyer, "Frauen im österreichischen politischen System," in *Handbuch des politischen Systems Österreichs: Zweite Republik,* ed. Herbert Dachs et al. (Vienna: Manz, 1996), 185-202.

6. Anne Phillips, *Engendering Democracy* (University Park, PA: Penn State University Press, 1991), 85.

7. Statute of Organization of the SPÖ (1993): "§ 16 (2): Both, at the election of officials of the SPÖ and drawing up candidates on the lists of the SPÖ should be made sure that there are no fewer than forty percent of women and no fewer than forty percent of men represented."

8. The Declaration of Principle of the ÖVP: "The equal representation of women and men in society has to be accompanied by an equal representation of women and men in politics. Equal rights are to be driven forward by a minimum quota of a third for public office and a women-friendly political culture."

9. Neyer, "Frauen im österreichischen politischen System," 186.

10. Rosenberger, *Frauenpolitik,* 108.

11. Ibid., 75.

12. In Austria the major interest groups, the "social partners," are very much involved in governmental politics. The social partnership consists of members of the unions, the Chamber of Labor, the Chamber of Commerce, and the Chamber of Agriculture. These four interest groups are eligible to send representatives to the Commission on Equal Treatment.

13. In general, establishing the equality agenda at the state level is less advanced than at the federal level. But in comparison to regional and municipal Equal Treatment Agencies in Germany, for example, most of the Austrian states are backward. It was not until the end of the 1980s that institutions to support the equal treatment of women and men were established. Similar delay exists regarding equal treatment legislation for public employment.

14. See Brigitte Geiger and Hanna Hacker, *Donauwalzer und Damenwahl. Frauenbewegte Zusammenhänge in Österreich* (Vienna: 1989).

15. See Erika Weinzierl, "Kirche seit 1970," in *Der österreichische Weg,* ed. Erich Fröschl and Helge Zoitl (Vienna: 1986), 239-48.

16. For example, the Social Insurance Act grants the wife of an insured husband health insurance. See Gerda Falkner, Sieglinde Rosenberger, Emmerich Tálos, and Karl Wörister, "Sozialpolitik und Frauen. Tradition - Probleme - Perspektiven," in *Bericht über die Situation der Frauen in Österreich* (Vienna: Bundesministerin für Frauenangelegenheiten, 1995), 387-429.

17. See Constanze Kren, "Geschlechterdemokratische Fortentwicklung von Recht und Rechtsanweisung," in *Feministische Jurisprudenz. Blicke und Skizzen*, ed. Ursula Floßmann (Linz: Trauner Verlag, 1995), 56.

18. Margit Wiederschwinger, "Qualifikation, berufliche Tätigkeiten und Berufslaufbahnen," in *Bericht über die Situation der Frauen in Österreich*, (Vienna: Bundesministerium für Frauenangelegenheiten, 1995), 241.

19. The proportion of working women in Denmark is 60 percent, in France and Portugal, the rate of working women is about 45 percent; and in Italy it is about 35 percent (1989). Brigitte Schramm, "Entwicklung und Struktur der Frauenerwerbstätigkeit," in *Bericht über die Situation der Frauen in Österreich*, (Vienna: Bundesministerin für Frauenangelegenheiten, 1995), 227-36.

20. Silvia Siegmund-Ulrich, "Zur Ambivalenz des gleichen Rechts," in *Österreichische Zeitschrift für Politikwissenschaft* 2 (1994) 445-68.

21. See Gerda Falkner and Emmerich Tálos, "Politik und Lebensbedingungen von Frauen. Ansätze von 'Frauenpolitik' in Österreich," in *Der geforderte Wohlfahrtsstaat. Traditionen - Herausforderungen - Perspektiven*, ed. Emmerich Tálos (Vienna: Löcker-Verlag, 1992), 195-234.

22. See Julia Eichinger, *Rechtsfragen zum Gleichbehandlungsgesetz: Mittelbare Diskriminierung - Sexuelle Belästigung - Beweislastverteilung* (Vienna: Orac Verlag, 1993).

23. Mary Frank Fox and Sharlene Hesse-Biber, *Women at Work* (Mayfield, 1984).

24. Falkner, Rosenberger, Tálos, and Wörister, "Sozialpolitik und Frauen," 390.

25. See Inge Rowhani, "Frauenzeit - Männerzeit," in *Feministische Politikwissenschaft*, ed. Erna Appelt and Gerda Neyer (Vienna: Verlag für Gesellschaftskritik, 1994), 183-218.

26. For a critique, see Nancy Fraser, "Talking about Needs: Interpretive Contests as Political Conflicts in Welfare-State Societies," in *Feminism and Political Theory*, ed. Cass R. Sunstein (Chicago: University of Chicago Press, 1990), 159-184.

27. Inge Gross, Beatrix Wiedenhofer, and Werner Vötsch, *Die wirtschaftliche und soziale Rolle der Frau in Österreich. Analyse statistischer Daten* (Vienna: Bundesministerium für Arbeit und Soziales, 1994).

28. The agreement of the SPÖ and ÖVP coalition government (March 1996) includes the purpose of opening military careers for women.

29. Decision of the European Supreme Court of 17 October 1995, Nr. C-450/93 related to Provision 177 EC-Treaty.

FORUM
AUSTRIA AND THE GHOST OF
THE NEW EUROPE

Introduction

Since 1986, Austria's image has changed. Waldheim's successful presidential campaign gave Austria an almost completely new image, especially in the United States and in Western Europe. The country of Mozart and the Trapp family had become the country that was responsible for Adolf Hitler. Since 1986, a common joke defines Austria as the country which made the world believe that Beethoven was Austrian, but Hitler German.

The role Waldheim played in the 1980s has been taken over by Haider in the 1990s. This does not seem to follow logic: Waldheim represents postwar Austria, especially the political culture of consociational democracy, of grand coalition, of social partnership. Haider represents the fundamental opposition to this political system of post-1945 Austria which gave stability the highest possible priority—especially priority over innovation and participation. Waldheim was always an insider of this system. Haider was always an outsider. Waldheim stood for one of the two major traditions, the political culture that consociationalism was built upon—he was a product of political Catholicism: he spoke for the Christian-conservative camp. Haider stands for the tradition of Austrian Pan-Germanism which had every reason to feel completely excluded by the Austrian type of consociationalism.

However, a second view can explain this parallel between the role Waldheim and Haider share. Both seem to contradict the Austrian claim to be Hitler's first victim: Waldheim indirectly, by "forgetting" to speak openly about his years with the *Wehrmacht* on the Balkans, and Haider directly, by defending the "war generation's" experience (a code for Austria's involvement in Hitler's war and in Hitler's rule). Waldheim seems to represent postwar Austria as it is caught in its half-truth. Haider is accusing postwar Austria for not standing openly (and proudly) for its involvement. Waldheim stands for tampering with the historic truth. Haider is proud of this truth, even when he is avoiding any clear position concerning the Holocaust and the responsibility for World War II. Involuntarily, Waldheim has brought the postwar era to an end, especially this era's dominant understanding of history. Haider is now exploiting the end of taboos which had concealed the least palatable aspects of contemporary Austria.

Tony Judt reflects the principal critique that most historians and social scientists, who are doing research on contemporary Austria, express with regard to post-1945 Austria. However, this critique becomes part of the picture itself—the picture the critique wants to explain. To define Jörg Haider as the dominant figure of Austrian politics today is a kind of self-fulfilling prophecy. The more this viewpoint is published, the more it becomes reality. Mass media and academia have a certain kind of responsibility for making Haider important. Of course, that does not mean that anyone—may he be Haider or Waldheim, Vranitzky or Klima—should be judged by considering the political effects of such a judgment. But these effects have to be part of an overall evaluation.

Tony Judt's article throws down the gauntlet for Austrians and for Austrian intellectuals. His analytical approach is typical of the attitude Austria has had to face intellectually and academically ever since the Waldheim debate started. There cannot be a univocal response. To incite a controversy, four Austrian intellectuals—two historians, a diplomat (and lawyer), and a political scientist (and diplomat)—have been invited to respond to this challenge. They have been invited because all of them had already participated in the discussion about Austria's coming to terms with its past. Seen together, their responses also represent the peculiarities of Austrian *Lager* thinking among intellectuals.

In 1995, *Gabriele Holzer* published a book that provoked a passionate response in Austria.[1] In her answer to Tony Judt, she is using the approach she had already developed in that book: she emphasizes the ambivalence of Austria's past and contradicts the main critique as expressed in Judt's article.

Holzer's main argument is that any evaluation of Austria must not be based only on the darker sides of the country's twentieth century history. There has been the Austrian Nazi Party, and there has been Austrian Pan-Germanism. But there has been resistance also—by the

Austrian government and by important segments of Austrian society. The Anschluß was not only an event welcomed by many Austrians. The Anschluß was also a violation of international law; it was a military occupation. In that respect, Austria was a victim—as a sovereign state. Were there Austrian roots of Nazism? Yes, but what would have happened to Hitler's career without his success in Germany, without the German roots of Nazism?

It is interesting that Holzer refers to Daniel Goldhagen's book to make her point.[2] This is an important detail, because Goldhagen underlines the German responsibility for the Holocaust—the responsibility of German society. As his book does not use any comparative approach, he does not mention any specific Austrian roots, or Austrian responsibilities, just as he does not mention Polish or French or Croatian responsibilities either. In that respect, he can be used as a witness for Holzer's argument only indirectly. He does not say anything about Austria, but he does present many decisive arguments for specific German roots, for a specific German responsibility that is deeply ingrained into German history and society.

In some respects, Holzer's critique is persuasive first, the Waldheim affair was not the beginning of a completely new chapter of Austrian consciousness. Other "affairs" have preceded the Waldheim debate: Taras Borodajkewycz, Friedrich Peter/Bruno Kreisky/Simon Wiesenthal, Walter Reder/Friedhelm Frischenschlager. But the Waldheim affair had a new quality: Austria itself. Austria's self-perception came into the fire of international but also domestic criticism. Second, Austrian nationalism—if defined as the strong feeling of an Austrian separateness—has been and still is distinctly antithetical to any kind of German nationalism. Because Austria's distinctiveness is threatened by Pan-Germanism as by no other ideology, the Austrian version of German nationalism contradicts Austrian nationalism from a principal point of view. Haider's dictum of the Austrian nation as an "ideological monstrosity" ("*ideologische Missgeburt*") is the best proof for this antagonism. From Georg von Schönerer to Jörg Haider, Austrian Pan-Germanism has nothing to do with Austrian patriotism or Austrian nationalism.

Judt could have used and quoted some of the literature which underlines that point—the books written by historians like Felix Kreissler and Ernst Bruckmüller, the books written by social scientists like Albert Reiterer and Max Haller. They all emphasize that Austrian identity, as a specific identity, separate from any other national identity, has been developed in contradiction to German nationalism.

Nevertheless, Holzer seems to overlook one point: in his latest developments, Haider tries to reconcile Austrian patriotism with his brand of Pan-Germanism. In his political fight against Austria's memberhsip in the European Union, Haider not only uses a pseudo-Marxist vocabulary, arguing against "huge multi-national corporations," he also uses a vocabulary that stands traditionally for Austrian patriotism— arguing in favor of defending "Austrian identity." For Schönerer and for the founders of Haider's party, the latter argument would have been an anathema. The Waldheim affair seems to be a kind of turning point for Austrian patriotism: the logical contradiction between Pan-Germanism and Austro-Patriotism became completely overshadowed by Waldheim's dictum about his "duty" in the Greater German *Wehrmacht*. If it had been a duty to serve in the *Wehrmacht*, and not just the result of force, if it still had been a duty for an Austrian, who (like Waldheim) did not represent Austrian Pan-Germanism, and if this perspective was instrumental for Waldheim's success, then Tony Judt got it right.

Holzer is writing from a perspective which is very critical of Judt's understanding. *Brigitte Bailer* and *Wolfgang Neugebauer*, on the other hand, represent an approach which can be called almost parallel to Judt's. Holzer criticizes Judt's perception of Jörg Haider as the dominant figure of Austrian politics. Bailer and Neugebauer concede that Haider's rise is of extreme significance for Austria. They agree with Judt's conclusion about Haider's European significance: he is the "trend-setter" for a Europe that is becoming more and more ethno-nationalistic and xenophobic.

In tandem with their publications about Neo-Nazism and other right-wing phenomena in Austria,[3] Bailer and Neugebauer analyze Haider's background, his career within the FPÖ, and his tactics. Despite his variations of "camouflage," Haider is the most recent descendant in the species of anti-democratic, anti-humanistic, and anti-liberal politicians. Bailer and Neugebauer's article pictures the development of the FPÖ as a party which tried to overcome its Nazi roots but ended up with Haider. The "liberals"—liberal in the sense of gaining credibility for having broken with the party's Nazi-background—have left the party. What is left is the amalgam of old and new Nazis, of opportunists and mavericks.

But why is this party so successful on the electoral level? Bailer and Neugebauer try to answer this question by referring to the analytical concepts of "de-alignment" and "re-alignment." Of course, the rise of the FPÖ from a 5 percent to an (almost) 25 percent party has something to do with the radical restructuring of Austria's party system. But why is this process, which Bailer and Neugebauer convincingly put into a European perspective, working in Haider's favor to such an extent? Why is Haider—as a vote-getter—more successful than Gianfranco Fini or Jean Marie LePen? There must be some specific Austrian conditions which are able to explain this.

Thomas Nowotny's approach is somewhat between the other two responses. He criticizes Judt for his neglect of some facts. Judt could have used easily available data (economic structure, political financing, etc.) for his article—if it was designed to be primarily an academic one. By stressing some factual errors, Nowotny indirectly clarifies what Judt's article is not—an analysis, based on the broadest possible knowledge of data and literature, that not only contemporary history but also social sciences could have provided. Additionally, Nowotny makes clear, what Judt's article is—an intellectual provocation.

Nowotny agrees with Judt about the specific role Austria and Austrians have played within the Nazi regime. He agrees that many Austrians were instrumental in preparing Austria for the Anschluß. He especially agrees with Judt that post-1945 Austria did not confront the Austrian responsibilities for Nazism with an open mind. But Nowotny also emphasizes that the picture is more complex. By quoting Helmut Qualtinger's "Herr Karl," he stresses that there has always been an Austrian opposition against Austria's disregard of its involvement in Nazism.

Thomas Nowotny, who as a political scientist has published extensively about aspects of social democracy in Austria,[4] made a point which seems to be of special importance. For an analysis to be more than mere provocation, one must use the tools of comparison to be convincing. Austria's responsibilities for the rise of Nazism must be seen in the context of Germany's responsibilities. Post-1945 Austria's tendency to picture Nazism as a pure German product must be seen in comparison with post-1945 France's tendency to ignore the real dimensions of French collaboration. Austria's treatment of Holocaust survivors must be seen together with the international lack of ablitity to understand the uniqueness of the Holocaust.

Tony Judt's article is helpful in many respects. Judt forces Austrians to confront their routine knowledge and the facts. Indirectly, Judt's critique helps to correct perceptions of Austria by Austrians— even if some have to confront Judt with a more complex picture of Austria than his provocation is able to offer.

Anton Pelinka
Stanford University
February 1997

NOTES

1. Gabriele Holzner, *Verfreundete Nachbarn: Österreich-Deutschland. Ein Verhältnis* (Vienna: Kremayr & Scheriau 1995).

2. Daniel Goldhagen, *Hitler's Willing Executioners: Ordinary Germans and the Holocaust* (New York: A. Knopf, 1996).

3. See especially, *Handbuch des österreichischen Rechtsextremismus*. Ed. Stiftung des österreichischen Widerstandes (Vienna: Deuticke, 1994).

4. See, for example, Thomas Nowotny, *Bleibende Werte, verblichene Dogmen* (Vienna: Böhlau, 1985).

Austria and the Ghost of the New Europe*

Tony Judt

Vienna

On Sunday December 17[, 1995,] two parliamentary elections were held in Europe. In Russia, the subcontinent's largest country, the Communists and their allies were victorious, emulating similar successes by Communist and ex-Communist parties in Hungary, Poland, and elsewhere in the former Eastern bloc. In Austria, one of Europe's smallest states, nothing much happened: the governing majority was once again returned to office, fighting off a challenge from right-wing opponents. But the circumstances of the Austrian election may prove the better, and also the more disturbing, guide to the European situation in coming years.

On the face of it that proposition may seem unlikely. It has been a long time since Austria mattered much for anyone who doesn't live there.[1] Since the State Treaty of 1955, when Allied occupation forces withdrew, and Austria entered the UN and declared itself permanently neutral, the Alpine Republic (as it likes, somewhat misleadingly, to be known) has become a stable and prosperous country at the center of Europe. Its eight million people (a quarter of whom live in Vienna) derive their income in large measure from tourism, and employment in nationalized industries and the state bureaucracy, and have been governed since the first post-war elections by two political parties, normally in coalition. The People's Party, heir to the Christian Social Party of the pre-war years, with close links to the Catholic Church, was the senior member of the governing alliance from 1945 to 1966 and then governed alone between 1966 and 1970. Since then the Socialists, formerly the junior coalition partner, have been the larger party and have governed in unbroken sequence either alone or supported in their turn, since 1986, by the People's Party. Only briefly, from 1983 to 1986, has this "large coalition" been abandoned for a "small coalition" between the Socialists and the right-wing nationalist Freedom Party, of which more later.

This remarkable political continuity is further sustained by the social peace enforced through the system of "social partnership" set up in 1957. Just as the coalition partners distribute ministries, patronage appointments, and money according to their respective electoral strength—a system known as *Proporz*—so unions, chambers of commerce, and representatives of industry have for forty years discussed and ironed out social and economic disagreements under a de facto corporatist system in which conflicts between capital and labor are muted. Political and economic strategies are decided in a complex series of formal and informal meetings, of which parliament itself is perhaps the least significant, serving only to rubber-stamp decisions made elsewhere and brought to it by the leaders of the governing parties, after consulting with union and company officials. In a country whose earlier history was marked by geographical amputation, economic collapse, civil war, occupation, and defeat, Austrians were on the whole pleased with the stabilizing benefits of these conventions.

But in 1994 the foundations of Austria's post-war system began to crumble. In the parliamentary elections of that year the two ruling parties between them lost 12 percent of their vote, much of it going to the Freedom Party under its new leader Jörg Haider. The People's Party especially did badly: its share of the vote, in steady decline since 1970, fell to 27 percent, just five points ahead of Haider's party. The Socialists remained the leading party, but with 35 percent of the vote (compared to 51 percent at their peak in 1979) they, too, were losing ground. The coalition government survived, its majority much reduced.

But the new leader of the People's Party, Wolfgang Schüssel, interpreted the results as a warning: his party's longstanding alliance with the Socialist Chancellor Franz Vranitzky was costing it votes and the time had come to make a break. Now that Austria had entered the European Union the country was under pressure to reduce its budget deficit in line with the requirements for adopting a single currency.

Schüssel seized the occasion to charge the Socialists with economic mismanagement and took his party out of the government. The People's Party would fight the resulting election on a program of economic reform, offering Thatcherite proposals for sound money and reduced public spending.

As an election issue this was unconvincing. Austria's budget deficits are small by European standards and neither of the major parties would risk serious cuts in the complex and impressive system of public services and social security that benefit all their constituents. Austrians, for example, can count on excellent, inexpensive public transport, unusually comprehensive children's benefits, and generous old-age pensions. The real dilemma is that since the Sixties the social bases of Austria's two-party system have changed, while the political parties themselves have failed to reflect this. The Socialists can no longer look to secure blocs of votes from industrial labor, government employees, and "Red" Vienna, whose citizens have a long tradition of backing Socialist candidates. The People's Party, with its strength in the rural, Catholic regions to the south and west of the capital, has been undermined by urbanization and secularization. As the longtime junior partner in government the People's Party is vulnerable to criticism for tax-and-spend policies over which it has limited control. And having been (like the Christian Democrat parties elsewhere in Western Europe) in the forefront of the move to join the European Union, it bears the brunt of popular disappointment with the European Union's accomplishments and fears over the costs of membership. The People's Party, in short, needed to get out of government. But if it were to come back into office without the Socialists it could only realistically hope to do so through a coalition with the right-wing Freedom Party, something Schüssel refused to exclude—"a change," he remarked, "will do our country good." And the implications of this strategy became the true issue of the 1995 election.

The Austrian Freedom Party was founded in 1956, heir to the League of Independents. The League, formed in 1949, was the direct descendant of the faction that promoted pan-German nationalism for Austria both under the Habsburgs and in the years following World War I. Since the major political goal of the German nationalists in Austria had been union (Anschluß) with Germany, and since Anschluß is expressly forbidden in Article 4 of the State Treaty, the League and the Freedom Party had long lacked a defined political program. Their supporters consisted of ex-Nazis, monarchists, and others nostalgic for a forbidden past, together with conservatives whose anti-clericalism kept them hostile to the People's Party and small businessmen, retired professionals, and others resentful of the large, cozy, state-protected sector from which they felt excluded.

Initially reluctant to welcome the terms of Austrian independence, especially the neutrality clause, the Freedom Party chose instead to take a pro-European position as a substitute for identification with Germany. Because there was no other political group espousing free-market, pro-(Western)Europe and even libertarian views in Austria, the Freedom Party also eventually came to include a liberal wing resembling the Free Democrats of the Federal Republic of Germany. But the two tendencies were always uneasy with each other, since the party's origins were never wholly abandoned: its first two leaders were respectively a former member of Chancellor Arthur Seyss-Inquart's post-Anschluß Nazi cabinet of 1938 and an ex-SS officer.

Until recently the Freedom Party was a marginal part of Austrian public life. Its predecessor, the League of Independents, scored around 10 percent in the elections of 1949 and 1953; thereafter the FP received between 4 percent and 7 percent of the national vote, though it did better in the southern province of Carinthia, where, ever since the 1920 referendum that attached the region to Austria, German nationalists have made political capital out of local animosity toward the Slovene minority and fears of Yugoslav irredentism. But in 1986 the Freedom Party obtained 9.7 percent of the vote in the parliamentary elections, in 1990 16.6 percent, and in 1994 nearly one in four Austrian electors voted for it. This was all the more striking because in 1993 the liberal wing of the party, unable any longer to tolerate the sharp rightward direction of the party's leadership, particularly the racial overtones of its attacks on immigrants, had broken away to form a new group, the Liberal Forum. The panic that overtook many Austrians in 1995, when Schüssel and his party broke with their Socialist partners, was induced by the vision of public life and politics being placed at the mercy of the rising radical party of the right, and in particular at the prospect of the growing influence of its young leader.

Jörg Haider was born in Upper Austria in January 1950, and thus had what he calls *"die Gnade der späten Geburt"*—the good fortune of a late birth; in other words, he cannot be tarred with the brush of Nazism and isn't responsible for Austria's past. But he comes from a good Nazi family—both his parents were active party members and he speaks often of the need to put an end to the "criminalizing of personal histories." His rise through the ranks of the Freedom Party has been rapid: he took over the party organization in Carinthia in 1983 and has been head of the national party since 1986. He is good-looking in the manner of the host of a sleazy game show, and does well on television, benefiting from the growing importance of electronic showmanship in Austrian politics.[2] His election posters emphasize that he is not responsible for the promises of past governments—"He has not lied to you"—and play upon the theme of honesty and directness, contrasting Haider's character with that of the establishment politicians—"Simply honorable, simply Jörg."

Direct he unquestionably is. Under Haider the Freedom Party has just three themes, upon which its leader plays with studied insistence. The first is Austrian nationalism, a theme which retains the substance of German-national nostalgia while updating its form. Thus the FP used to identify with "Europe," but Haider is now against membership in the EU and has made it the main tenet of his polemic against the government. The time has come, he says, to put "Austria first," to end immigration, withdraw from the European Human Rights Convention, tighten the laws against foreigners and repatriate those already in the country. In his base in Carinthia he attacks the laws according language and cultural rights to the tiny Slovene-speaking minority and warns—with surreal implausibility—of Austria becoming a "multi-cultural society." In fact, foreigners make up less than 9 percent of the population, an fewer than three in one hundred foreigners receive Austrian citizenship each year. The number of foreigners (or dark-skinned people, since Haider has nothing against Western tourists) has risen sharply with the temporary influx of Bosnian and Croatian refugees—in 1990, non-citizens were only 5.3 percent of the total population. Austria has few Gypsies, most of them concentrated in Vienna and the Hungarian frontier region. It is a country in which it is notoriously difficult for non-citizens to get a work permit; the requirements are more stringent than anywhere in Europe outside Switzerland,

and non-citizens have fewer political rights than in any other member-state of the European Union. Many Austrians fear a coming wave of eastern and southeastern European migrants, but this has not yet happened.

Still, there is no doubt that Haider can call on considerable popular backing for such views: one third of all those polled in 1995 believe that guestworkers and other foreigners in Austria have too many benefits and privileges. There has been a series of letter bombs and deadly booby traps aimed at Gypsies and other minorities and at public figures known for their work with Bosnian and other refugees. When one of the Austrian victims, the refugee advocate Maria Loley, was being given first aid following a bombing in October 1995, neighbors in her village of Poysdorf were heard to comment that she had it coming. She had gone too far and "broken the rules." One woman remarked that "she doesn't realize what she is doing to us. One day these foreigners will be marrying our children."[3]

Haider's second theme is a populist attack on the beneficiaries of Austria's system of social benefits. In Haider's world the country is rotting from within, burdened with the cost of supporting *Sozialschmarotzer*—social-parasites, among whom he includes not only government employees and pensioners but also the cultural "swine" (*Schuft*) in Vienna who take subsidies from the state for musical, artistic, and theatrical productions, sell the country short in their criticism of Austria's conservative tendencies and its murky past, and lack national feeling. Here Haider plays on suspicion of Vienna and claims to count on an "quiet understanding" among the ordinary "decent" people. Austria is a small country but quite a long one—it is some seven hundred kilometers from east to west—and the Viennese traditions of social-democratic administration and cultural cosmo-politanism are still as deeply distrusted in the little towns of the remote countryside today as they have been since the late nineteenth century. Haider benefits, too, from the support of the *Neue Kronen-Zeitung*, Austria's biggest-selling daily, with 41 percent of the national readership, an unpleasant tabloid rag that has played up Haider's claim that Austria's system of corporate government and subsidized culture is destroying individual responsibility and leading the land to moral decadence.[4]

Haider's third theme concerns Austria's past. On its far right wing the Freedom Party has always had supporters who were linked with neo-Nazi violence and nostalgia, but hitherto its main spokesmen have tended to avoid identifying too closely with Austria's Nazi past. Under Haider this has changed. The most notorious instance came just before the recent elections, when German television showed a video of Haider addressing a recent gathering of Waffen-SS veterans in a southern Austrian town. The film was not shown on Austrian television before the vote, but it is doubtful whether it would have made a marked difference to the outcome. At the meeting Haider addressed his audience as his "dear friends," describing them as "decent men" of "spiritually superior" character. He contrasted them favorably with the "work-shy trash" and others who receive government support, and praised them for remaining true to their convictions in the face of opposition.

But Haider's views have never been a secret. Ten years ago he told a similar meeting of former SS men that their sacrifices saved Western Europe. Our times, he said, need men like you, for whom Homeland (*Heimat*) still means something.[5] In that same year he praised Walter Reder, the Austrian SS officer responsible for the wartime murder of civilians in the Italian town of Marzabotto, as a soldier who "did his duty." On June 13, 1991, he told the Carinthian regional assembly, whose leader he then was, that Nazi employment policies had been "sound," unlike those of the present-day government in Austria. This outburst cost him the support of the local People's Party, and thus his regional office, but he was unchastened, describing himself instead as a "near-victim" of the *Verbotsgesetz*, the Austrian law forbidding support for Nazism and Nazi policies.

If Haider and his party have done increasingly well in Austrian elections in recent years it is probably not because of his manifest sympathies for former Nazis but in spite of them. A large minority of Austrians may well be drawn to Haider's views of the Nazi past, but he gets their votes for a different reason.[6] Some of his criticisms of the state ring true, notably his attacks on corruption, which has steadily increased, perhaps inevitably so in a system where a single party or a coalition of parties has been in power for decades. Some aspects of Austrian patronage procedures closely resemble the practices of Italian public life, except that they are more efficient. (Building companies may exploit party connections to get state contracts, but the projects are solidly constructed and on time.) Haider's offer of a "Contract with Austria" (blatantly borrowed from Newt Gingrich) appeals to those voters who believe they are being taxed to pay for benefits and privileges from which they are excluded, and who fear that economic changes, and particularly pressures from the European Union, may threaten Austria's cozy isolation. In a situation where the two mainstream parties have together monopolized public office and the perquisites of patronage, the mantle of protest and opposition inevitably falls upon the only available candidate.

But Haider's promised "Third Republic" (replacing the Second, which was established after the war) did not come about in the December 17 election. Schüssel's gamble failed—the fear of economic instability brought voters back to Vranitzky's Socialists, while the People's Party and the Freedom Party stayed at about their previous levels.[7] The new government will inevitably be a coalition of the two big parties (since neither has anything close to an absolute majority), with the Socialists even more dominant than before. The "Haider-panic" is apparently over, and the irresistible rise of Austria's "yuppie-fascist" has been at least temporarily halted. Why, then, does the Austrian election matter, and what does it mean?

In Austria itself the election and the rise of Haider mark the end of the comfortable post-war consensus. As many commentators have noted, post-war Austria was constructed on a mendacious myth rooted in ambiguity. In November 1943 the Allies declared Austria to have been Hitler's "first victim," although in fact Austrians had been eager collaborators with Hitler and no less criminal in their treatment of Jews. The announcement conferred on Austria a bogus legitimacy, even though it was followed after the war by a ten-year occupation implicitly acknowledging that Austria, with Germany, was a defeated enemy. But thanks to Austria's ambiguous status, and perhaps also to the Western Allies' obsession with the "Prussian" origins of Nazi rule, Austrian de-Nazification was even milder than that undertaken in Germany. The result was that until the Waldheim affair in 1986 there was no national discussion of Austria's Nazi past. Because the quasi-fascist regime headed by Kurt Schussnigg between 1934 and 1938 had been over-thrown by Hitler, it, too, was subjected to little retrospective scrutiny,

and the Christian-Social and Social Democratic camps, violently antagonistic between the wars, constructed between them an amnesiac
post-war republic shorn of any usable past. It took the revelations that
Waldheim had lied about his wartime military service under the Nazis
to shake Austria's political class out of its comfortable lethargy and
into an uncomfortable process of self-questioning.[8]

The country was also disturbed by the collapse of Communism in
1989. Post-war Austria was consciously conceived, notably by Bruno
Kreisky, the Socialist chancellor from 1970 to 1983, as a country
whose identity would henceforth derive from its geographical situation
between east and west, its neutrality during the cold war, and its role
as intermediary between first and third worlds (Austria under Kreisky
had a particular sympathy for nationalist and anti-colonial movements
in the Middle East and Africa). This sat oddly with Austria's past, but
of what else could "Austria" consist? There had never been an
"Austrian" nation—alone of the many regions of the former Habsburg
Empire it harbored no nationalist aspirations. After the Imperial
monarchy collapsed in 1918, union with the rest of German-speaking
Europe was the logical and sentimental goal of nearly all Austrian
politicians, even Socialist. Only in 1933 did the Socialist Party remove
from its program the demand for Anschluß with Germany, and as late
as 1937 Otto Bauer, the Party's leading thinker, dismissed the idea of
an Austrian nation as grotesque; in Austrian nationalism he saw only
the specter of a union of the Catholic Church, Habsburg tradition, and
feudal Baroque culture.[9]

After 1989, with the disappearance of Communist Eastern Europe
and the end of the cold war, Austria's newfound identity effectively
disappeared, and its future lay inexorably in the European Union, as an
autonomous appendix to a united Germany. The only distinctive
meaning attaching to "Austria" now had to be found somewhere in the
layers of its checkered history. A creation of the post-World War II
settlement, Austria is a victim of the collapse of that settlement, and
one characteristically "Austrian" sentiment today is thus indeed the one
expressed by Haider—resentment and fear at the rapid transformations
taking place in Europe, a confused sense that these will bring change
to Austria, and a natural resort to defensive pride in what has been

lost.[10] (Haider himself may demand all manner of changes, but change, of course, is just what his voters fear most.)

This makes Austria very different from Germany. Unlike Austria (whose present constitution is that of 1920, as revised in 1929), the Federal Republic of Germany started afresh in 1949, with a Basic Law whose prime function is to emphasize and guarantee the break with the past. Austrians no longer seek an Anschluß—indeed, many of them fear absorption into a German-dominated Europe—but Germany is always on their minds, whereas Austria is a topic of almost no sustained interest in Germany itself. It probably never has been—Anschluß was primarily an Austrian demand, after all, not a German one. And the rise of Haider is a reminder of just how different the situation of the two countries has become; his politics of *ressentiment*, of fear of the future, and of ambivalence over the Nazi past lack the popular appeal in Germany that they now have in its southern neighbor. It is very difficult to imagine someone with Haider's opinions and policies scoring nearly 23 percent in a German national election.

Another comparison may be more revealing. During the last weeks of the Austrian election the strikes in France against measures to limit pensions and reform the welfare budget were on everyone's mind. The social costs of economic reform—the price of fiscal tightening as a prelude to carrying out "Maastricht 2," the next stage of the European Union agreement, were just what Vranitzky warned against in posters promising "We won't let them take away pensions, nor women's rights," among other guarantees. Haider in his last election advertisement was even blunter—"Austria mustn't got the way of France!"[11] The two politicians meant slightly different things, of course; Vranitzky's Socialists want to preserve the welfare state, the *état providence* whose defense brought the French onto the streets in December. Haider—who regards the *état providence* as inimical to the national spirit—was warning against the internal turmoil that Austria's integration into Europe would bring. But the common message was clear—Austria has social peace—"Austria is too precious for experiments" as the Socialist posters put it—and France does not. And France is our future if we are not careful.

France, moreover, is the only other European country in which the charismatic leader of the far right has captured a significant portion of the voters—though if Jean-Marie Le Pen were ever to do as well as Haider he would be leading the second political party in the country. In France, as in Austria, the past has become a source of national unease and controversy, and for rather similar reasons. Le Pen's deputy, Bruno Mégret, shares Haider's view that the time has come to break with post-war taboos on those who collaborated with Vichy and the Nazis; for their own reasons both men want to "liberate" a right-wing national past that has been buried under the heap of prosperous post-war self-congratulation.[12] Of course Haider lacks Le Pen's credentials as a student streetfighter and French Algerian extremist, but that, as he half admits, is just a matter of age. And in France as in Austria it is fear and hatred of immigrants (in France from the south, in Austria from the east, in both cases from lands over which they once ruled) that has replaced overt anti-Semitism as the emotion that binds the far right.[13]

The French, moreover, have been deeply disturbed by the end of the agreeable post-war arrangement whereby France pretended to be the leading European nation and Germany pretended to believe it. But if the French share the ensuing mood of self-questioning with Austrians, the sentiment is also widespread in Europe as a whole. The promise of an ever broader, ever deeper, ever more prosperous Europe may still hold charms for Eastern Europeans—though it is highly doubtful whether they will ever get to benefit from it in its present form. But in much of Western Europe that promise has now come down to the chimeric prospect of a single currency accompanied by the all-too-real expectation of deep cuts in government spending, cuts that threaten the social services and welfare systems that have been a part of the European dream since the onset of post-war prosperity. Such cuts are now seen as necessary to avoid the inflation in national economies that would undermine a single currency.

If the recent events in France, then, are a warning shot across the bows of a European vessel steaming into the unknown, Austria is a metaphor for Europe in the waning days of its happy post-war slumber. For Austria is a shrunken land with a confused identity, overshadowed by its heritage and fearful for its future, reluctant to abandon real social gains but convinced it can no longer afford them, happy at the end of the division of Europe but worried by the loss of this role in that division. But is this not also in varying measure the condition not just of France, but also of Italy, of Britain and other countries besides? Is it just a coincidence not only that Haider and Le Pen have merged during the Eighties and Nineties but also a new generation of Flemish nationalists as well as separatists and re-programmed ex-neo-fascists in Italy?

All of these stand to profit from the disappointments and fears that will flow from the effort to unite Europe along the fiscal principles of the German central bank, in which low inflation, tight money, and reduced deficits are a prerequisite; and all can be relied on to invoke national sentiments and antagonisms, past and present, real and imagined, in their rhetoric and their programs. Even the laudable attempt to make it easier for goods and people to cross frontiers within the European Union, the so-called Schengen program, carries the corollary of ever higher fences at Europe's perimeter to keep out unwanted migrants. The Schengen program has the unintended effect of helping to legitimize the theme of national xenophobia at the heart of right-wing rhetoric.[14] Here, too, the Austrian elections have something to teach Europe.

It is tempting, and some Austrian commentators have indulged the thought, to see in Jörg Haider and his party some kind of renascent fascism or even a sort of para-Nazims. But that is actually too reassuring, since it is easy to demonstrate why Haider (or Le Pen, or Gianfranco Fini in Italy) do not simply represent a return to the bad old days, an echo of the ghosts of Europe past. They are not totalitarian ideologues. If they were, we could probably ignore them—and anyway they would not be the successful populist politicians they now are. But just because an opportunist like Haider lacks principles, it does not follow that he has no deeply held and widely shared prejudices. As the European Union fiddles with "Maastricht 2" while its margins burn, Haider and his like stand for something far more serious: they are the ghost of Europes yet to come.

January 18, 1996

NOTES

1. With the exception of East European refugees and Russian Jews, for whom it was the nearest safe haven and first taste of freedom during the dark years (although most of them moved on to Israel and other countries). For that reason, and perhaps from some nostalgia for the milder days of the Habsburgs, even the descendants of the national minorities of the Empire showed, and still show, a certain respect for Austria and an inclination to overestimate its present importance and capacities.

2. He looks a bit like Tony Blair, the British Labour leader, and cultivates the same youthful, post-ideological image—except that where Blair has a straightforward and somehow innocent look Haider is distinctly *louche*.

3. See *Der Standard*, October 30, 1995. Whenever he is asked for his views on the series of bomb attacks in eastern Austria that began in 1993 and continue to the present without anyone being found responsible, Haider merely retorts that it is probably a matter of score-settling between criminals and drug-users and that the problem would be resolved if the victims were sent "home." For the immigration debate in Austria, and Haider's baleful influence on the policies of the other parties, see Richard Mitten, "Jörg Haider, the Anti-immigrant Petition and Immigration Policy in Austria," *Patterns of Prejudice,* April 1994, pp.27-47.

4. Sigrid Löffler, writing in the *Frankfurter Allgemeine Zeitung*, described the *Neue Kronen-Zeitung* as "the all powerful street voice and central organ of all the sick instincts of the Austrian soul." *FAZ*, October 25,1995.

5. See *Kärntner Nachrichten*, October 19, 1985, quoted in Brigitte Bailer-Galanda, *Haider Wörtlich* (Vienna: Löcker Verlag, 1995), p. 102.

6. That Austria has a problem with its past is of course well known. Recently an exhibition on the war crimes of the Wehrmacht came to Vienna, having previously been shown in Germany. The photographs and text are moving and terrible, but they show nothing new, and in Germany there was no notable response and certainly no public denial. In Austria, however, the exhibition provoked outrage, with charges of "fabrication" and "slander." The *Neue Kronen-Zeitung* called the exhibition "satanic." A member of parliament from Haider's party, John Gudenus, took part in a televised debate on the subject and was asked for his views on the existence of gas chambers: "I believe everything that is dogmatically prescribed," he replied, making quite clear that he did nothing of the kind. Haider confined his own public comment to a

remark before his "dear friends" of the Waffen-SS, noting that the state could not afford to do anything for them but had enough money for such exhibitions.

7. Though Haider and his party continue to score well in the provinces: in the city of Salzburg he obtained 27 percent of the vote; in Klagenfurt, the capital of Carinthia, he got 33 percent; and in some smaller towns of Carinthia the "dear friend" of the Waffen-SS veterans received two out of every five votes cast.

8. For an excellent discussion of these matters, see Richard Mitten, *The Politics of Anti-Semitic Prejudice: The Waldheim Phenomenon in Austria* (Westview, 1992).

9. Certain regions of the country, notably the western Länder of Tirol and Vorarlberg, have quite distinctive identities of their own—the Vorarlberg has even at times talked of separating itself from the rest of the country and joining Switzerland. Salzburg and its hinterland were only definitively acquired by the Habsburgs in the last century, while both the eastern and southern frontier regions have strong historical links with their Magyar and Slav neighbors across the border. Only Vienna and the adjoining districts of Lower and Upper Austria are historically "Austrian"—and as any glance at the Vienna phone book will confirm, a significant part of their population is of (recent) immigrant origin.

10. The comparison with former Communist countries may be suggestive. As the Austrian demographer Rainer Münz has noted, Austria often feels a bit East European—tight, closed, paternalist, backward-looking, undynamic. In some respects the country is even run the way Communist states once claimed to function, with the notable added benefits of prosperity and individual freedom. And the sort of people who vote nostalgically for former Communists in Hungary or Poland might well be tempted, in other circumstances, by someone like Haider.

11. See *Der Standard*, December 13, 1995.

12. In the aftermath of public debates over the "Vichy syndrome" Le Pen and many other Frenchmen would doubtless subscribe to Haider's belief that "no people can live over the long period with a criminalizing of its own history, and in Austria too there must be an end to it" (in *Neue Freie Zeitung*, January 15, 1992, quoted by Bailer-Galanda in *Haider Wörtlich*, p. 91). The French have even had their own "forgetful" president, admittedly in a lower register of ethical discredit.

13. Not that there is anything philo-Semitic about Jörg Haider. But like Jean-Marie Le Pen he reveals his prejudice indirectly, by naming—as examples of whatever it is in public life that offends him—people who just happen to be Jewish.

14. "We Austrians should answer not to the EU, not to Maastricht, not to some international idea or other, but to this our Homeland." Haider in *Junge Freiheit*, October 20, 1995. See Bailer-Galanda, *Haider Wörtlich*, p. 56.

Haider Business

Gabriele Holzer

Tony Judt's article on Austria is a skilled mixture of information and wide-spread misunderstandings, half-truths and clichés.

"Bogus Legitimacy"

One of the most disturbing clichés depicts Austrian identity as being based on questionable grounds. Judt resorts to it by referring to the country as "constructed on a mendacious myth rooted in ambiguity," as having a "bogus legitimacy" and an "ambiguous status." To support such judgments he argues, as others have, that within Austria after 1918, there was a strong movement to unite with Germany and that many Austrians were Nazis and most were in favor of the 1938 "Anschluß."[1] According to this account of Austrian history there had been little or no repentance or "cleaning-up" after 1945, and Austria's Nazi past had only come to the fore of consciousness with the events surrounding Waldheim's election as Austrian president in 1986.

Anschluß as a Primarily "Austrian Demand"

These arguments are a mixture of truths, misrepresentations, omissions, and erroneous conclusions. True, in the aftermath of the trauma of 1918 and for some time, aspirations by Austrian elites to unite with Germany were widespread. But after the take-over of Germany by the Nazis in 1933, the Austrian "quasi-fascist regime," as Judt calls it rather simplistically, put up strong if ineffective and misguided resistance against the enormous economic, political, and terroristic pressures by Nazi Germany (which, for example, had supported the murder of the Austrian Chancellor Engelbert Dollfuss in 1934). The take-over of Austria by Germany in 1938, the invasion by some 100,000 soldiers and 16,000 policemen starting on 12 March, was an act of force and a flagrant violation of international law. Unlike their present-day counterparts, U.S. ambassadors in Vienna and Berlin and the international press of the time (such as the *New York Times*) clearly considered these events as typical German aggression, condoned by the appeasement-minded Western powers. The Czech government readily understood the threat that was in the air. These observers interpreted the Anschluß as having been triggered by the foreseeable, namely pro-Austrian, outcome of a public referendum on Austrian independence. The Austrian chancellor Kurt Schuschnigg had scheduled it for 13 March with the intention of fending off Nazi Germany once and for all. The Austrian Jewish community—certainly not oblivious to traditional anti-Semitic tendencies in Austria, and hardly partisan to the ruling clerico-authoritarian regime—strongly supported Schuschnigg's attempts to save the country from Nazi Germany's grip. Its spokesmen mobilized for his referendum, arguing that as long as Austria remained independent, Jews would have nothing to fear. After all, many German Jews had by this time found refuge in Austria. It is a falsification of history to deny German aspirations of Anschluß which, by the way, long preceded Hitler. Initially, the Nazis had put all the "blame" for the Anschluß on the Austrians. Their heirs continue to do so to this day. Judt seems to be ignorant of these facts.

"Mendacious Myth: First Victim of Hitler"

The *state* of Austria was indeed the first victim of Nazi Germany, despite the fact that there were many Austrian Nazis. True, many cheered Hitler and some committed crimes. A "regime" was not "overthrown by Hitler," as Judt puts it; rather, a state was eradicated by outside military intervention of another state. The "referendum" staged by the Nazi regime in April 1938, which is often referred to as proof of legitimacy of the Anschluß, was, of course, a farce. Austria had already ceased to exist. This farce resulted in a 99 percent majority favoring the Anschluß, a result typical of totalitarian "elections." True, resistance in Austria remained weak. But, in the eight years of Austria's non-existence, it nevertheless cost about 40,000 people their lives. Austria's status as first victim was not in doubt at the time. The State Department reconfirmed this in 1946, at a time when the extent of Austria's collaboration, while under German rule, certainly was no secret, if it ever had been one.

Austrian Origins of Nazi Rule?

By pointing out the "Western Allies' obsession with the 'Prussian' origins of Nazi rule," Judt refers to the well-known allegation that Nazi ideology, especially murderous anti-Semitism, was actually invented in Austria and from there imported into Germany, which thus became a victim of Austria. This is absurd and only serves to obliterate German responsibility. Ideological and political figures of the early twentieth century, such as the often mentioned mayor of Vienna Karl Lueger, and the radical German nationalist Georg Schönerer, can also be found by the dozens in German history of the nineteenth and twentieth centuries. This includes the first German Chancellor Otto von Bismarck, a skilled manipulator of anti-Semitism, and Emperor Wilhelm II, whom Schönerer praised as the only hope against Jews. Recently, Daniel Goldhagen[2] described the socio-political climate in Germany long before Hitler was granted rule. Brigitte Hamann[3] pointed out that Hitler, in his early years in Vienna, had no success with his radical theories and behavior. He hated and despised his country of origin which he deemed unworthy of his grandeur. He left Austria twenty years before he became the "Führer" of Germany. His declared models were not only Lueger and Schönerer but also Germans, such as Heinrich Clasz, the long-time president of the "*Alldeutscher Verband*," and the best-selling author Dietrich Eckart.

"Disproportionate Share in Mass Murder"

Along this ideological line of shifting blame to Austria, it has become fashionable to claim that Austrians were more ferocious Nazis than the Germans and bear a disproportionate direct responsibility for the mass murders of European Jews. There is no reason to doubt that quite a number of Austrians committed atrocities. There is, however, no evidence as to whether their share of blame was greater, equal to or smaller than that of Germans, the Dutch, or others.[*] Such evidence would presuppose more public, political, legal, and historical interest and research about the identity of the perpetrators than has hitherto

* Editor's note: For differing views see Hans Safrian, *Die Eichmann-Männer* (Vienna: Europa Verlag, 1993); Walter Manoschek, *'Serbien ist judenfrei:' Militärische Besatzungspolitik und Judenvernichtung in Serbien 1941/42* (Munich: R. Oldenbourg, 1993).

been accomplished by scholars. Daniel Goldhagen was not the first one to point out that the vast majority of murderers have gone unidentified (and unpunished), in Germany and elsewhere.

"Postwar Amnesia"

Facts stand in contrast to the cliché of total "amnesia" in postwar Austria, another claim serving to substantiate Austria's "bogus legitimacy." Based on *Austrian* anti-Nazi legislation, criminal proceedings were initiated by *Austrian* authorities in 136,000 cases. There were 13,607 persons convicted of Nazi-crimes by Austrian courts created especially for this purpose between 1945 and 1955. Forty-three convictions included death sentences. Also, Austrian "denazification" affected about half a million people, the vast majority of former Austrian members of the Nazi party. They were, depending on the case, imprisoned, removed from office and jobs, forced to clean the rubble left by Allied bombing in the streets of Vienna, subjected to financial penalties, and stripped of their political rights. A large majority of postwar Austrian politicians were clear opponents of the Nazi regime; many of them (for instance about two-thirds of the parliamentarians) were former inmates of Nazi concentration camps and prisons and were members of the Austrian resistance. The question of how to deal with the great number of "small" and "big" Austrian Nazis remained a matter of public concern and debate for a number of years. True, measures of punishment, undertaken also by the Allies, were highly insufficient, often a perversion of justice and only temporary, lasting for a few years in the worst cases. It is, however, more than "amnesia."

Tony Judt and others depict (Western) Germany as fundamentally different, namely better than Austria in respect to penalizing collaborators. However, *less* has been achieved in this respect by (West) German authorities and courts, not only in relative but in absolute terms. For example, criminal proceedings were undertaken in about 100,000 cases, and resulted in convictions of about 6,500 Nazi criminals. Additionally, "denazification" penalties were enacted against a total of about 610,000 persons (about 1 percent of the population and only a small part of the former German members of the Nazi party). Germany's acceptance of its successor status to the Third Reich was not purely motivated by recognition of responsibility, as many, including Simon Wiesenthal, have pointed out. This acceptance constituted an "entrance ticket" to the civilized world. Surprisingly, it also meant the reinstallation of practically all former (Nazi) officials in the bureaucracies. Libraries have been filled with books, by German and other authors, deploring the lack of justice, insight and acceptance of responsibility by a great majority of Germans in the first decades after the war. The same applies to Austrians. Others are only now "discovering" dark spots in their national past during the Nazi period. Still others have yet to bother "discovering" them. Singling out Austria's inadequate handling of the past is misleading and distorting.

No Austrian *"Wiedergutmachung"*

True enough, Germany officially accepted, had to accept, obligation to "*Wiedergutmachung*," a questionable term coined by Germans referring to financial restitution to (Jewish) victims. So far about DM 100 billion were spent on this account. In contrast, about DM 130 billion were spent for the victims of Allied bombing and ethnic Germans forced out of their original home countries after the war. Regardless of their shortcomings, these reparations are unparalleled in history. Austria passed "restitution" and "compensation" laws and so far spent about ÖS 40 billion on this account. All of these sums and the procedures many of the victims were subjected to in *both* countries are totally inadequate and often inhumane, even if only seen from the perspective of material losses. This remains a deplorable fact even if one considers that Israel (in 1952) and the Jewish Claims Conference (in 1961) explicitly did not ask Austria for "*Wiedergutmachung*" but for "compensation" (*Entschädigung*). The term *Wiedergutmachung* implies *state* responsibility, thus denying the illegality of the Anschluß. It is therefore not officially used for payments to victims and their heirs or representatives in Austria.

Public Opinion and "Slumber"

Contrary to the now popular stereotypes about their country, educated Austrians and those old enough to remember did *not* learn only ten years ago that there had been Nazis in their country—among them some prominent criminals. Admittedly, apart from historical research and inclusion in school curricula, there had not been much public, controversial, and continuous discussion of these matters, except on certain occasions, such as the airing of the movie *Holocaust*. True enough, in Austria, only part of the population is interested in history and public affairs of the past. True enough, many people preferred to "forget," to keep silent, or blame others. Here too Austria is not unique. It has been known for a while that few Nazi criminals were punished and some even had postwar careers. It was no secret that victims had received no respect, inadequate compensation, and little justice. These facts had been available and frequently described and deplored in literary and scientific works long before Waldheim. For example, *Herr Karl*, the biographic monologue of an Austrian opportunist, became a minor classic in the early 1960s. Questionable claims of ignorance and innocence by many former Austrian Nazis was a matter of sarcastic jokes among educated people. Few of them knew *The Sound of Music*, and fewer would have shared its political message about Austria.

Bogus "Revelations"

What surprised Austrians in 1986 and thereafter was not a "discovery" of a dubious past, but the international attacks on a man who had twice been elected Secretary-General of the United Nations by the international community. This had happened with the consent of the four occupation powers who, unlike Austria, had Waldheim's war records on file. It astonished many that Waldheim was barred from entering the United States, which had transplanted prominent Nazis to their country after 1945 and helped, for example, Klaus Barbie to escape. What surprised Austrians was not the "discovery" that there are politicians—in Austria and elsewhere—who do not always disclose their history including mistakes and misdeeds. It seemed astonishing that one politician received exemplary punishment for lack of honesty, while others were welcomed and some even received posthumous honors by the very same governments which had previously denounced them as serious war criminals (as was the case at the Emperor of Japan's funeral, attended by U.S. diplomats). What surprised Austrians was that their whole country became equated with a man whom only a minority had elected (more than usual did not vote at all), and for reasons which had nothing to do with the past (Waldheim had been ahead in the polls all along). True enough, the Waldheim events triggered new discussions and encouraged historical research. People who previously had no interest and little knowledge of history were educated about basic facts concerning the past. This was a positive effect. But some confused their personal ignorance with an overall ignorance and proudly proclaimed themselves as pioneers of enlightenment.

Cui bono?

To portray Austrian identity as based on lies and amnesia is factually unjustified. It is unwise to forget that denying Austria's (historical, cultural, ethnic, national, moral) legitimacy has always been a tool of the Pan-Germanic expansionists in Austria and outside of the country, who strove for the abolition of the country for the benefit of a larger German state. Thus it should not be ignored that Jörg Haider more than once claimed that Austria is an artificial creation based on lies, that most Austrians were in favor of the 1938 Anschluß, and that they avoided common responsibility in 1945, abandoning their German brothers by artificially and maliciously creating a state and identity of their own. This claim serves only to support the world-view of unrepenting Pan-Germans.

History Explains All?

True, some Austrians are uncomfortable with the past. Some, for instance, do not like to know the truth about the *Wehrmacht*, the German army, parts of which were involved in crimes, as Judt points out. But some Germans are also uncomfortable about knowing the truth. The latest exhibition about *Wehrmacht* crimes aroused strong emotions in both countries. On the other hand, the victims of Nazi military "justice" (at least 30,000 death sentences), especially deserters from the *Wehrmacht*, have not been rehabilitated to date in (Western) Germany. With very few exceptions, none of the thousands of Nazi judges and prosecutors have been brought to justice. Most of them continued their careers in (Western) Germany. Their cruel sentences are still legally valid in that country, regardless of repeated efforts to change them. Honorable German politicians such as the Honorary Chairman of the CDU/CSU-parliamentarians, Alfred Dregger, publicly questioned in 1995 whether Germany's defeat in 1945 should be commemorated as liberation from the Nazi regime. Some German authorities refuse to, or are slow to, re-name streets named after prominent Nazis and anti-Semites. But who would therefore conclude that "Germany" as a whole is uncomfortable with its past and therefore has "bogus legitimacy," as

Judt does with Austria? If radical clean-up after a criminal past were
to be considered the indispensable basis of sound, unambiguous, un-
questionable legitimacy of a country, how many countries could be
considered legitimate? If myths—erroneous, historically inaccurate self-
conceptions—were to de-legitimize social entities and nations, how
many could claim legitimacy? Such self-conceptions or identities are
the rule rather than the exception in the process of nation-building.

Austrian Nationalism and "German National Nostalgia"

Austrian "nationalism" today does not "retain the substance of
German national nostalgia," claims Judt. On the contrary, if there is
one lesson Austrians have learned from history, in particular the
experience of 1938-45, it is that they are not German and, with all due
respect, do not want to be part of Germany. Anschluß is out of the
question—in Austria and in Germany—not because it is prohibited, as
Tony Judt appears to insinuate. Austrians do not *wish* their country to
be a mere annex of Germany. But it should not be ignored or omitted
(as Judt does) that there are many Germans who—based on the
predominantly ethnic-cultural-linguistic concept of nationhood—still
question or deny that Austria is a nation, even as they do not question
its existence as a state. True, Germany plays a very important role,
both in real terms and in the memory of many Austrians. Many have
retained a partly fearful, partly jealous, partly self-righteous inferiority
complex. The benign neglect of Austria by many Germans, the
imbalance in the degree of mutual attention, is, however, quite normal
between neighbors of such disproportionate size and power.[4]

In sharp contrast to altitudes prevalent in the 1920s and 1930s,
today most Austrians have no problem with their nationality. Haider's
excursions into Pan-Germanic rhetoric deter voters rather than attract
them. He recently appears to have cast off this aspect of his political
rhetoric and now presents himself as an Austrian nationalist. Given his
background and past as a German nationalist—his embrace of a
profoundly anti-Austrian ideology— such a sudden conversion invites
suspicion. Haider is on record as having termed the Austrian nation a
"monstrosity" (*Mißgeburt*). It is grotesque to equate a German nationalist (*Deutschnationaler*) with Austrian "nationalism," as Judt does. The
other political forces, however, for whatever reasons, *de facto* appear

to have abandoned the "national" theme, thus leaving it to Haider. In the absence of competitors, Haider ironically now acts as the true spokesman for the *Heimat*. He gains strength by posturing as an Austrian patriot against Brussels—the David slaying the anonymous Goliath forces of the European Union threatening Austria. This political ammunition was involuntarily delivered to Haider by the massive governmental disinformation campaign preceding the vote on EU-membership on 12 June 1994. Haider almost overnight shifted from a long-nourished pro-European Community stance to opposing it. But his opponents failed to gain anything from this shift. Judt simplistically mentions none of this, explaining Austrian identity in terms of an allegedly "Austrian" nationalism, which he sees represented by some-one whose world-view is, in essence, anti-Austrian.

Purposeful Invention of Austria as "Neutral"

Judt claims that the vision of Austrian identity as neutral (between East and West) was an artificial and opportunistic construction, "sitting oddly with Austria's past." Such judgment reveals considerable ignor-ance. Due to its geopolitical situation at the crossroads of European cultural, ethnic, and religious realms, instances of *de facto* neutrality and a politics of mediation are found in the early history of what is now Austria. The recurrent experience of involvement in complex and futile affairs, of domination by neighbors more powerful and resolute, of ending up on the losing side in most military confrontations, have nourished a sociopolitical climate which is the basis of neutrality. The idea of neutrality had already been on the minds of Austrian politicians before 1933/38, and definitely grew between 1945-55. This idea trans-lated into international legal terms in 1955, during the Cold War. This neutrality is anything but artificial and reflects ancient experiences.

As do other ancient peoples, Austrians retain a memory of genera-tions sent to battlefields for allegedly good purposes. Neutrality also strongly symbolizes the willingness to achieve self-determination as a result of the experiences of 1938-45. It stands for pursuing a distinctive path—distinguishable from the German one, in particular. Neutrality is thus an important ingredient of Austrian national self-perception and self-respect. It is no coincidence, therefore, that neutrality was viewed with suspicion and disappointment at its inception in 1955 by the Adenauer government, and refuted by the predecessor of Haider's

Freedom Party. Haider himself now urges for Austria's North Atlantic Treaty Organization (NATO) membership, which would translate into the definite abandonment of neutrality. Judt mentions none of this.

"What Else Could Austria Consist of?"

Judt insinuates that Austria lost its sense and purpose of national existence which, according to him, was "consciously conceived," by Bruno Kreisky, as being situated between "East and West." This judgment too betrays ignorance of the facts. It wisely suggests that Austria had been adrift. Furthermore, Judt's analysis omits the fact that the country has always been firmly imbedded in the West. His finding discards the fact that national loyalty has more to do with social peace, political stability, and economic success than with the international positioning of one's country. This judgment of an artificially created and then forgotten purpose is furthermore based on the assumption that every country must have a purpose or mission, possibly along the lines of the "American dream." In the case of Austria, Judt ignores or is ignorant of the disastrous role of such "mission mentality" in the past. The loss of a catholic, imperial mission after 1918, coupled with the refusal by mission-craving elites to accept a small post-1918 Austria, were the roots of the 1938-45 disaster. The acceptance of a small, non-missionary Austria after 1945 had marked the beginning of productive cooperative politics within the country and in its relations with other nations. The urge to be an Empire or part of one has been absent from the current world-view of most Austrians. This is, however, no longer the case for some of their political elites, ridiculous as this may seem given the real prestige of the country. Austrian politics *vis-à-vis* former Yugoslavia and the unconditional drive for EU membership are cases in point. Judt mentions none of this. Instead he falls into the trap of missing the purposes of Austrian national existence, certainly a favorite theme of Pan-Germanic nationalists. But who, on the other hand, needs, for example, England, Norway, France, or New Zealand, and for what purposes? If nation-states can only exist on grounds of a purpose, God save them, and us from them! For good reasons, namely from bad experiences, many ordinary people retain a profound distrust of nations with missions and strong national purposes. Changes in the macro-political field, such as the implosion of the Soviet Union, obviously create uncertainty and require political reorientation. It would be desirable if these processes could be concluded with greater dedication, skill, and speed. Austrians have not been more puzzled or paralyzed on this account than others. These changes have not, as Judt insinuates, eliminated what he obviously considers the main and bogus foundation of national existence and thrown the country off course. If Austria appears to be waffling, this is primarily due to the present lack of political leadership among the great powers.

Counterproductive Exaggerations

In the aftermath of the alleged discovery of an Austrian Nazi past, it became fashionable to denounce the whole country as based on lies, and to denounce its inhabitants as notorious, and even genetic, criminals and liars. It became acceptable to explain each and every unpleasant event and negative development as resulting from unrepented crimes of the past. It became common to do penance in public, along the German model. Most of these (self) accusations have done nothing to change the realities of xenophobia or anti-Semitism. But they at least earn Austria, and especially the accusers, some international applause. They are particularly welcome in the German *feuilleton*.

It also became fashionable to not only criticize and question political and social habits and institutions, which is justified and necessary, but to denounce them and urge for their destruction without recommending any substitute. Thus, Haider as well as some of his leftist critics justifiably criticize cases of corruption and patronage, and shortcomings in democratic life and in the social partnership. But they also claim that such deficiencies are typically Austrian. They proclaim that Austria is uniquely backward, hopelessly provincial, a corrupt country. This is often coupled with the belief that all is much better in Germany. Such ignorance nourishes the revival of the traditional Austrian inferiority complex. These exaggerations discourage serious attempts at change. These Austro-centric findings are (totally and) often deliberately ignorant of the rest of the world and hence profoundly provincial. Judt reiterates them without reflection.

"There Had Never Been an 'Austrian' Nation"

Pan-Germans, also in Haider's entourage, would certainly rejoice if they read in Judt's article that "there had never been an 'Austrian' nation," and that "Austria's new found identity effectively disappeared." They would welcome utterances such as "one characteristically 'Austrian' sentiment is the one expressed by Haider." They would certainly agree that "in some respects the country is even run the way Communist States once claimed to function." Haider said so himself repeatedly! On the basis of the (Pan-Germanic) ethnic/cultural/lingual concept of nation, one may doubt Austria's identity. This, however, should not be done in ignorance of German neo-nationalistic tendencies. The consequences of such conceptions should be applied to other nations and nation-states, including Germany. All of them are by nature artificial constructs. On the basis of history, it is legitimate to question the territorial integrity and national existence of every single country in the world. Judt points out that the constituent parts of Austria preceded the Austrian state of today and retain distinctive identities. He seems to indicate that Austria is therefore a piecemeal, politically unstable construction. Is such a history of contemporary nation states not the norm? Which *Länder* (of Germany), for instance, were part of today's Germany 130 years ago and do they not retain "distinctive identities"? Of course they do, just as the former Western and Eastern parts of that country retain their identities.

Confused "Identity"?

Austria—like most countries in Europe and elsewhere—is undergoing and facing changes more rapidly than used to be the case. Many countries are at a loss. New ways and methods have not been found. Some of Austria's intellectuals therefore have been diagnosing an "identity crisis" which they date back to Waldheim and the alleged discovery of history. They deplore a lack of "identity" and claim that Austria's identity consists only of suppressed and unrepented crimes as well as lies about history. In their search for something especially Austrian, possibly a mission justifying its existence, they discover nothing but a nightmare. Judt appears to reiterate this sentiment of some Austrian intellectuals. It is futile if not dangerous. Austria has no one single identity, but many, and it has no need for one. Austria is multi-ethnic and multi-cultural in substance. Its national foundation is not one of ethnicity, as in the Pan-Germanic ideology, constitutional reality, and political practice. This foundation is a mixture of the Western concept of nationhood (everyday *volonté de tous*, or political will to live as a nation) and the awareness of sufficient distinctions from neighbors on historical and cultural grounds.

Small and Backward?

Austria is not nearly as sensationally interesting as its critics describe it. Also, it is not "one of the smallest countries in Europe"; quite a few European states are smaller or have fewer inhabitants. The idea of "smallness" is a remnant of nostalgia for Austria's "great" past, and is not shared by most contemporary Austrians. They do *not* primarily live on tourism, nationalized industries and state bureaucracies—another pejorative cliché—but on industry, manufacturing, and services, like most modern European countries (see the Nowotny article in this forum). These erroneous disclosures only serve to reinforce the overall picture of contempt, prevalent in Judt's portrayal of Austria and alien to reality and the self-conception of most Austrians. According to all international ratings, Austria is among the most stable, democratic, and economically viable countries of the world.

Haider

Three quarters of Judt's article is more or less directly devoted to Jörg Haider, the leader of the Freedom Party. This is a common media technique. Haider—or the mere image of him, right or wrong—is always sure to gain attention. Some of his most dedicated opponents in the Austrian press use the same strategy to get attention: Haider on the cover or in the headlines, even if there is nothing new to report, ensures sales. The more outrageous, scary (for instance as in Judt's article, Haider as Hitler), the better. The effect of this Haider cottage industry is public relations *for* Haider, certainly unintended by many. But being in the news is primarily what counts, irrespective of substance. Judt follows this line.

Haider: "Just Three Themes"

Judt reduces Haider's politics and success to just three themes: xenophobia, anti-socialism, and Nazi sympathies. This is a huge distortion of reality. While all of these themes are found or can be extrapolated from Haider's repertoire, they are not the only and especially not the *decisive* ones. Decisive for Haider's rise are his populist political style,[5] conforming to and supported by the media, and the persistent inability of others, especially leading figures in the two strongest political parties, to redress shortcomings within their spheres of influence. To portray Haider, let alone those who vote for the Free- dom Party, as neo-Nazis, is inaccurate, ineffective, and counter- productive.

Xenophobia and Anti-Semitism

Judt's attempts to prove Haider's xenophobia and anti-Semitism are much less skillful than Haider's scapegoating techniques. Haider does not only slander persons who happen to be Jewish but many other groups as well. One of his favorite skills is to quote in the affirmative opponents and people who would have nothing to do with him or his views, among them many Jews such as Theodor Herzl and Bruno Kreisky. One can be pretty sure that he quotes Tony Judt to his advan- tage, especially Judt's findings about Austrian Nazi "amnesia," "bogus legitimacy," "slumber," and "communist-like-run-country."

To conclude that Haider's electoral successes indicate wide accep- tance of xenophobia in Austria is, at best, short-sighted. Fear and dislike of foreigners is not remarkably stronger in Austria than in most other countries. Vienna harbors about 20 percent foreigners. Many citi- zens are foreign-born or second generation Austrians; many live in mixed marriages—without creating major social tensions. The extent of extremist violence by the right in Austria is considerably lower than in many European countries. Until the wave of letter bombs and the murder of four gypsies (presumably originating from a single criminal or a rather small group of conspirators), nobody had been killed, and very few people were injured in Austria, as opposed to dozens killed in Germany and in other European countries. There are no mass gatherings of right-wing extremists and no cheering onlookers of right- wing extremist crimes as elsewhere. It is, of course, possible to find people anywhere who will pronounce stupid and inhumane views about their fellow human beings. Judt quotes a neighbor of a letter bomb victim who voices understanding for this crime. Many others with op- posing views could also be cited. Judt does not quote them. The largest postwar political demonstration in Austria (about 250,000 people in Vienna alone) was directed against Haider's tactics of stirring up xeno- phobia. Judt does not mention it.

Statements about limiting the influx of foreigners and denouncing the disadvantaged as abusing the social system are a recurrent feature in the rhetoric of successful and respectable politicians and political parties in many countries. Some of these pronouncements originate with the likes of Pat Buchanan and Ross Perot in the United States (not to mention of David Duke[6]). Some emanate from parliamentarians and members of government in the presently ruling parties in Great Britain and France, to mention just a few. Some are shockingly apparent, as in the ruling parties in Germany (like in the Bavarian CSU). Their aim to integrate the right fringes of society into mainstream parties was publicly proclaimed. Some Germans are sensible enough to bless heaven and earth for the fact that Haider cannot run for office in Germany. They know that Haider or someone like him would have a good chance in Germany too, especially if the politicians were to react as inadequately as they do in Austria. The resemblance of Haider's views to those of some respectable German and other international politicians is striking. It would certainly be unfair and irrelevant to characterize, for instance, Germany in terms of some political statements uttered during the prolonged "asylum debate," or the United States by way of some notorious opposition leaders or the rhetoric around the bombing in Oklahoma City. Resentment of foreigners and fear of rapid transformation are not limited to Austria, nor to Europe, nor to right-wingers.

"Austrian Sentiment" Best Expressed by Haider

Haider's political advance was clearly stopped at the elections of December 1995. As before in 1994, three-quarters of the Austrian electorate voted for parties that were distinctly anti-Haider. The same applies to the EU parliamentary elections in October 1996. The ÖVP and SPÖ together lost more than a million votes, but Haider also lost many thousands of votes (because of non-voters), a fact hardly reflected anywhere in the Austrian or international press. Therefore, three-quarters of Judt's article should have been devoted to other politicians rather than Haider. But this would not have served any clichéd agenda and would, moreover, have been less sensational. The foundations of Austria's postwar system did not begin to crumble in 1994, but much earlier. Both "big" parties, the People's Party (ÖVP) and the Social Democrats (SPÖ), had been steadily loosing support and influence since the early 1980s, a process of de-alignment within the traditional political systems which was common to many European countries (*vide* Italy). Haider's advance will, however, be stopped not if he is criminalized and his voters are denounced as neo-Nazis, but only if their concerns are taken more seriously. These concerns cannot be adequately described merely as xenophobia, Nazi-nostalgia, social envy, and fear of the future. Chances for productive change would be greatly enhanced if the often unconscious and certainly involuntary complicity ceased: between Haider and some of his critics, especially in the media, who exaggerate even his exaggerations and thrive on the outrage on which he relies. Judt's article is one example of this ignorant and innocent complicity. Some of the most detrimental "Haider effects" on (Austrian) politics have been polarization, a simplistic worldview, deterioration of (verbal) political culture, and a blockade of productive reforms and constructive opposition. It is by now detrimental to one's reputation not to equate Haider with a perennial Nazi-Austria and not to be frightened to death, but to take a dispassionate look at contemporary Austria. Judt's article operates along convenient, simplistic, and therefore largely useless lines.

Austrian Model?

It used to be fashionable in Austria to portray this country as a model of social peace and stability. For some time now it has been fashionable to portray Austria as a new model, one of evilness in the past, in the present, and in the future. For Judt, Haider, whom he implicitly equates with Austria, stands for the ghost of Europe yet to come. Nothing more flattering could ring in *Haider's* ears. This Austro-megalomania and the "Haider business" have economic foundations. They certainly do not promote, rather they hinder, a realistic critical view of Austria. If all or most Austrians are inherently or genetically Nazis, there is every excuse to do nothing about it and to abandon all hope, efforts, and the country itself. It would certainly be more fruitful to take notice of tendencies toward a rise in nationalism in almost all European countries (Austria's national pride has rather declined by contrast). The marginalization not only of outsiders but also of insiders (such as the weak, non-achievers, non-winners, non-mainstreamers) is apparent. Tendencies toward growing polarization, an antagonistic and simplistic worldview, and the relationship between the media and politics deserve more attention. Judt's article is hardly a contribution to this inquiry. Should one not become aware and alarmed and discuss the on-going weakening and dismantling of social and political institutions, such as those, hitherto widely accepted, that addressed social responsibility (*Sozialstaat*) in many European states? Are these institutions, admittedly often ineffective, to be replaced by an aggressive system of "survival of the fittest" or "winner takes all"?

Most of these tendencies are not alien to Austria, and Tony Judt accurately points in this direction. Nevertheless, his Haider-fixated field study more resembles a caricature than a portrait of contemporary Austria. Equating Haider with Austria and with "the Ghost of New Europe" is doing justice to none: neither to Haider, nor to Austria, nor to Europe.

NOTES

1. Anschluß is put under parentheses as the events of 1938 constituted a violent eradication of Austria by Nazi Germany and not the peaceful and voluntary joining that many among the Austrian (and German) elites had aspired to between 1918 and 1933.

2. Daniel Jonah Goldhagen, *Hitler's Willing Executioners: Ordinary Germans and the Holocaust* (New York: A. Knopf, 1996). See also the review of Goldhagen's book in this volume.

3. Brigitte Hamann, *Hitlers Wien: Lehrjahre eines Diktators* (Munich: Piper, 1996).

4. Herald von Rickhoff and Hauspeter Neuhold, eds., *Unequal Partners: A Comparative Analysis of Relations Between Austria and the Federal Republic of Germany and Between Canada and the United States* (Boulder, CO: Westview, 1993).

5. See, for example, Max Riedlsperger's essay and Peter Pulzer's review of the *Handbuch des Österreichischen Rechtsextremismus* in *Contemporary Austrian Studies* IV (1996): 351-74.

6. See, for example, Anton Pelinka and Susan Howell, "Duke and Haider: Right Wing Politics in Comparison," *CAS* II (1994): 152-71.

Judt Business

Thomas Nowotny

Tony Judt comments on the recent Austrian elections and on the rather strong showing of Jörg Haider, a Populist, right-wing politician. Judt's main conclusion is certainly to the point. The election results should not be taken lightly: Haider articulates fears, spite, and resentments that undermine not only the hold of traditional parties but the political system as such. The forces unleashed are likely to lead politics in a dangerous direction. These forces spell trouble not only for Austria, since Haider has his counterparts in other European nations. He thus represents tendencies that threaten the hidebound political process all over Europe.

Professor Judt uses various arguments to substantiate his conclusions, and 95 percent of them are factually correct. One could leave it at that, if the remaining five percent were random errors, which they are not.

Let us start with the innocuous claim that Austrians "derive their income in large measure from tourism and employment in nationalized industries and in the state bureaucracy." One need not be an economist to recognize that this cannot be so. Though tourism is important, and employment in the state sector relatively high, the main sources of employment are, of course, other than the above. Yet apart from this factual error, there is an innuendo which is difficult to ignore: the suggestion that Austrians are not very entrepreneurial. In addition, there is also the implication that the Austrians are among the most wealthy peoples of Europe by sheer accident. Actually, they have worked hard at becoming wealthy. The investment rate in Austria is one of the highest among economically mature countries.

Here is another example of evident bias: Judt finds it difficult to see how the inflow of foreigners could have become a political issue.

After all, "foreigners make up less than 9 percent of the Austrian population." The figure is roughly correct (it is actually 10 percent). Another fact is missing, however. Namely, this percentage is the highest in the European Union.

There is also a sweeping aside that "*Some* aspects of Austrian patronage procedures closely resemble the practices of Italian public life" (my emphasis). This makes one wonder what is meant by "some." Judt goes on to state that the Austrian and Italian systems are basically alike, with one exception: the Austrian system is still more efficient ("building companies may exploit party connections too...but the projects are solidly constructed and on time"). Others will certainly step in to defend the Italian construction industry. It is reputed to be among the world's best. I will, however, question the comparison between Italian and Austrian politics. Does Judt really believe that parties in Austria are mainly financed through kickbacks, that organized crime has penetrated politics, and that these politics are under the control of clans of retainers?

The system of the Austrian "*Proporz*" is difficult to explain to outsiders. Its reach has shrunk, and it is now limited to a few areas. Still, a number of key posts are reserved for (professionally qualified) members of particular groups. While that system does not apply to the vast majority of jobs, it still is valid, for example, for headmasters of schools, for the boards of the National Bank and of some utilities, and for various advisory groups, among others. Certainly, there is a trace of Southern Europe in this—something of the notorious Southern European "clientelism." But, to a greater extent, "*Proporz*" has elements that can also be found in other European countries which—like Austria—were riven by violent religious, political and ethnic divisions in the past. There is also a suggestion of the U.S. "group entitlements." Political scientists—and Tony Judt is one of them—have defined such societies as "neo-corporate." The Netherlands and Switzerland, for instance, are neo-corporate. Would Judt compare them to Italy?

There is a lengthy account of a speech given by Jörg Haider to members of the former *Waffen SS*. The event was videotaped by a German participant, and it was later shown on German television. After Austrian television had carefully investigated the authenticity of the tapes, it showed them as well. But this was after the last national elections. Judt believes it to be "doubtful whether it would have made a marked difference in the outcome" of these elections if the video tapes had been shown before the voting. How does he know? Did he do some polling that we don't know about? As it happened, after the showing of the tapes, there was a vast outcry, with some members of Haider's own party defecting from their leader. Polls taken later showed a further and rather substantial decline in Haider's popularity since that date. Many observers relate this change to the airing of the tapes.

Tony Judt has written,

Austria was consciously conceived, notably by Bruno Kreisky, the Socialist Chancellor from 1970 to 1983, as a country whose identity would henceforth derive from its geographical situation between the East and the West, its neutrality during the cold war, and its role as intermediary between first and third worlds...of what else could Austria consist? There has never been an Austrian nation.

But what is a nation? The answer is not always as evident for those who don't have the good fortune of a "manifest destiny" from "sea to shining sea." The best answer is still that a nation is a group of people who believe themselves to be a nation, who regard their association as legitimate, and who support their political institutions.

These things can be measured. According to such empirical findings, Austrians do not doubt that they are a separate nation. They do not see themselves as just an "appendix" to Germany. For Judt this is not enough. He believes that only those nations should exist who can claim some special "mission" which reinforces their identity. The pervasiveness of this magnificent thought has caused quite some trouble in Europe's past. So what is wrong with aspiring to nothing more than just being a state that functions well, is democratic and—as Chancellor Bruno Kreisky said—is a "good home to its citizens." Kreisky's legitimacy and political success was not due to his foreign policy (though it was a sensible and rather successful one). It was due to the fact that he liberalized and modernized Austria, and yes—also made its society more equitable.

As mentioned, foreign policy was not instrumental in his success. But as one of Kreisky's former aides, I would like to correct an impression that Judt has conveyed, that Kreisky tried to position Austria *between* East and West. I have differed with Judt on this issue before. He still has not substantiated his claim. Kreisky never called the "western" quality of the country into question. Nor did he entertain the illusion that the two competing systems would ultimately merge peacefully. He did, however, strive to minimize the risks inherent in the inevitable confrontation, and he pleaded with other Western countries to maintain some contacts with the East so as not to foreclose its eventual return to Europe.

On the other hand, Kreisky was the only one at the 1975 Helsinki summit to observe that an ideological compromise between the two systems would be impossible, and that the confrontation was bound to continue. He added prophetically, one might add, that in his view history would be on the side of the democracies. Nothing comparable was offered by any other Western diplomat.

Judt is also quite dogmatic in his judgments on the era between 1938 and 1945 when Austria was part of Hitler's Germany and on Austria's reckoning with this past. Much depends on how these facts are evaluated. Hopefully, we can at least agree on what really happened.

According to Judt, the union with Germany—the Anschluß—was "primarily an Austrian" and not a German initiative. He is right insofar as, in the 1920s, Austria's desire to unite with Germany was more pronounced than Germany's desire to unite with Austria. The situation changed, though, with Hitler's seizure of power in 1933. From that time on, two of the three major Austrian political forces, that is the Socialists and the Christian Democrats, opposed the Anschluß. Obviously, they did not relish the idea of joining a state where their sister parties had ceased to exist. Now, it was Hitler who made the Anschluß one of his main goals. A coup instigated by the Nazis failed in 1934. Thereafter, more subtle methods were employed. The Austrian government—authoritarian at the time—resisted. It lacked international backing, however. This was still the time when Britain and France thought it possible to appease Germany.

After yielding some terrain to Hitler in 1936, new demands were made upon the Austrian government in early 1938. If Austria had accepted these demands, the sovereignty of the Austrian state would, for all practical purposes, have ceased to exist. Austria decided to resist. Austria called for a referendum on the Anschluß that would have resulted in a 60 to 70 percent vote for continued Austrian independence. Hitler decided to prevent the vote from taking place and invaded the country.

The statement that Austria was the first victim of Hitler is therefore not a "mendacious myth." But it is equally true that once the Anschluß occurred, Austrians did cooperate with the new regime—and some quite enthusiastically. They did "their duty" in Hitler's army and a number of the more prominent war criminals were Austrian.

The postwar government nonetheless perceived itself to represent a population that had escaped the German yoke. Three factors (aside from sheer opportunism) make such a stance plausible:

1. One half of the government, and 70 percent of the newly elected parliament, consisted of former inmates of concentration camps. It would have been difficult to persuade them that they had been accomplices and not victims of the Nazi regime.

2. The vast majority of the population was of the same view. They might have seen things differently in their own and not too distant past. On the other hand, it is evident that Austrians increasingly resented the Germans and perceived them not as kin but as occupiers.

3. Some of the politicians came from the Austrian resistance movement. Austrian resistance was certainly less effective than French or Yugoslavian resistance, for example. It was not negligible, though, and it suffered heavy losses due to German countermeasures.

Professor Judt claims that "Austrian de-Nazification was even milder than the one undertaken by Germany." I know that similar claims have now been repeated so often that it has become established truth. But I still search for evidence to support them. As an Austrian, I am a bit hesitant to excuse whatever wrong might have been done by pointing to failures of other nations. But in a less than ideal world, people and nations will have to be judged not against an abstract moral standard but against how others behave in similar circumstances. One thing is clear: war crimes were prosecuted rather vigorously, as demonstrated by the large number of death sentences pronounced by special courts. As for the rest—I am waiting impatiently for Tony Judt to provide me with primary sources which show that the Austrians were worse than the others.

There can be no question, though, that Austria has failed to deal adequately with its past. This has come back to haunt our country. But, as a political scientist, Judt must answer the question as it pertains to "compared to whom," and "by which criteria."

A large part of the Austrian past—war literature, for instance, deals extensively with these questions of guilt. There is, for example, *Herr Karl*—a widely shown and devastatingly revealing play written in the 1960s. It targets the mean opportunism and mendacity of the "average guy." In the time between 1943 and 1955, the protagonist neatly switches sides whenever it proves useful. He is morally callous, completely self-centered, and full of prejudice and barely suppressed hostility. Nonetheless, he is also full of self-pity for all that he has been made to suffer. I know of no counterpart to this play in other countries that had come under the spell of the Third Reich.

These questions concerning Austria's past are evidently important both to Judt and to myself. Yet, they are not really central to the issue. All in all, I would agree with Judt when he maintains that Haider succeeds, not because of his excusing or even extolling Austria's Nazi past, but in spite of it. This is the really troubling aspect, and here too, I agree with Judt. Haider is scary not because he is a powerful politician in a uniquely amoral and decadent country of uncertain democratic credentials, but rather because he has become so prominent in a country that can claim to be rather successful, stable, decent, and democratic.

The FPÖ of Jörg Haider—Populist or Extreme Right-Winger?

Brigitte Bailer
Wolfgang Neugebauer

In his admirable article, Tony Judt has succeeded in portraying the essential characteristics of postwar Austrian politics, including the main problems of the country's domestic and foreign affairs. He has also dealt with the status and function of Jörg Haider's FPÖ, and attempted to place all these dimensions of Austrian political life in a European framework. While finding no fault with Judt's narrative or analysis, we consider it worthwhile to illuminate some key aspects of the development, structure, and politics of Haider's FPÖ. This is a democratic necessity, as Haider is adept at camouflaging his hidden agenda by dressing up his policies in democratic Austrian garb, thus deceiving not a few politicians and scholars at home and abroad. In the following pages, we attempt to show Haider's movement in its true colors, revealing the specifically Austrian contours of this "Ghost of the New Europe."

1986: The Shift Towards Racism
and Right-Wing Extremism

The Innsbruck party congress of the FPÖ in September 1986 must be seen as a milestone in Austrian domestic politics. The change in the leadership of the FPÖ signaled a marked shift of that party to the extreme right, led to the termination of the SPÖ-FPÖ coalition government, and affected the ensuing general election, which produced a socialist-conservative administration of the SPÖ and ÖVP. Since then, Austrian politics has been characterized by an increasingly sharp and effective onslaught on the part of Haider's FPÖ against the government of the day. The attacks of the FPÖ are directed at the political system as a whole and have brought the party unprecedented electoral success and considerable political influence. The perspective of Haider's party coming to power by means of the electoral process cannot be excluded. It is therefore of enormous significance for the future course of Austrian politics to examine the origins, structure, and goals of today's FPÖ, including its position in the political landscape. Countless evaluations of the Haiderite FPÖ have been published by politicians and scholars; the following summarizes our views.[1]

The Complete Elimination of the Traditionally Liberal Wing in the FPÖ

Following the Innsbruck congress, the liberally-inclined group led by Norbert Steger was forced out of the party. Those liberals who did remain in the FPÖ finally left in 1993. Under the leadership of Heide Schmidt and Friedhelm Frischenschlager they formed a new party, the Liberal Forum. Ultimately, they split from Haider over his initiative to launch a xenophobic referendum on the question of foreign workers in Austria.

Restructuring the FPÖ from a Members' Party to an Authoritarian Movement under Haider's Diktat

Whereas the pre-1986 FPÖ was characterized by rival groups and political personalities in their own right, Haider's present dominance of the party is not in dispute, mainly because of the electoral gains attributed to his name. He demands unquestioning loyalty, and callously removes any (even potential) rivals (for example, his former Chief Whip, Norbert Gugerbauer) or even those who promoted his political career for many years (Friedrich Peter, Mario Ferrari-Brunnenfeld, and Kriemhild Trattnig to name a few). All leading posts in the FPÖ are filled according to his whims, usually with people of low political caliber. Haider also decides the party line, and changes it abruptly and frequently. The 96 percent vote of acclamation he received as party leader at the Feldkirch congress of the FPÖ in November 1996 demonstrates that Jörg Haider is truly a "Führer" personality.

The Integration of Extreme Right-Wing and
Neo-Nazi Elements into the FPÖ

In the last ten years, there has been a reunification of sorts within the FPÖ's extreme right-wing Pan-Germanic groups, which had not been united for the preceding twenty years. Many persons mentioned in the *Handbuch des österreichischen Rechtsextremismus* can be found today in the FPÖ, including those who have made a career in the party or represent it in elected bodies at all levels. As the entry of such extremists into the FPÖ did not occur without the knowledge or consent of the domineering party leader, it is imprecise to speak here of infiltration tactics. In fact, it was more the case that traditional right-wing extremists were integrated into the FPÖ. Links between the party and neo-Nazi activists became evident. For example, it emerged that the youths who had desecrated the Jewish cemetery in Eisenstadt in 1992 (daubing the headstones with the swastika, the SS symbol and *"Heil Haider!"* slogans) were well-known to the then General Secretary of the FPÖ, Karl Schweitzer, subsequently removed by Haider. The accused had been taught by Schweitzer in secondary school, were members of the FPÖ youth organization (*Ring Freiheitlicher Jugend*), and one of them had stood for the FPÖ at elections. Many FPÖ politicians, not least Haider, received their political socialization in the Pan-Germanic *Burschenschaften* and other student or academic bodies, all of which consider the *Aula* magazine (published in Graz) to be their mouthpiece for propaganda and ideology. After the *Aula* manager had been convicted in court for neo-Nazi activities (Holocaust denial), Haider denied any links between the magazine and the FPÖ, despite the fact that he had supplied *Aula* with no less than twenty-five interviews or articles up to that juncture. The latest highpoint in the fusion of the extreme right with the FPÖ was an event to commemorate the one-thousandth anniversary of the first mention of Austria (*Ostarrichi*) in a historical document. The *Festkommers* was organized by FPÖ members, the Pan-Germanic *Burschenschafter*, and other extremist representatives of the "Third *Lager*," that is, those groups or parties not aligned to either the Left or Catholic conservatism. Haider was billed to speak at the *Festkommers* on 30 November, but declined under pressure. Many of the FPÖ parliamentary group were prominently in attendance and the party subsidized the spectacle with a large sum.

The FPÖ Moves Right: Haider
Becomes Outspoken

The change of course in the FPÖ towards the far right is not only visible in terms of party personnel, but also in the utterances, actions, and policies of Haider himself. For our purposes, it suffices to refer to some of his better-known statements which disclose his extreme right-wing and neo-Nazi sympathies: defamation of the Austrian nation as "an ideological monstrosity," his praising of "the proper employment policies of the Third Reich," interpreting the world war Hitler launched as Europe's war of defense against "Bolshevism," finding words of praise for the traditions of the *Waffen-SS*, and condemning the verdicts passed at Nuremberg. Two key areas of Haider's agitation have a special significance in connection with his public statements.

Haider's Critique of Democracy

The permanent, systematic, and radical criticism of the "system" of representative democracy and of the political parties refounded at the beginning of the Second Republic in 1945 is of the utmost significance. At the heart of Haider's fundamental opposition to the democratic system lies an anti-pluralistic concept of what politics should be, best expressed in his vision of an authoritarian "Third Republic" with built-in plebiscitary correctives. In spreading his views, Haider uses an aggressive political style which does not shrink from making unjustified, defamatory remarks or naming the victims of his vituperation in public.

The Anti-Foreigner Policy of the FPÖ

This aspect of Haiderite politics has overtly racist traits and aims similar to those pursued by the letter-bomb terrorists and neo-Nazis: the rejection of a multicultural society, a stance which has contributed greatly to a climate of latent or open violence against foreigners or those held to be friendly towards them. Haider rejects universal human rights unequivocally and on principle—he has demanded that Austria withdraw its acceptance of the European Human Rights Convention. Presenting the FPÖ as a new "workers' party" and calling for the establishment of trade unions under his control are two policies which Haider shares with Le Pen's *Front National*.

In this context, one must address the question whether parallels exist between the policies of the FPÖ and those of National Socialism, not so much in respect to the mass murder carried out by the Nazi regime, but in the image the NSDAP projected before it gained state power. The historian Franz Schausberger, now Governor of Salzburg Province, has written a precise analysis of how the NSDAP helped to destroy the parliamentary system in Austria by means of the systematic agitation its elected members carried out in the provincial assemblies (*Landtage*) during the years 1932-33. These methods are quite similar to those used by the FPÖ: moving countless emergency motions in Parliament, tumultuous behavior in the Chamber, dramatizing real or alleged scandals and cases of corruption, campaigning against the salary scales of politicians or the privileges of the Austrian bureaucracy, attacking the cultural politics of central and local government, and making political capital out of cases of social welfare abuse. Other unmistakable characteristics of FPÖ politics are the leader-cult, the presentation of issues with propagandistic fanfare, and, of course, social demagoguery. The primarily anti-Semitic racism of the Nazis corresponds to the xenophobic campaigns of Haider, which are his best instrument for mobilizing voters at election time. Finally, but not con-clusively, the dynamic of the NSDAP's growing influence up to 1933 can be compared to the successes of the FPÖ since 1986. In evaluating the policies of the Haiderite FPÖ, it is important to inquire whether Haider has moved away from his original political position, which was formed by the ex-NSDAP milieu of his youth and family. Peter Michael Lingens, a columnist in the Vienna daily newspaper *Der Standard*, who long believed that Haider was capable of changing for the better, wrote an article on this question under the title "A Run-of-the-mill Young Nazi." The piece, which Haider did not make the basis for a libel action although threatened to do so, contains the following key passage: "Haider is only pretending. When he speaks from the heart, he says things like those in his speech in Krumpendorf. Then he has to keep his hand firmly on the lectern, otherwise it would shoot up to salute."

In addition, Bruno Kreisky, in whose footsteps Haider maintains he himself is now treading, stated in 1988: "Then there are real Nazis, highly dangerous types.... In my opinion, Jörg Haider has become one of them."

The Camouflage as "Statesman" and "Austrian Patriot"

In reaction to the criticism voiced against the aggressive style and extreme right-wing content of Haider's policies, which impair his public image and suitability as a partner in a coalition government, the FPÖ leader now and again announces his conversion to a moderate politician and statesman, thereby winning the approval of gullible parliamentary colleagues and journalists. His tendency to camouflage his real political intentions is most apparent in his newly-discovered "Austrian patriotism." The traditional Pan-Germanism which molded the FPÖ since its inception—and Jörg Haider in his childhood—is still included in the FPÖ's party program. The Pan-Germanic core of the "Third *Lager*" has proven to be a major stumbling-block in political debate, particularly as it now attracts only the stagnant segment of FPÖ traditionalists and is counterproductive in regard to the winning over of new voters. Haider realized this, deposed his ideological watchdog Andreas Mölzer, and stated that he rejected "jingoistic Pan-Germanism." However, an analysis of his statements, those of his colleagues, and those from journals close to the FPÖ, indicates that this is not the case. According to the 15 November 1996 issue of *Junge Freiheit*, Haider, when renewing the traditional vow of his *Burschenschaft* (Silvania), said that one "must stand up for the preservation of German customs and traditions." Hitherto, neither Haider nor his party have ever openly stated their allegiance to an independent Austrian nation fully detached from Germany, a statement which is a matter of course for all other political parties. Moreover, his utterances on Austrian patriotism are implausible, empty phrases, a playing with words.

The Austrian "patriotism" Haider now proclaims has two main political functions: first, to deceive the public about the consistently Pan-Germanic, and in the last instance, anti-Austrian, basic stance of the FPÖ; second, to mobilize or utilize xenophobic attitudes in the population. The fact that Haider's right-wing politics dominate the FPÖ should not be taken as implying that the entire party or its voters share such views, nor that his electoral successes are primarily due to extreme right-wing politics or propaganda. Essentially, extreme right-wing positions within the FPÖ are held by old Pan-Germanic elements, by students, and by those extremists, mentioned earlier, who have been integrated into the party since 1986. On the other hand, many of the new party members have a hazy political profile and say that they are motivated by Haider's personality and policies. His attractiveness is mainly based on the talent to present himself well in public, especially on television, where he slips into the role of crusader, fighting against shortcomings, corruption, and the system of privilege in public life, arguing like an advocate of the man in the street against all the injustice in the world. As many of the critical points he makes have substance and are, to a certain extent, subsequently rectified, he can easily promise what he, as an opposition politician, will not have to fulfil. He thus finds great resonance among voters who are deeply troubled by the many changes in modern society or who have become the disadvantaged victims or "losers" of modernization.

Haider offers simple solutions for complex problems of a personal or economic nature. With its smear and hate campaign against foreign workers, who are portrayed as criminally inclined and who are unfavorably compared to the "decent, hard-working Austrians," the FPÖ can latch on to authoritarian and racist feelings which are widespread in the country. With the assistance of the yellow press, the FPÖ can appeal to such prejudice and heighten its tone. In contrast, the anti-fascist criticism of the FPÖ, shared by only a part of the media, is obviously not getting across to the general public.

Haider knows that he will never gain power on his own strength, but will do so only in a coalition with others. He also knows that his lack of "respectability" is the greatest obstacle to this end. Apart from projecting himself as a democratic Austrian, Haider is also at pains to play the active Catholic, courting the favor of the right wing of Catholicism, that strain in the Austrian Church personified by Kurt Krenn, the Bishop of Sankt Pölten and a sympathizer of the FPÖ. On the other hand, Haider attempts to portray himself as Kreisky's rightful heir, currying favor with frustrated social democrats. At any rate, Haider is determined to broaden the political spectrum of the FPÖ and has had some success in persuading respected personalities to stand for the party at elections—sportsmen, journalists, businessmen, managers, and judges, to mention a few. The candidature of Peter Sichrovsky, a journalist of Jewish origin, to stand for the FPÖ at the European Elections on 13 October 1996, was part of this new strategy. This candidate did not go down well with the FPÖ rank-and-file, but Haider hoped that the surprise of Sichrovsky would help the FPÖ to break out of the quarantine imposed on it by liberal, left-wing, and Jewish circles. The ploy was also designed to refute the charge of anti-Semitism leveled at the party and repair the negative image it has abroad. In this sense, the FPÖ can be seen to belong to the "New Right," as an extreme right-wing party which is outwardly modern, but still disseminates the old message and slogans and endeavors to overcome the political stigmatization under which it has been placed since Haider's ascendancy, so that it can win partners for a political alliance and increase its overall influence.

We admit that there are other evaluations of Haider's FPÖ.[2] The extreme left, for example, is sometimes of the opinion that Haider is an ordinary politician within the capitalist system, whose policies differ only slightly from those of the government; the formal anti-fascism of the State uses Haider as a decoy, in order to divert attention from the unsocial, anti-worker politics of the ruling coalition. Some social democratic politicians want to end the strategy of excluding Haider from democratic participation. They hope that the ÖVP would then be weakened, and do not rule out the prospects of some political deal between Haider and their own party which would consolidate the position of the declining SPÖ. Bourgeois commentators state that the FPÖ is a normal middle-class party, Haider just a populist without a political program or aims who wants to enter the government at all costs.

Such individual opinions do not stand up to rigorous analysis or answer the following question: What will happen when Haider is in power? The expectation that such a politician will sooner or later fail because of insoluble problems was the grave mistake made in Hitler's case and had disastrous consequences. Haider's contempt for humanity, specifically his targeting of party "rivals," political opponents, and foreigners, demonstrate what he now stands for in his oppositional role. We can only imagine with dread the wide-ranging measures he would put into effect as head of government: a profound change in Austria's political climate, the introduction of inhuman policies against foreign workers, and restrictions on the democratic rights of native Austrians. Haider has already announced what lies in store—forced labor for the unemployed and curtailing the freedom of the press, to give but two examples.

"The Ghost of the New Europe?"

By winning over 28 percent of the votes cast at the European Election last October, Haider's FPÖ has established itself as the most successful, extremely right-wing party in Europe, thus becoming a model for the far right in the other states of the European Community. Even if one does not agree with our estimation of the FPÖ as an extremely right-wing party threatening the contemporary political system, but maintains that it is a populist movement of the right striving to gain power by mobilizing as many voters as possible in order to enforce profound political change, there is little disagreement about the content and style of the policies of the FPÖ at the moment. The following components of right-wing policies apply to Haider's movement, or serve as models for less successful parties of a similar political complexion:

* ethnocentrism, nationalism and chauvinism;
* smear and agitational campaigns with strong racist overtones against foreign workers, emigrants, and refugees, especially those from southeastern Europe, Asia, and Africa;
* rejection of the European Community, the Maastricht Treaty, and the common currency, the Euro;
* a permanent debasement of the parliamentary party system and of representative democracy, authoritarian tendencies, and hostility to pluralist politics;
* a social demagoguery which exploits the unpopularity of politicians and utilizes fears held by the population about the present and future economic climate;
* law-and-order sloganeering, overdramatizing criminal statistics in order to whip up fear and emotion;
* the charismatic leader, the cult of the leader, and propagating the need for "strongman" government;
* portraying the world in black and white, propagating hatred and images or objects of hatred;
* an aggressive and offensive manner when confronting political opponents or enemies;
* staging politics like a show, especially during television appearances and appealing to the lowest instincts of the masses as practiced by the yellow press.

What political scientists call "de-alignment" in Western Europe, that is, the erosion or collapse of the traditional links between parties and their voters and the "decline of great parties," has reached a climax in Italy. In Austria too, great inroads have been made into traditional voting patterns, a development which owes a great deal to the agitation of Haider's FPÖ. This process can be reversed. However, no signs of it are present just now. "The Ghost of the New Europe" is indeed present in Jörg Haider's policies, in his reconstructed FPÖ. This perspective of a dangerously unstable political scene does not augur well for Austria's future.

NOTES

1. For greater detail, see Brigitte Bailer-Galanda, *Haider wörtlich, Führer in die Dritte Republik* (Vienna: Löcker Verlag, 1995); *Handbuch des österreichischen Rechtsextremismus*, ed. Stiftung Dokumentationsarchiv des österreichischen Widerstandes (Vienna: Deuticke Verlag, 1994); Brigitte Bailer-Galanda and Wolfgang Neugebauer, *Incorrigibly Right: Right-Wing Extremists, "Revisionists," and Anti-Semites in Austrian Politics Today*, (Vienna: Stiftung Dokumentationsarchiv and New York: Anti-Defamation League, 1996).

2. See Gerd Kräh, *Die Freiheitlichen unter Jörg Haider. Rechtsextreme Gefahr oder Hoffnungsträger für Österreich*, (Frankfurt: Peter Lang Verlag, 1996); Markus Wilhelm, "Haider=Vranitzky," *Foehn* 21 (1995): 3-81; Max Riedlsperger, "The FPÖ and the Right," *CAS* IV (1996): 351-68; and Peter Pulzer's review of *Handbuch des Österreichischen Rechtsextremismus*, ibid., 369-74.

HISTORIOGRAPHY ROUNDTABLE
PLACING JOHN BOYER'S WORK IN AUSTRIAN HISTORIOGRAPHY

Introduction

These papers were presented at the annual conference of the German Studies Association in Seattle, Washington (10-13 October 1996). Judson and Beller revised their GSA presentations, Pelinka and Hanisch did not. We would like to thank the Austrian Cultural Institute in New York and Dr. Peter Mikl for generously supporting this panel.

While Carl Schorske's work on the *fin-de-siècle* culture of Vienna has attracted immense interest in Austria and abroad, John Boyer's massive and erudite volumes on turn-of-the-century Viennese politics have been largely ignored outside the immediate purview of specialists in the field.

Naturally, the Austrian public prefers to dwell on the glories of its great cultural past rather than confront the netherworlds of its problematical political past. Boyer's work makes vital contributions to the rise of the conservative politics in Cisleithanian Habsburg Austria (and the demise of liberalism), the emergence of Lueger's populist Viennese machine politics, and adds to *Bürgertumsforschung* in Austria. Boyer also places Habsburg Austria—often marginalized to the periphery— into the mainstream of European historical scholarship. Boyer's findings on the nature of Christian Social politics and ideology also add tremendous insights to a more sophisticated understanding of the political history and the political culture of the two Austrian Republics. These four essays place Boyer at the *center* of Austrian political historiography where he belongs.

These essays should be read in conjunction with Allan Janik's brilliant analysis of Austrian *fin-de-siècle* historiography (his Kann Memorial lecture) "Vienna 1900 Revisited: Paradigms and Problems," *Austrian History Yearbook* 28 (1997), 1-27.

Günter Bischof

John Boyer's Work in a Comparative Context

Pieter M. Judson

Among the four panelists asked to assess the historiographic importance of John Boyer's work, my particular role was to add a comparative European dimension to the proceedings. In these brief comments I will indeed evaluate some of Boyer's more important claims and accomplishments in comparative terms, but I have deviated somewhat from my assignment in my choice of comparisons. I believe it is crucial to make Imperial Austria itself one of the contexts for comparison if we are to understand the distinctive nature of Boyer's achievement. I will start by discussing his work in terms of *urban* political culture throughout the Austrian monarchy and then conclude with a brief look at work on developments outside of Austria.

In the past half century, an unfortunate, if understandable, tradition among historians of politics, culture, economy, and society in Central Europe has too often read the political and cultural history of Vienna as the history of the monarchy as a whole. This tendency resulted partly from the state of research into the social history of the monarchy, partly from regional biases that confused important trends in today's Austria with those of yesterday's empire, and partly from the long term influence of postwar theories of backwardness and modernization. Making imperial Austria itself a point of comparison for Boyer's work helps to avoid confusing this work with a definitive work on Habsburg domestic politics and political culture at the turn of the century, as some have tended to read it. It also aids in locating the special nature of Boyer's accomplishment. He has carefully limited his sights to giving an exhaustive account of Viennese politics during a key period of upheaval, transformation, and restabilization. It is an account that draws from expertise on countless related subjects so as to convey to the reader the multi-layered complexities of Viennese political life. Boyer's account also lends a useful perspective to those working to explain apparently similar political transformations that occurred elsewhere in Central Europe around 1900. All these qualities tempt us to read the work as paradigmatic for the monarchy as a whole, a temptation which, if I read him correctly, Boyer himself would strongly reject. A close examination of events and political transformations in other parts of the monarchy help us to see Viennese exceptionalism and how it fits into the larger trends transforming Austrian political life at the turn of the century.

Boyer's first book, *Political Radicalism in Late Imperial Vienna*, showed us the broken ring of a new political coalition in Vienna, one that eventually replaced the ruling Liberal Party in municipal government. The spectacular success of this Christian Social coalition derived from its ability to integrate far greater numbers of Viennese into municipal political processes. It also derived from the Christian Socials' ability to reproduce this mobilization over time through the manipulation of highly effective rituals, symbols, and organizational structures that gave far more people a sense of ownership in the administration of their city. This coalition controlled its potentially dangerous social mobilization through the careful regulation of the terms on which this new political community would be based. Thus for Boyer, the most crucial ideological accomplishment of Karl Lueger and his emerging party was the political reconstitution of a socially fractured *Bürgertum*. It was in the context of this revived identity, that the Christian Social mobilization could ultimately be viewed as a stabilizing political force.

This development in the 1890s was not exactly mass politics as we know it; after all, it took place within the confines of a still quite limited corporate electoral system. But, for Boyer, it represents the recognizable beginning of something new and qualitatively different in Vienna, and he argues passionately that we should recognize in his subject the foundations of modern mass politics.[1] We all have our favorite foundational moments for modernity. As an historian of Austrian liberalism, I might argue that the liberals invented a recognizable mass politics long before Lueger. Others, like Bill Bowman, have suggested that the organizational foundations necessary for the political mobilization of Catholics in Vienna largely predate Lueger.[2] Be that as it may, let us not quibble over who invented modernity. For the purpose of evaluating Boyer's accomplishments, let us accept his argument in full so that we may better understand both its scope and its limitations.

In asserting that the Christian Socials represent the key transition point to a new type of politics, Boyer wants to show us the logic, coherence, and detailed structures underlying a political transformation that for too long had been considered sudden, surprising, anti-rational, emotional, and even illogical. The so-called politics-in-a-new-key, once viewed in psychological terms as the unleashing of the masses galvanized by emotional ideologies like anti-Semitism, is revealed by Boyer in the humdrum terms of political coalition building, selective contextual pitches made to various social groups, and the revitalization of the idea of a unitary *Bürgertum* hearkening back to the heroic days of March 1848. This latter idea, and not anti-Semitism, not political Catholicism, and certainly not nationalism, is what bound the various parts of the coalition together. In other words, it was their local cultural identity as *Bürger* that mattered most to them. The threatening outsider, on whose implicit enmity this political union was founded, turns out not to have been the Jew as was traditionally believed, but rather the anti-*Bürger*, the socialist. In framing the history of the Christian Social movement in these terms, Boyer draws attention away from anti-Semitism, the traditionally distinctive characteristic of Lueger's party, to show how the coalition functioned as an anti-socialist alliance of worried *Bürger* from all parts of the Viennese social spectrum.

In both his books, Boyer masterfully conveys the uncertain foundations on which this coalition rested and the ways that these fragile foundations shifted over time. He shows that no single interest (clericalism, catholic identity, German identity, anti-Semitism, Catholic labor) was paramount for very long within the movement, and he argues that the economic and patronage-based success of the party usually managed barely to outweigh potential conflicts among competing partners within the coalition. This ongoing process is fundamentally altered in his second volume, *Culture and Political Crisis in Vienna*, as the Christian Social movement became an important provincial and then parliamentary party in the monarchy. As such it struggled with its identity, particularly with the need to integrate the interests of new factions from other regions and provinces with those of its traditional, urban, Viennese clients.

The attentive reader follows Boyer's sure grasp of Vienna ward politics to gain an appreciation for Lueger's structural political accomplishments and for the larger historical significance of his party. But this is not all that the attentive reader learns. Embedded throughout Boyer's analysis, there appear several complex, often insightful, discourses on the nature of the Austrian state, the bureaucracy, and especially on Lueger's opponents: in his first volume on the liberals, and in the second volume on the socialists. Boyer keeps each of these diverse subjects within his sights at all times—he has something important to say about each of them and about their roles in this complex story.

This series of ongoing digressions forces the reader to experience the same story on three or four simultaneous levels—make that five or six if the reader follows the informative endnotes—and it increases the reader's appreciation for Boyer's detailed mastery of Austrian and Viennese political history. But it is also at this point that problems arise. This multi-layered, confidently empirical approach tempts the reader, confronted by so much information, to believe that the larger story as presented, is in fact watertight, internally coherent, and hermetically sealed. Since the author has indeed covered more bases in these two volumes than might be considered humanly possible, in close to nine hundred pages of text and three hundred of notes, it is often difficult to remember that this remains, nonetheless, a very limited subject. As brilliantly as they de- and then re-construct the Christian Social movement, these volumes are not, after all, the final word on the rest of Austrian history during this period, although any reader caught up in this fascinating narrative may be forgiven the temptation to believe so. Boyer's uniformly confident style unintentionally reinforces these greater paradigmatic claims, since he rarely suggests explanations about the more peripheral subjects like liberalism, socialism, or the bureaucracy; rather, he states them with the same unquestioned certainty that he gives his main subjects.

Consider for a moment Boyer's work in the context of new urban-based forms of politics in other parts of the Austrian monarchy. Boyer quite rightly sets his history of Christian Socialism in the larger context of Central European politics from the very beginning of the first volume. He is an historian of Central Europe, not simply or exclusively of Austria. Yet, of course, he is also eager to highlight the distinctiveness of Christian Social, particularly Lueger's, accomplishments. While most European historians will recognize the themes of popular mobilization from their own fields, Boyer makes the Christian Socials the prime, and, occasionally, by default, the sole purveyors of this new politics in the monarchy. In his desire to highlight the distinctiveness of Lueger's accomplishments in the first volume, for example, Boyer encouraged the reader to view the new politics as a Christian Social creation.

This is a complicated problem. Clearly the various crises experienced by the Viennese *Mittelstand* and *Mittelbürgertum* in Boyer's account occurred similarly in other cities of the monarchy. But they often gave rise to very different kinds of political solutions. While we can say that mass mobilization was a common phenomenon throughout the monarchy and Europe, I don't think we can say that the particular constellation of elites and challengers, victors and victims, in Vienna is necessarily paradigmatic for the monarchy. To Boyer's credit, if the first volume ends with the triumphant invention of mass politics by the Christian Socials, the second volume begins with more modest claims for their distinctiveness. Boyer himself maintains consistently that the books are primarily about Vienna. Nevertheless, in both the books themselves, and more particularly in their reception, and even on the charge to this panel, important unacknowledged slippages occur and Vienna comes to stand for the monarchy as a whole.

These slippages, this eliding of Vienna with the monarchy are understandable if we consider how few works on Austrian history are read by a larger scholarly audience and how many aspects of

Austrian history Boyer calls upon authoritatively to enrich his narrative. Yet we must struggle to keep Boyer's particular subject in mind as we read his work, so tempting are his digressions on liberalism, socialism, the bureaucracy, and the Imperial system, among others. Perhaps one way to do that is to ask how Boyer's particular contribution looks when the focus is moved from Vienna and placed on the emerging political culture among German-identified activists in Prague, Graz, Liberec (Reichenberg), Brno (Brünn), Oppava (Troppau) or Jihlava (Iglau). Or one could take a further step and view the achievements of the Christian Socials in the context of emerging mass parties among the Czechs, with whom Boyer does occasionally compare the leadership strategies—(but not the popular mobilization strategies)—of Christian Socials in his second volume. If we look at developments outside of Vienna in the 1880s and 1890s, particularly in Bohemia, Moravia, and Silesia, but also in Styria and Carinthia, we see immediately that other German-identified groups were also busy trying to effect mass mobilizations on rather different models from Lueger's. Several of these groups also attempted to transcend regional parochialism by linking movements from the north with those in the west. The Viennese Christian Socials were neither alone, nor were they particularly original, although they were certainly extraordinarily successful. They were not even the first to initiate this set of trends which other groups might then have copied.

But of what did the innovations of this new politics consist, and what is their ultimate significance? For Boyer there can be no question that the new mass politics confronted an older system controlled largely by the liberals, what he characterizes as the hybrid liberal-absolutist system of 1867. For Boyer, the new politics in Vienna was *organizationally* anti-liberal in nature, if not *psychologically* anti-liberal as the older explanation had it. If Boyer were not writing primarily about Vienna, however, he might have seen the new politics in much different terms. How would Boyer explain the phenomenon of liberal nationalists themselves initiating a successful mass mobilization when it became clear to them that the central state could no longer be considered either an ally or even (to them) an impartial force in politics? Even more interesting, what about the way these liberal nationalists also transformed the cultural concept of German *Bürgertum* into a universalist category in order to unite potentially clashing groups against the increasing threat of socialism? This was very much the case both in Bohemia and in Styria. And these new liberal nationalist movements were anchored in a dense web of semi-political popular interest groups and national defense organizations whose members perceived their cultural tasks in political terms and their political opponents in cultural terms.

Boyer has remarkably little to say, even in his endnotes, about these liberal nationalists and their popular mobilization before 1907, or even about the more explicitly *Mittelstand* nationalists such as Otto Steinwender's *Volkspartei* in the western Alpine regions of the monarchy. While the extremely radical *Schönerianer*, a pretty marginal group in terms of numbers—if not rhetoric—appear frequently in his account, the much more significant, larger movements of German nationalists (as opposed to their parliamentary leaders) hardly are mentioned. This is understandable because the liberal, nationalist, political revival did not occur in Vienna or Lower Austria. But it did occur in the monarchy, and it is important to understanding why, for example, in Austria, unlike in Germany, popular German nationalism was to be found more on the left of the political spectrum than on the right. One schizophrenic exercise that will help reveal the degree of this problem follows: juxtapose Boyer's *oeuvre*, for example, with Lothar Höbelt's recent political history of the German nationalist parties in Imperial Austria.[3] The latter work focuses on the rise of mass parties and politics in the western and northern provinces of the monarchy. In Höbelt's book Steinwender is more often the heroic focus in the 1890s, Lueger merely a minor player, and Christian Socialism ultimately a local phenomenon. Or juxtapose Boyer's work to Gary Cohen's, Cate Giustino's, Scott Spector's, or even Bruce Garver's work on Bohemia, or Peter Vodopivec's on Slovenia, or Hanns Haas' and Robert Hoffmann's on Salzburg. The astute reader might well ask whether we are even in the same monarchy.

Boyer is certainly not to blame if historians continue to read Vienna as Austria, and the rise of a new politics as a rejection of liberal cultural, political, and social values. That is an unfortunate legacy of popular misreadings of Carl Schorske's important work. And Boyer frequently warns the reader in his second volume of the need for more local and regional studies even of the Christian Social movement, before larger conclusions may be drawn. But, by blurring the lines in his own study through his tendency to make hermetically sealed claims about almost every aspect of Austrian history during this period, Boyer himself unwittingly perpetuates this myth, reading the collapse of Viennese liberalism as somehow exemplary for the entire monarchy.

There is a related problem here, and that is the often unintended teleological character of the tasks Boyer has set for himself in both volumes. Some of his most interesting ruminations in the second volume, for example, relate the struggles within the Christian Social Party to that movement's later role in the first and second Republics. These observations help the reader to understand the precise nature of the *Reichspartei's* legacies to contemporary Austrian politics. But these observations pose the danger that both Boyer and his readers may easily place too much importance on those particular pre-1919 developments that prefigure the party of the 1920s, 1930s, or 1950s. But why should this be a problem? Once again, such a strategy exaggerates the importance of Vienna within the context of the pre-1914 monarchy. It draws our attention away from the crucial political and cultural contributions of, say, the Reichenberg nationalists or of the so-called Moravian *Sprachinseln* liberals, without which Austrian history around 1900 makes little sense. Even though we may agree with Boyer that Vienna was becoming more politically important than ever in the decade before the First World War, we can not consider Vienna outside the political context of those regions, if the goal is to understand Austrian rather than Viennese history. Historians and political both tend to forget that only the division of the German-speaking communities to the north and east from post-1919 Austria, those areas where the liberal nationalist legacy had been strongest, made the Christian Social and Social Democratic legacies appear so overwhelmingly dominant while other crucial political legacies became invisible at a stroke.

This criticism may seem beside the point in view of the specific task Boyer has set for himself, and in view of Boyer's own admirable warning in the second volume that the "history of the Christian Social Party can be seen only within the limits of its time and judged within the context of its time."[4] Nevertheless, both his books and their reception rest on an underlying and fundamental tension between the context of the monarchy and the context of post-1918 Austria. Furthermore, the extent of Boyer's authoritative claims about almost every aspect of Austrian history (beyond Christian Socialism *per se*), claims made not as suggestions but as necessary pieces of a larger argument, and the extent to which others have received his reading of Viennese history as a new paradigm for Austrian history (hardly Boyer's fault), make it necessary for me to raise these points.

If Boyer's contribution to Austrian history can only be measured taking non-Viennese political culture into account, the distinctiveness of his approach becomes more apparent when it is placed in a larger European context. Part of this is due to the peculiarities of Austrian historiography and its state of development when placed alongside British, French, or even German historiography. Of course, Boyer was not writing in a vacuum, far from it. Yet the relatively backward state of the field gave him the opportunity I noted above, to range confidently over several crucial topics extending well beyond the rise and development of the Christian Social movement. What I alluded to as an attempt to contextualize events, and partly as the temptation to subsume them under a broad, encompassing, and hermetic new theory of Austrian history, makes Boyer's books distinctive in terms of scale, when they are placed within a larger European context.

In terms of writing a political history of the *Mittelstand*, Boyer's work should be seen as part of a larger attempt, dating from the 1960s, to explain the rising involvement of European lower-middle class groups in politics at the turn of the century. Thus, it makes sense to see at least his first volume in the context of works by scholars familiar to the English-speaking world, like David Blackbourn, Gary Cohen, Geoff Eley, Robert Gellately, Hermann Lebovics, Arno Mayer, Philip Nord, and Shulamit Volkov, to name a very few who have studied the *Mittelstand* mobilizations produced by moments of economic and social structural crisis. But Boyer also differs substantially from others in his overriding fascination for the nuts and bolts of urban ward politics. More than any of these other historians, Boyer always starts from a basic presumption of politics, rather than economy, society, or culture. No one who has given these books serious attention can deny Boyer's ultimate fascination with the detailed local neighborhood dramas of urban political movements. The thrust of his analysis focuses ultimately on the particularly political uses to which economic, social, or cultural crises can be put. He works backward to locate the specific socio-economic developments, technological advances, cultural traditions, legal changes, and government policies that gave men like Lueger the opportunity to develop new political strategies at the local level.

This is evident if we compare Boyer's methodology to Philip Nord's equally compelling work on the transformation of politics in late nineteenth-century Paris neighborhoods, work that culminated in the book *Paris Shopkeepers and the Politics of Resentment*.[5] Nord too documented the political shift to the right of artisans, small retailers and white collar employees from a leftist democratic tradition, those "who in the past had voted or in the future might have voted liberal."[6] Nord also explored the dimensions and uses of anti-Semitic rhetoric among these groups as a means of forging a new, populist, coalition movement. But Nord typically approached his subject far differently than Boyer, starting with the neighborhood dimensions of Paris, and not with neighborhood politics. Nord focussed far more of his analysis on the physical, social, and economic changes wrought by commercial development and city planning on artisan sections of Paris. From there he proceeded to analyze the various new forms of politics born of Haussmanization and later economic crisis in Paris.

A comparative view is even more useful for evaluating Boyer's expressed interest in culture in the second volume. Although, according to Boyer, this volume is even more a party history than the first, it does raise the question of culture in several interesting contexts. The title itself provocatively links questions of culture to the political crises and challenges experienced by Christian

Socialism in power, suggesting that cultural practice and cultural policy became increasingly central concerns for the now hegemonic party. Culture here, as always these days, means several things. On one level it refers to particular practices produced by Christian Social politics, the culture of the ward political organization, of party patronage, of membership, and of anti-Semitic or anti-socialist exclusion. But Boyer also goes well beyond this structural sense of culture to consider the political uses of cultural issues themselves, and the role of cultural politics for positing a specific future for Austria. To do this, he explores the all-embracing visions put forward, particularly by younger Social Democrats during this period, and the alternative visions developed by the younger generation of Christian Social activists. Both sets of visions about urban transformation were mutually exclusive, but Boyer shows how much they resembled each other in their all-encompassing breadth.

While Boyer succeeds beautifully in conveying these visions, notably in his central chapter on religion and nation, his largely political and instrumentalist approach by questions of culture fails to illuminate the important question of just how these discourses, these visions of the future were received, understood, and processed by Christian Social voters. Boyer wishes to show how important cultural issues became for the Christian Social Party during this later period. The actual process by which certain tools purvey those cultural visions, however, and reception of those visions at the local level, do not come into play in Boyer's account. This sets an enormous challenge for future historical work in this area, since the Christian Social Party, as Boyer has frequently pointed out, relied heavily on rituals, symbols, images, and slogans, designed to convey a particular kind of vision of Vienna and its people.

The further study of Christian Social manipulation of cultural practices, and the *popular response* to those manipulations will be critical for dealing convincingly with the crucial question of anti-Semitism. While it was a major achievement that Boyer managed to place bourgeois anti-socialism on the agenda, he has not dealt convincingly with the particular meanings and popular attractions of Christian Social anti-Semitism in Vienna. He analyzes anti-Semitism largely as a strategic instrument in order to differentiate its opportunistic use by Lueger from its use by a convinced anti-Semite like Schönerer. Boyer's account is almost troubling at times. He argues unquestionably that anti-Semitism is indeed a terrible thing and makes the point that Lueger resorted to this instrument on particular occasions, when it would prove politically effective. Boyer reminds us that it was never Lueger's intention to deprive Jews of citizenship rights, and this helps differentiate between types of anti-Semitism and the varied uses to which they were put. Of course, Boyer does not wish to excuse Lueger, merely to prove that Lueger was not a *true* or *convinced* anti-Semite. But does this really matter anymore? Did not Lueger's and his party's invocation of anti-Semitic rhetoric, themes, and stereotypes, whether he meant it or not, contribute ultimately to a normalization of anti-Semitism in Viennese political culture around 1900? The question we need to answer is not whether Lueger or the Christian Socials were indeed anti-Semitic, but rather, how in cultural terms they helped create the popular normalization of anti-Semitism.

Here I was struck by the useful approach of Michael Burns' work on how the national politics of the Boulanger and Dreyfus affairs were both brought to and understood by local French peasants.[7] Burns explored: (1) what visual symbols or narrative structures with long-term historical meanings were used to convey the message of General Boulanger or the story of Dreyfus in ways that most peasants would find relevant to their lives, and (2) what constructions peasants themselves gave to those symbols, how peasants occasionally made them their own, or how they used them to gain advantage in ways hidden from national politicians. Several other recent works, most notably David Blackbourn's *Marpingen: Apparitions of the Virgin Mary in Bismarckian Germany*,[8] have also wrestled productively with this question of the intersection of local and national agendas through contests over symbols and the very different meanings given those symbols by peasants, bureaucrats, journalists, or politicians. A study like Michael Burns', which investigated just what anti-Semitism meant to different social groups in Vienna in terms of popular culture, would contribute enormously to Austrian historiography.

If John Boyer's work towers above its contemporaries in its breadth and its erudition, those elements should not necessarily be misread as constituting a new paradigm of Austrian history, although in some elements (the anti-socialist thesis) they do come close to it. Boyer's work fills several gaps and makes certain that future students of modern Europe will be less likely to treat Austrian history as a complete mystery. By placing Vienna firmly in Central Europe, Boyer has forced German historians to take Austria seriously, and Austrian historians, to pay more attention to the work of their non-Austrian colleagues. James Sheehan is absolutely correct that Boyer's *oeuvre* has already become a standard work, and that it contributes much to our knowledge of European history in this period. Boyer's fascination with the details of local politics, with the ins and outs of Austrian bureaucratic mechanisms, and with the workings of the Austrian system have also helped to place Austrian historical developments on the general European agenda. Nevertheless, his success only demonstrates the future need to treat the Vienna-Austria relationship with care. A comparison of Boyer's work with that of French and German historians suggests ways in which the cultural questions he addresses might be pursued to better advantage in even greater depth.

NOTES

1. John Boyer, *Political Radicalism in Late Amoral Vienna: Origins of the Christian Social Movement. 1848-1897* (Chicago: University of Chicago Press, 1981).

2. William Bowman, "Religious Associations and the Formation of Political Catholicism in Vienna, 1848 to the 1870s" in *Austrian History Yearbook* 27 (1996); Pieter M. Judson, *Exclusive Revolutionaries: Liberal Politics. Social Experience and National Identity in the Austrian Empire* (Ann Arbor, MI: University of Michigan Press, 1996).

3. Lothar Höbelt, *Kornblume und Kaiser Adler. Die deutschfreiheitlichen Parteien Altösterreichs 1882-1918* (Vienna: Böhlau, 1993).

4. Boyer, *Culture and Political Crisis in Vienna*, 462.

5. Philip Nord, *Paris Shopkeepers and the Politics of Resentment* (Princeton, NJ: Princeton University Press, 1986).

6. Boyer, *Culture and Political Crisis*, 461.

7. Michael Burns, *Rural Society and French Politics: Boulangism and the Dreyfus Affair 1886-1900* (Princeton, NJ: Princeton University Press, 1984).

8. David Blackbourn, *Marpingen: Apparitions of the Virgin Mary in Bismarckian Germany* (New York: Oxford University Press, 1993).

John Boyer's Fin-de-Siècle Vienna

Steven Beller

John Boyer's two volume history of Christian Socialism from its beginnings to the end of the Habsburg Monarchy is a formidable achievement of dedicated scholarship. The first volume, which appeared fifteen years ago, has already fundamentally changed our perception of what was happening in Vienna at the turn of the century, and the second volume contributes further food for thought which will likely lead to further historiographical shifts.

An attempt to assess the importance of Boyer's work for current scholarship on the Habsburg Monarchy, and the history of Vienna in particular, has to address two central tasks. It must delineate what the historiographical impact of Boyer's two volumes has been: how have the views of historians actually been affected and indeed changed by Boyer's work? It must, though, also address that work critically, and ask where it needs to be added to and modified, where, in other words, Boyer's views themselves could in turn profit from some changes.

From my perspective, the immense achievement of Boyer's work, especially the first volume, was that it fundamentally changed the picture of what happened to Viennese *society* in the 1890s. The view with most currency in 1981 was that of Carl E. Schorske, who, in a series of essays subsequently included in a famous volume, *Fin-de-Siècle Vienna: Politics and Culture*, had sought to explain Viennese cultural modernism by linking it to the political crises of the time, especially the rise of anti-liberalism (and hence the Christian Socials).[1] The link between politics and culture, which Schorske identified, was a liberal, educated middle-class or bourgeoisie, which was alienated from power by the collapse of liberalism first at the "national" and then at the municipal level. It was the scions of this alienated, liberal bourgeoisie who then sought refuge from a hostile political world in the "inner" worlds of art and the psyche. The transformation from *homo economicus* to *homo psychologicus* was thus accounted for by the political experience of a social class, the alienated, liberal bourgeoisie.

Boyer offered a radically different picture of what happened socially and politically in turn-of-the-century Vienna. Far from the anti-liberal forces of the Christian Socials having alienated the Viennese bourgeoisie, Boyer presented a picture of Karl Lueger and his allies reuniting the petty bourgeois and bourgeois wings of the Viennese *Bürgertum* to produce an anti-liberal, but still bourgeois coalition which protected middle-class power and interests against the threat of Social Democracy.

The Boyerian view seemed in stark contrast to that of Schorske, but it was clear that much of the apparent contradiction stemmed from the blanket use of such terms as "bourgeois"or "educated middle-classes" to describe a group or groups of people, whose social and ethnic complexity simply did not allow for such undifferentiated treatment. This led me to the thought, given the very high Jewish presence in the portion of Vienna's educated elite from a "liberal" socio-economic background, that a link between politics and culture on the Schorskean model was still very cogent. It was just that it was not so much a liberal bourgeoisie as a *Jewish* bourgeoisie, which had been alienated from power and retreated into the world of culture. For, if Boyer was correct, the only social group really alienated from political power in the 1890s was not any "bourgeoisie," but Viennese Jewry. Schorske, seen through the Boyerian prism, could thus be interpreted as offering a convincing explanation for why so much of modern culture in *fin-de-siècle* Vienna was produced by Jews, or people of at least partly Jewish descent.[2]

Boyer's social history of the impact of the Christian Socials is thus something for which he can be justly praised. Boyer's other major change, and what appears even more clearly in his second volume as the central thrust of his work, is his attempt to alter the received, Schorskean view of the Christian Socials from an irrationalist, reactionary—even proto-fascist—political phenomenon to an *emancipatory* movement that liberalized Austrian politics. The main theme of *Culture and Political Crisis in Vienna* is, indeed, that the Christian Socials tried, on the one hand, to democratize the Austrian state and open it up to modern politics and, on the other, tried to help the

Austrian Cisleithanian state function beyond the national question. Indeed, it was, in Boyer's opinion, the Christian Socials and Karl Lueger who were the direct ancestors of the nascent Austrian national/ supra-national identity, which is today dominant in the Second Republic.[3]

This view of the Christian Socials is a large challenge to the predominant understanding of modern Austrian history, and would necessitate a complete rethinking if true. I think there is a great deal here which does bear thinking about, for Boyer shows a political movement which is much more "reasonable," and in many ways much more "responsible," than might have been hitherto suspected. But here we come to the second task, the task of criticism, for there is much to Boyer's picture of an emancipatory Christian Social movement which does not ring true, despite all the evidence he presents.

One of the most striking things about these two volumes, especially the second, is that despite their great length there is a relative paucity of discussion and information about Christian Social anti-Semitism. To be fair, Boyer does squarely address the question of Christian Social anti-Semitism and condemns it. At the same time, though, he satisfies himself that the use of anti-Semitism by the Christian Social leadership was merely instrumental, not really meant as a matter of conviction, and Boyer leaves it at that. The content of much of Richard Geehr's biography of Karl Lueger, especially as regards the anti-Semitic rhetoric of the Christian Socials, and their various anti-Semitic ploys, such as the "Aryan Theater," is reduced to half a page in Boyer's second volume.[4] Karl Renner's accusation, from as late as 1910, that the Christian Socials only see Jews is simply not dealt with by Boyer.[5] Even if this sort of Jew-baiting was only meant rhetorically, as Boyer would assert, then he still has not adequately assessed the effect of this anti-Semitic rhetoric on the mindset of the Viennese and Austrian populace. Nor has he adequately addressed Peter Pulzer's claim about the way in which anti-Semitism's "domestication" in the mainstream of Austrian and German life before the First World War, in which the Christian Socials played a large role, prepared the way for the disasters of the inter-war period.[6]

One of the main reasons for this oversight on Boyer's part would appear to be that any emphasis on this particular aspect of the Christian Socials is upsetting to his view of the movement. For Boyer, the

Christian Socials were a party which combined "a mild clericalism and a moderate anti-Semitism," the mildness and moderation of which seems to prevent these aspects being taken all too seriously.[7] On the other hand, for Boyer, the Christian Socials were "universalist" in their politics, "pluralist," "inclusive," "emancipatory" and, when it came to the Czechs, "assimilationist."[8] They were almost, in this version, a perfect, democratic, mass party offering upward social mobility and social and political integration to a city full of immigrants, and wresting power away from the father-state and giving it to the people. The problem with this sort of description is that whenever Boyer mentions one of these "liberal democratic" qualities, he is silent about Jews. At times, it is almost as if he has forgotten that they were also a part of Viennese political life.

Certainly, Boyer's claims about the Christian Socials sound rather strange when the Jewish aspect is included. Hence one could perhaps, say that the Christian Socials had a "universal politics," except for Jews; were inclusive, except for Jews; were pluralist, except for Jews; and were "assimilationist," except for Jews. On this last point, Boyer defends the "assimilationist" practice of the Christian Socials when it came to the many Czech immigrants in Vienna, and goes so far as to say that the exclusion of the Czechs would have been "absurd" because Czech-speakers comprised 5 percent of the population. Yet he does not mention, in this context, that Jews, whom the Christian Socials perforce did exclude from their version of Vienna, comprised approximately double that number, roughly 10 percent.[9] We are thus left to assume that the exclusion of 5 percent of the population from political life would be absurd, but the exclusion of 10 percent was not.

Boyer chooses to compare Lueger in the second volume with the party bosses in the large cities in the United States of roughly the same period. While this is also instructive, an equally revealing comparison could have been made with other sorts of populist U.S. politicians, especially in the Deep South. The sort of combination of "democratic" political practice with mass discrimination against one group is something which a figure such as George Wallace and his predecessors would surely have understood all too well. Indeed, the comparison between Lueger and Wallace is rather close, I would say, but it does not make Lueger look as "emancipatory" as Boyer apparently wishes him to look.

Another aim of Boyer's work is to integrate Austrian history into the larger German historical framework. It is thus somewhat strange that Boyer does not make anything of the fact that the Christian Socials fit as well as any German political agent into the model of "negative integration" which has so dominated the historiography of the Wilhelmine Empire. How better to describe a political movement which aimed to reintegrate the middle class *Bürgertum* by identifying those who did *not* belong, the outsiders: the Jews and the socialists? Yet Boyer's wish to see the Christian Socials as on the "democratic" end of Austrian politics seems to have blinded him to this obvious, if not very laudatory, aspect to the movement.

If Boyer's handling of Christian Social anti-Semitism can be criticized as somewhat scanty, his copious discussion of the relationship between the Christian Socials and the liberals and socialists suffers from other problems, of balance and timing. What made the Christian Socials a remarkable political phenomenon was the rapidity with which they went from being virtual insurgents to being one of the strongest *staatserhaltend* (state-preserving) elements in the politics of the Habsburg Monarchy. Peter Pulzer noted this many years ago: "Never had poacher become gamekeeper so quickly and so successfully."[10] This is also the main thought running through Boyer's first volume and much of his second: that the Christian Socials gained power from the Liberals, but almost simultaneously were already looking to defend the power of the *Bürgertum* from the already apparent threat of the proletarian Social Democrats. This standoff between the Christian Socials and the Social Democrats, in Boyer's view, increasingly took on a cultural character, which proved much more resistant to compromise than a purely interest-driven politics would have done. It is this cultural-political dialectic between the two main "camps" of Viennese-Austrian politics which is seen by Boyer as the central theme of subsequent Austrian history. He is surely right in this, but his characterization and explanation for the development of this dialectic is not so convincing.

Boyer's suggestion is that the Christian Socials were not really the originators of this putting of cultural issues at the fore of Austrian politics; rather, their liberal and socialist opponents, united in their anticlericalism, were responsible for making educational, and hence cultural, issues the most prominent points of conflict between the parties. It was thus the socialist educational reformers, such as Karl Seitz and Otto Glöckel, who really made Austrian politics impossible by making the lines of division cultural and not interest-based. The Christian Socials were always reacting, in Boyer's view, to socialist initiatives and attacks. It was the threat of proletarian socialism which brought about the Christian Social unification of the *Bürgertum*, and it was the socialists who started the anticlerical campaign against the Christian Socials in the schools. This caused the Christian Social "clerical" reaction, which, in turn, was to lead to the unbridgeable *Kulturkampf* of the post-1918 era.[11]

Boyer argues his point on the basis that, again, the Christian Socials were only being instrumental in their use of religion, and were not, in their heart of hearts, truly "clerical," despite their rhetoric and policies. Thus, it was the socialists and their anticlerical liberal allies, such as Ludo Hartmann, who forced the Christian Socials into a "clerical" posture in reaction to such initiatives as the *Freie Schule*. As Boyer himself puts it, "The Social Democrats and the new Fabian Left-Liberals helped through initiatives like the *Freie Schule* to create what they insisted they wanted to destroy—a truly *Catholic* Christian Socialism."[12] This strikes me as a clever, but forced and unbalanced argument.

To argue that the Christian Socials were not "clerical" because they only had an instrumental understanding of religion, Boyer must have such a narrow definition of "clericalism" as to be quite unrealistic. Surely it matters much more that the Christian Socials knowingly *used* religion as a way of intimidating their opponents, than whether they believed in what they said or did, and Boyer shows that, from the beginning, they were fairly merciless in their use of religion to get at their socialist opponents. If the leadership later felt pressured into becoming more of a "real" Clerical party than they might have pragmatically wished, then this surely stemmed more from the logic of their own situation, from their own exploitation of religious and educational issues, and from their own purported "ideology" than from any Social Democratic or Liberal opposition.

Boyer does point to the fact that the Christian Socials consciously resisted using the word "Catholic" as self-description, because they did not want to alienate their significant and potentially anticlerical, German national constituency within the Viennese electorate. Yet the use of the word "Christian" was just as "culturally" loaded as "Catholic," though in a different way. One can glean how from a comment quoted by Boyer from the British diplomat, Sir Edward Goschen, when he described Christian Social efforts "to avoid identifying themselves with a completely Clerical policy...and to explain that they are a Christian (anti-Semitic) and a German rather than a Catholic party."[13] "Christian" was preferable to "Catholic" because it was essentially a codeword for a category larger than mere Catholicism: anti-Semitism. In other words, in 1907, if they were trying not to be completely "Clerical," the Christian Socials were instead trying to maintain the other "cultural" divide between "Christians" on the one side and "non-Christians" (Jews and their atheistic, socialist allies) on the other. It was just as "cultural" as "Clericalism" and even more divisive.

Indeed, Boyer's whole argument about the clerical/anticlerical dialectic of Austrian history, and his interpretation of who started the *Kulturkampf*, looks a little different when the "Christian" aspect of the Christian Socials is examined as a code word for anti-Semitism. Then it was clearly the Christian Socials who started the "cultural" divide in Viennese and Austrian politics, through their wildly successful use of the "cultural" card of anti-Semitism. Moreover, it was the Christian Socials themselves who made the infamous "cultural" connection between Jews and socialism. One notorious example was provided by none other than Karl Lueger, in a speech of late 1905, when he specifically linked Jews and socialist revolution in a speech about the revolution in Russia. Boyer cites this speech, and is clearly aware of some of its implications, but does not seem to appreciate what it does to his argument about the reactive role he claims the Christian Socials played in the "cultural" divide in Austrian politics. Here, at least, it was the Christian Socials actively creating a characterization of their opponents—the socialist-Jewish conspiracy—which was to be prove one of the most divisive of all.[14]

Another of Boyer's main arguments concerns the role of the Christian Socials in the demise of Habsburg politics before and during the First World War. In relating the story of how the Viennocentric party attempted to become a *Reichspartei*, and how it supported the attempt to make the democratization of imperial politics work, Boyer has opened up what is, for historians, even many Austrian historians,

almost virgin territory, a service for which we should be very grateful.
When explaining why this attempt to parliamentarize and democratize
Austrian/Cisleithanian politics from 1907 onward failed, Boyer comes
to a startlingly *traditional* conclusion, one which echoes Oscar Jaszi,
Josef Redlich, and even Henry Wickham Steed, as well as Otto Bauer.
Boyer argues, as they did, that it was the lack of political (democratic)
control over the bureaucracy which led to the co-opting of the
politicians by that bureaucracy, and vice-versa. It was this "politics of
the bazaar," typified by figures such as Rudolf Sieghart, which
corrupted the political process and led to the state of crisis in
Cisleithanian political life on the eve of war in 1914.[15]

The tragic "hero," as Boyer calls him, in this tale of the empire's
demise is now Albert Gessmann, for having tried—and failed—to
politicize the imperial government and administration. Boyer sees the
failure of Gessmann's *Arbeitsministerium* as a great, lost opportunity
for the parliamentarization of Austrian politics.[16] The "villains" in the
second volume, as in the first, are the Liberals. In the first volume, it
was the Liberals who accepted the command of the neo-absolutist
regime for the exclusion of the petty bourgeoisie from the municipal
franchise.[17] In the second volume it is the Liberals who are responsible
for acquiescing in the Habsburg system of governing, co-opting the
bureaucracy in the 1860s and 1870s, rather than reforming it radically.
It is also the "liberal" Josephist bureaucracy which is blamed, in effect,
for being too "nice," too accommodating, and thus not allowing the
strict Weberian distinction between "political and bureaucratic modes
of rule" to take effect.[18] Instead politicians were seduced into taking
"tips" instead of demanding real power as they ought.

The strong suggestion is that if the Christian Socials had been able
to take actual power, as they had in Vienna and Lower Austria, if they
had been able to master the bureaucracy and make it do their bidding,
then the political situation could have been more "democratic" and
hence better. Boyer therefore sees the Christian Socials as the best
chance Austria had for subordinating the administrative bureaucracy to
the political rule of the parliamentary parties, an outcome he now
appears to advocate.

This is, as I understand Boyer's relative positions, a large change
of mind from volume one. There he states, "The last thing the
[Cisleithanian] system needed was doctrinaire demands for complete

congruence between political parties and administrative power—this could have destroyed it."[19] Now, in contrast, he seems to think that *not* having this sort of congruence *also* destroyed the same system. This raises the question of what relationship between politics and administration would have been preferable.

Boyer himself uses the example of the United States, where politics and political parties existed prior to bureaucracy, to make his case that politicization of the bureaucracy would have been better than the bureaucratic hegemony that actually existed on the Cisleithanian level.[20] Boyer might want to consider the admittedly idealized remarks of Henry Wickham Steed about the British Civil Service, which, on the one hand, was not supposed to be politicized in the American manner, yet, on the other hand, *was* supposed to be subordinate to the general public.[21] In Austria, by contrast, there was a politicized and suborned municipal and provincial administration in Vienna and Lower Austria, with the Christian Socials in full control on American party machine lines. Yet, on the Cisliethanian level, there was a hegemonic state bureaucracy, which had, in effect, become its own interest group. Out of the combination of local politicization and state-level bureaucratic hegemony (and party political infantilism) arose the political irresponsibility, negativism, and corruption which—Boyer now agrees—was the curse of the Habsburg Monarchy.

The question remaining is to find out who or what was responsible for this sad state of affairs. Here Boyer's attempt to put most of the responsibility onto the Liberals, and to see the Christian Socials as largely the "good guys" becomes highly problematic. It was the Liberals who had tried to wrest power away from the imperial authorities for the sake of more representative government. It is true they had largely acquiesced in having to share power with Francis Joseph and his officials, but this was much more due to Francis Joseph's resistance than Liberal wishes. The one time the Liberals did seriously try to wrest more power after 1867 was in 1878-79, over Bosnia. In that constitutional crisis, they were soundly shown who was boss by Francis Joseph and his *Kaiserminister*, Eduard Taaffe, thus ending the last serious attempt to rein in the power of the imperial authority and its bureaucracy within the state. It was the ensuing period of the "Iron Ring" which saw the beginnings of the mushrooming of the numbers in, and power of, the bureaucracy, as well as the fragmentation of Cisleithanian politics.

Christian Social anti-Semitism and clericalism then added to the fragmentation within the German ranks, weakening yet further any Liberal attempt to provide a credible counterweight to the power of the bureaucracy. Lueger's approach to politics on the Cisleithanian level, as a source of favors to satisfy his local clients and hence enhance his power, encouraged precisely that "politics of the bazaar" which Boyer ends up so roundly condemning. Boyer praises Lueger for showing the "mark of a true statesman" in 1907, but it can well be argued that it was the tactics of this "true statesman" which before then had greatly encouraged the eventual breakdown of Austrian parliamentarism.[22] Who, finally, did most to encourage the members of the bureaucracy to see themselves as an interest group on their own, with no higher loyalty to the general good? One need only read Boyer's detailed treatment of this subject in volume one to see the answer: the Christian Socials.

Boyer claims in his conclusion that the Christian Socials "became the last and perhaps 'best' hope" for the Austrian bourgeoisie. I disagree. They might have been the last hope, but they were far from being the best. They were really far more divisive than Boyer admits, far more divisive of the Austrian bourgeoisie than they were ever unifying. But then this depends on what one understands by the bourgeoisie and who was and was not an Austrian. Boyer describes the Eucharistic Congress of 1912 as an attempt to show the power of Catholicism to unite Austrians "while respecting ethnic diversity."[23] This was fine for ethnic diversity among Catholic Austrians. But what of the non-Catholics? What of the non-Christians?

Boyer's book is full of most interesting comparisons, with the German *Zentrum* party, and with U.S. political machines and party bosses. I would suggest the addition of only two more individual comparisons. I have already mentioned one, George Wallace. The other I would suggest is a somewhat more sympathetic figure, Joseph Chamberlain. For a subject in which populist politics, municipalization, and the transition to the imperial stage are such prominent features, it seems odd that Chamberlain is not once mentioned in Boyer's two volumes. This is a pity, for I think the Chamberlain parallel most instructive.

Chamberlain had a great deal in common with Lueger (and Gessmann). He too was the mayor of a major city, came from the same sort of "democratic," radical liberal background as Lueger. He also engaged in large-scale municipalization of city services, and used his local power base to launch himself on the national stage. He was even faced with the same sort of political crisis concerning the unity of his empire, although the main antagonists in his conflict were not Germans and Czechs but British and Irish. His situation in that crisis, and his responses to it, were similar but different to those of the Christian Socials, for he sided much more decisively with those seeking to preserve in its entirety the Union, rather than cede home rule, splitting from the Liberals in the process. In his subsequent politics, he pursued trade protectionism, and it was essentially his Unionism that created the modern Conservative Party, which shared many characteristics in terms of policy and constituency with the Christian Socials. Yet, there was also a great deal which differentiated Chamberlain's heritage from that of Lueger's. Chamberlain might have similarly ended up being pro-capitalist and pro-imperialist, but he was not even instrumentally a "clerical" and he was not anti-Semitic. Unlike Lueger, he was neither proto-fascist nor Baroque.[24]

This comparison is worth thinking about for another reason, as well. In 1902, Theodor Herzl had an interview with the British Colonial Secretary, Joseph Chamberlain. Herzl had for years been engaged in his campaign for a Jewish state, a campaign which had originated largely in the shock of the victory of Lueger's anti-Semitic Christian Socials in Vienna in April 1895. In 1902, Herzl appealed for help from Chamberlain to find a suitable territory in or near Palestine. Chamberlain responded positively. Even if nothing came of that meeting at the time, the negotiations then started were eventually to lead to the Balfour Declaration. Perhaps such strange linkages are not mere coincidence. Perhaps a comparison of the histories of Joseph Chamberlain's Conservative and Unionist Party and Karl Lueger's Christian Socials would tell us something interesting about both, and perhaps, as a result, the pernicious nature of the latter's influence on turn-of-the-century Austrian politics would be that much clearer than, for all their remarkable scholarship, it is in John Boyer's two volumes.

NOTES

1. Carl E. Schorske, *Fin-de-Siècle Vienna: Politics and Culture* (London: Weidenfeld, 1980).

2. See Steven Beller, *Vienna and the Jews, 1867-1938: A Cultural History* (Cambridge: Cambridge University Press, 1989).

3. John Boyer, *Culture and Political Crisis in Vienna: Christian Socialism in Power, 1897-1918* (Chicago: University of Chicago Press, 1995), 213.

4. Richard S. Geehr, *Karl Lueger, Mayor of Fin de Siècle Vienna* (Detroit: Wayne State, 1990); cf. Boyer, *Culture and Political Crisis*, 63.

5. Cf. Geehr, *Lueger*, 204.

6. Peter Pulzer, *The Rise of Political Anti-Semitism in Germany and Austria* (London: Halban, 1988), 281-321.

7. Boyer, *Culture*, 51.

8. Ibid. 164, 170, 216, 239, 298, 318, 329.

9. Ibid., 214.

10. Pulzer, *Anti-Semitism*, 182.

11. Boyer, *Culture*, 210-11.

12. Ibid., 170.

13. Ibid., 198.

14. Ibid., 77-8.

15. Ibid., 352-6.

16. Ibid., 447.

17. John Boyer, *Political Radicalism in Later Imperial Vienna: Origins of the Christian Social Movement* (Chicago: University of Chicago Press, 1981), 418.

18. Boyer, *Culture*, 351-53.

19. Boyer, *Radicalism*, 416.

20. Boyer, *Culture*, 351.

21. Henry Wickham Steed, *The Habsburg Monarchy* (New York: Fertig, 1969), 59.

22. Boyer, *Culture*, 116.

23. Ibid. 324-5.

24. Cf. Boyer, *Radicalism*, 314.

John Boyer and Austrian Twentieth-Century History

Ernst Hanisch

Schorske or Boyer?

In the Robert A. Kann Memorial Lecture, Allan Janik accused Austrian historical scholarship of methodological and theoretical deficiencies.[1] He described it as being more monographic than interpretive, and characterized more by a fixation upon source material than an orientation toward models and interpretations. Janik also stated that it lacks new hermeneutic strategies. These charges contain an element of truth, and, among other factors, this is most certainly connected with the powerful tradition of the *Österreichische Institut für Geschichtsforschung*. These deficiencies account for the success of two American historians, Carl Schorske and John Boyer.[2] These are without a doubt the two most prominent names in the field of research dealing with the final decades of the Habsburg Monarchy. Schorske is well-known and highly esteemed in Austria, where his work is available in translation and widely discussed; John Boyer, however, is generally unknown. This may well have to do with their respective topics. Schorske brought *fin de siècle* Viennese art to the attention of the world, thereby supporting the Austrian quest for celebrating brilliant epochs in its own history and the process of establishing an Austrian identity. On the other hand, Boyer's subject, the rise of Karl Lueger and the Christian Socials, was tainted with the stigma of anti-Semitism—the Christian Socials bore responsibility for the destruction of democracy, and Lueger was damned by the praise of Adolph Hitler. It may likewise be connected with the matter of style: Schorske's elegant descriptions offer a stark contrast to Boyer's plodding prose in which the discovery of occasional stylistic brilliancies is an arduous task indeed. It may also be connected with the rather leftist political orientation and "moral correctness" of scholarly research in modern Austrian history, which has displayed scant interest in a comprehensive and multifaceted analysis of the Christian Socials.

In a highly sophisticated fashion, Janik has read Boyer's first volume as a challenge to and a critique of Schorske. This has to do with the idea "the failure of liberalism." Concurring with Boyer, Janik makes the case that the Austrian liberals were not so very liberal at all. Their social welfare policy orientation was a narrow one, they did not cultivate contacts to the petite bourgeoisie, and they abandoned the ideals of 1848—the civic revolution and the establishment of a civil society. This is now truly one of the central questions of twentieth century Austrian history.

The Weakness of Liberalism, the Weakness of the Laicistic Republican Bourgeoisie

Compared with other western nations, Austria in the twentieth century is marked by the conspicuous absence of a strong, bourgeois, liberal, republican tradition. By the end of the nineteenth century, liberalism had already virtually evaporated, replaced to a large extent by German Nationalism. It was not until the 1990s that a liberal party, led by Heidi Schmidt, broke away from Jörg Haider's Freedom Party (FPÖ). An historical elucidation of this phenomenon calls for an extremely wide-ranging approach.

First, viewed in the context of Stein Rokkan's geohistorical model, the shift of the center of the international capitalist economy to the Atlantic rim meant a weakening of the urban belts along the Rhine and the Danube, and brought with it a deceleration of their economic dynamism. In other words, there existed substantial structural impediments to the development of an economic bourgeoisie.[3]

Second, the specific Austrian process of state formation placed the bureaucracy in a central position. During the liberal phase in the 1860s, bourgeoisie and bureaucracy cooperated extremely closely. Boyer stresses the fact that this liberal state was a hybrid, displaying elements of centralism and absolutism.[4] A liberalism, associated with the reign of Joseph II, in the tradition of an enlightenment from above, took shape in Austria, characteristics of which continue to be exhibited by the bureaucracy which is its modern-day successor. Bureaucratic liberalism was forced to think in terms of conflict avoidance, whereas it was precisely this conflict and competition which constituted, for economic liberalism, the driving force behind social development.

Third, as the liberal historian Richard Charmatz succinctly formulated it, "During this epoch, the concept 'liberal' meant nothing more than the word 'anticlerical.'"[5] John Boyer expanded upon this argument: the Catholic Church as the object of liberals' criticism was a mere pretext, since liberals did not dare to directly attack the authoritarian state.[6] On one hand, anticlericalism was necessary, because only in this way could Austria be modernized and the influence exerted upon society by the rigid, absolutist church be broken. Moreover, anticlericalism was the only way by which civic society could be emancipated, fundamental rights formulated, and clerical influence upon the schools and universities eliminated. On the other hand, all political conflicts thus became highly emotionally charged issues of opposing *Weltanschauungen*. As Boyer concluded, anticlericalism became "one of the major leitmotifs of Austrian politics."[7] This liberal anticlericalism was passed down through Georg von Schönerer to the German Nationalists and the National Socialists in one line of development, and to the Social Democrats in another. The anticlericalism of the Social Democrats served the party as a means of integration, functioning similarly to the opposition to Socialism among the Christian Socials.[8] In any case, the clericalism/ anticlericalism line of conflict was one of the major disputes of the First Republic. Its ramifications continued to be felt even after 1945, for example, in the case of the integration of anticlerical National Socialists into the Socialist Party.

But there was an additional problem: clericalism could not be simply equated with Catholicism alone. To name just a few of its forms, there also existed the episcopate of Joseph II, the inflammatory "rabble rousing chaplains," the secularizing Catholicism (with the "Lord God in heaven") of the Viennese Christian Socials, the new Catholic lay intelligentsia, and the traditional Catholicism of the rural peasantry. Moreover, in the last third of the nineteenth century, Catholicism itself began to utilize democratic forms and to reorganize the Catholic populace.

Fourth, when it came down to defending democracy in Austria in 1933-34, the Social Democrats stood alone. There no longer existed a liberal bourgeoisie that would have been prepared to join the struggle on their side. What was left of the liberal bourgeoisie—in the press, in business, and in the arts—were predominantly individuals of Jewish descent, and thus emerged the dilemma of the lesser evil. In comparison to Hitler, Dollfuß was a more or less acceptable alternative.

Who were the "Liberal Bourgeoisie"?

Steven Beller and Allan Janik have taken exception to Schorske, maintaining that he has neglected the Jewish segment of the "liberal bourgeoisie." Beller estimates that Jews comprised 71 percent of the Viennese "liberal bourgeoisie" at around the turn of the century.[9] I would like to state my case on this issue in slightly different terms. Perhaps this is only a matter of linguistic conventions, but from the point of view of German-language *"Bürgertumsforschung,"* the concept "liberal bourgeoisie" is inadequate. Here, more exact differentiations are necessary.[10]

First, there was the traditional "urban bourgeoisie," the *"bodenständige,"* long-established urban dwellers with deep roots in the local community, who were so indefatigably courted by Lueger. This included, for example, the social stratum made up of influential property owners who, as Boyer has shown, comprised the last social grouping to join the anti-liberal coalition of the Christian Socials.[11] The *"bodenständige"* urban bourgeoisie was organized politically into clubs, such as the association in Vienna with which German Nationalists and Christian Socials were affiliated.

Second, there was the "economic bourgeoisie," the true bourgeoisie, including the large "financial bourgeoisie" that actually was predominantly Jewish, and the "industrial bourgeoisie" whose social and religious composition awaits definitive analysis.[12] The extent to which the economic bourgeoisie was still liberal during the phase of "organized capitalism" is a question which remains open.

Third, there was the *"Bildungsbürgertum"* of highly educated middle-class intellectuals. As Beller has demonstrated, it was precisely this social stratum in Vienna which included a high proportion of Jews in the self-employed professions, including attorneys and physicians. Nevertheless, urban and rural dissimilarities must also be taken into account here. In the provincial regions of Austrian, in Bohemia and Moravia and in Alpine areas, it was these very same self-employed professionals who were so quick to take up the cause of German Nationalism and, in the 1930s, to form the intellectual basis of support for National Socialism. This *Bildungsbürgertum* was also comprised of civil servants from the upper and middle levels of the bureaucracy. Jews were for the most part excluded from this inner core of governmental authority. The upper-level bureaucracy within the government ministries upheld the liberal tradition of Joseph II, but the middle and lower levels switched their allegiance to the German Nationalists and the Christian Socials. John Boyer is to be highly commended for having provided, in his second volume a comprehensive and precise analysis of the brutal politicization of the Viennese municipal administration and the bureaucracy of the Province of Lower Austria in the direction of the Christian Social Party. The most dramatic example of this is provided by the school system.[13]

Finally, at around the turn of the century, there emerged a new Catholic *Bildungsbürgertum*, many of whose members rapidly achieved tremendous career success through their involvement in the *Cartellverband* fraternity during the First Republic. The attempts at artistic expression undertaken in connection with this Catholic renaissance are intellectually rather inferior and, as a result, have not yet been sufficiently integrated into the panorama of the *fin de siècle*.[14]

Fourth, there was the rather vaguely defined "petite bourgeoisie" which included master craftsmen, tradesmen, and small shopkeepers. It was in this social stratum that the anti-liberal, anti-Semitic protest movement of the Christian Socials first articulated itself.[15]

In short, I enter a plea on behalf of a paradigm "liberal bourgeoisie" which is more fully elaborated and takes more precise account of its various aspects.

Austrian Identity in the Age of the Nation-State

The structural preconditions of the multi-ethnic state complicate the process of formation of national identities. Prior to the creation of a national state, there existed a *Reichspatriotismus* which originally bound subjects to the Holy Roman Empire and which, over the course of the nineteenth century, was transferred to the Habsburg Monarchy.[16] In the center of this Austrian identity stood the dynasty, the consecrated person of the *Kaiser* as the guarantor of the unity of the empire. But there then occurred strong *processes of nation building* along linguistic lines. The newly-formulated question for scholarly investigation of the Germans thus emerges. Was there a unitary German process of nation building which subsumed both the *Reichsdeutschen* of Germany itself as well as Germans of Austria? Or, as Ernst Bruckmüller plausibly argues in his latest study, did two separate processes of German nation building take place—a German one, the cumulative result of which was Bismarck's *Reich*, and a German-Austrian one?[17]

In any case, the outcome of this process was that the Austrians of the Habsburg Monarchy and the First Republic displayed a multiple identity.[18] In the case of the Christian Socials, John Boyer has shown this by means of an example. In their view, it was a matter taken completely for granted that Vienna was a "German" city; at the same time, though, Vienna was an "Austrian" as well as a "Christian" city.[19] This sentiment is expressed in the words of Karl Lueger: "Good German, good Austrian, good Christian, always and forever."[20] The Germanness of Lueger was thus articulated quite differently than the Germanness of the Social Democrats, which was bound up with the Enlightenment, the classical epoch of Weimar culture, and the German Revolution. For the city's non-German inhabitants, for the Czechs and to a certain extent for the Jews, a "German" Vienna meant the offer of either assimilation or struggle to the death.[21]

The idea of a Greater Austria largely characterized Christian Social thinking during the first half of World War I; "German" dominance gained increasing allure during the second half of the conflict. A vehement German Nationalism then re-emerged, and the Austrian Revolution of 1918-19 followed the "German way." The enemy was named Habsburg; the enemy was Austria. During the phase of stabilization, an Austrian myth once again began to establish itself, centered around the person of Ignaz Seipel. During the authoritarian phase, this myth was instrumentalized in the struggle against National Socialism.

Boyer's most surprising statement follows: "The history of late Imperial politics thus ended not in November 1918 but in April 1945, and perhaps more fundamentally in May 1955."[22] Applied to the question of identity, this means that the tensions between "German" and "Austrian," this ancient legacy of the monarchy, began to subside only in the Second Republic.

However, there is yet another perspective. Regarded in the context both of the nation-state as a structural form and of modern nationalism, the double identity which characterized the Austrians of the monarchy was an antiquated, pre-modern type of identity formation; viewed today, in terms of the possibility of a multicultural society, even taking into account all of the associated problems, it was perhaps rather modern.

Democratic or Authoritarian?

The Christian Social Party was the essential driving force behind the transition to the dictatorship of the "Corporatist State"; thereafter, the party dissolved itself. This ignoble end is the image of the Christian Social Party which has long been imprinted in the collective memory. John Boyer is the first to succeed in drawing a detailed and comprehensive picture which painstakingly brings to light both its authoritarian and democratic characteristics. The Christian Social Party arose as an, indeed, vulgarly populistic but, nevertheless, democratic party. It supported the voting rights reform legislation of 1906-7. For Lueger, the parliament was the elixir of life; Albert Gessmann, the key figure in the second phase of the party's development, resolutely maintained that the basest form of parliamentary rule would be preferable to no parliament at all.[23] The group centered around Ignaz Seipel and Heinrich Lammasch can be placed in a liberal-Catholic context: rightist positioning and leftist thinking.[24] Large segments of the Christian Social Party supported and took part in the Austrian Revolution of 1918. That was one side of the coin. The other, however, was the party's susceptibility to authoritarian solutions, such as those repeatedly brought to bear by the circle surrounding the heir to the throne—in the form of the *Staatsstreich,* a *coup d'état* delivering a blow both to parliament and to the other political parties. The authoritarian form of government instituted during World War I was supported by the Christian Social Party; Mayor Richard Weiskirchner reigned as the Dictator of Vienna.[25] Ignaz Seipel, who had shrewdly led the party into the Republic, was, by the late 1920s, an embittered intriguer who paved the way to dictatorship. In the major cultural questions of the day, the party submitted to the totalitarian tendencies of the Catholic Church. John Boyer has painted this picture on a grand scale—it is filled with individual portraits and sketches of highly problematic subjects, suffused with starkly contrasting colors, and presents a thoroughly ambivalent depiction.

Which lines of continuity were set in motion by the chief protagonist, Dr. Karl Lueger? The one leading to Dollfuß? The one leading to Hitler? Or some other? John Boyer has made his position clear: "...the line runs from Lueger to Dollfuß, not to Hitler."[26] However, I would like to introduce into consideration a third, highly current variant: the line running from Karl Lueger to Jörg Haider. Haider's FPÖ cannot properly be categorized as a radical right-wing party; rather, it is a radical rightist political movement which takes advantage of the latent dissatisfaction of the population, accumulates and concentrates these aggressive forces, and deploys them against the existing political system. If one accepts this premise, then it becomes apparent that there are a number of remarkable analogies between the rise of Lueger and that of Haider. Both organized a protest movement which brought together highly diverse segments of society; both directed this protest against the same demonized object, the existing political system; both played the part of the charismatic leader imbued with aesthetic qualities ("handsome Karl," Jörg Haider's myriad outfits bespeaking the very height of fashion); both activated aggressive images of their respective foes (Jews for the former, foreigners for the latter); both stylized themselves as the advocate of the little guy (modern in its forms, whereas the content at the core evoked the primitive hostility of a barroom dispute); both liked to get out and meet the people (one in the pubs, the other in the discos); both possessed a burning political ambition and an alert instinct for power; both sought out individuals as targets of their attacks, stylizing them into the very embodiment of corruption; both were great actors who imparted a theatrical quality to politics.[27] Once he had attained power, Lueger came to terms with the system and transformed his persona into that of a father figure, but, at this point, the analysis comes to an end.

Theory and Method

Boyer's first volume is a social history of politics. The second volume, with a narrower methodological scope, is a classic structural history of politics: tightly linked to the source material, containing a wealth of fresh insights, properly balancing explication and analysis. What it lacks, however, is a true theoretical concept. Rudolf Hilferding's theory of "organized capitalism," for example, would have made it possible to also take into consideration the system of modern

Interessensverbände (chambers of labor and commerce, representative associations and unions) which began to form at around this time.[28] Modern Austrian social history (Josef Ehmer's and Albert Lichtblau's research) has been accorded little attention. If one regards this work in the context of international debates in the field of historical scholarship, it is truly striking: not the slightest trace of the approaches employed in historical anthropology, not even a hint of uncertainty as a result of the "linguistic turn." Boyer has done a solid job in his work with sources and analysis.

Both volumes, however, offer a refreshing contrast to the Austrian tendency to moralize in the writing of history.[29] Boyer's methodological approach is enunciated in the final sentence of the second volume: "The history of the Christian Social party can be seen only within the limits of its time and judged in the context of its time." This approach constitutes the foundation for any effort to achieve fairness in the writing of history.

NOTES

1. Allan Janik, "Vienna 1900 Revisited: Paradigms and Problems" (The Robert A. Kann Memorial Lecture,1995), *Austrian History Yearbook* 28 (1997), 1-27.

2. Carl E. Schorske, *Fin-de-Siècle Vienna: Politics and Culture* (New York: Vintage Books, 1980); John W. Boyer, *Political Radicalism Late Imperial Vienna: Origins of the Christian Social Movement* (Chicago: University of Chicago Press, 1981); idem, *Culture and Political Crisis in Vienna. Christian Socialism in Power, 1897 - 1918* (Chicago: University of Chicago Press, 1995).

3. Ernst Hanisch, "Das politische System Erste Republik/Zwei Erklärungsversuche," *Handbuch des politischen Systems Österreichs. Erste Republik 1918-1933*, ed. Emmerich Tálos (Vienna, 1995), 1-7.

4. Boyer, *Culture and Political Crisis*, p. xi.

5. Richard Charmatz, *Österreichs innere Geschichte von 1848 bis 1907* (Leipzig, 1911), 117.

6. Boyer, *Political Radicalism*, 29.

7. Boyer, *Culture and Political Crisis*, 208.

8. Ibid., 173.

9. Steven Beller, "Soziale Schicht, Kultur und Wien Juden um die Jahrhundertwende," *Eine zerstörte Kultur*, ed. Gerhard Botz (Buchloe, 1990), 75.

10. Hans-Ulrich Wehler, *Aus der Geschichte lernen?* (Munich, 1988), 161-90; *Bürgertum im 19. Jahrhundert. Deutschland im europäischen Vergleich*, 3 vols., ed. Jürgen Kocka, (Munich, 1988); *Bürgertum in der Habsburger-Monarchie*, ed. Ernst Bruckmüller (Vienna, 1990).

11. Boyer, *Political Radicalism*, 299.

12. Michael Pammer, "Umfang und Verteilung von Unternehmervermögen in Wien 1852 - 1913," *Zeitschrift für Unternehmergeschichte* 41 (1996), 45. Here, in reference to an increase in the proportion of Jews.

13. Boyer, *Culture and Political Crisis*, 52-54.

14. Erika Weinzierl, ed., *Der Modernismus. Beiträge zu seiner Erforschung* (Graz, 1974).

15. Josef Ehmer, "Ökonomischer und sozialer Strukturwandel im Wiener Handwerk - von der industriellen Revolution zur Hochindustrialisierung," *Handwerker in der Industrialisierung*, ed. Ulrich Engelhardt (Stuttgart, 1984), 78-105.

16. Hans-Ulrich Wehler, "Nationalismus, Nation und Nationalstaat in Deutschland seit dem ausgehenden 18. Jahrhundert," *Volk-Nation-Vaterland*, ed. Ulrich Herrmann (Hamburg, 1996), 269-77.

17. Ernst Bruckmüller, *Nation Österreich. Kulturelles Bewußtsein und gesellschaftliche-politische Prozesse* (Vienna, 1996), 286-94.

18. Ernst Hanisch, *Der lange Schatten des Staates. Österreichische Gesellschaftsgeschichte im 20. Jahrhundert* (Vienna, 1994), 154-64.

19. Boyer, Culture and Political Crisis, 217.

20. Ibid., 558.

21. Ibid., 244.

22. Ibid., 459.

23. Ibid., 395.

24. Ibid., 412.

25. Ibid., 374.

26. Ibid., 26, 476.

27. Richard S. Geehr, *Karl Lueger. Mayor of Fin de Siècle Vienna* (Detroit, 1990). See also the Forum section in this volume.

28. Ernst Hanisch, *Der lange Schatten*, 183-209.

29. Ernst Hanisch, "Die Präsenz des Dritten Reiches in der Zweiten Republik," *Inventur 45/55*, ed. Wolfgang Kos and Georg Rigele (Vienna, 1996) 33-38.

John Boyer and Austrian Political Culture

Anton Pelinka

Austria's political culture can be described as the transition from *centrifugal* to *consociational* to *competitive democracy*.[1] The *collapse of the First Republic* in 1934 was the consequence of a lack of basic consensus. It was exactly this consensus, which political elites were able to establish from 1945 on, that characterized the Second Republic. It is the increasing awareness of this consensus which is the reason for the shift from consociational democracy to a more competitive form of political culture.

Fragmentation is the basic assumption behind this typology. To understand the transformation of contemporary Austrian political culture, it is necessary to analyze its roots. Those are deeply ingrained in the era between 1867 and 1918, when Habsburg Austria was a semi-parliamentary, semi-constitutional system with strongly developed political parties. The beginning of this party system set the stage for the fragmentation that was so typical for pre-1945 Austria.

The party system of the late nineteenth century is responsible for the party state which dominates post-1945 Austria. Understanding the beginning of modern parties, which arose out of the political radicalization of late Habsburg Austria, helps to explain the party state of post-1945 Austria.

The Second Republic is a party state that developed to the extreme. It is a political system in which parties tend to become identical with the constitutional government and to dominate all of society. The political parties and institutions established by the Constitution are virtually identical. Austrian parties have much greater control over the government than parties in other democracies. The parties which founded the Republic and framed its constitution created contemporary Austria. The party system, with its three traditional parties, goes back to the 1880s, when, as a consequence of modernization movements in society, three "camps" (*"Lager"*) and three corresponding parties evolved:[2]

1. The socialist camp was politically organized as the Social Democratic Workers' Party since 1891, which re-named itself the Socialist Party of Austria (SPÖ).
2. The Christian (or Catholic) conservative camp was politically organized as the Christian Social Party. After 1945 it became known as the Austrian People's Party (ÖVP).
3. The pan-Germanic camp is the third camp and was first organized from several smaller parties. In 1949 it became the League of Independents (VDU), and in 1956 was renamed the Austrian Freedom Party (FPÖ).

The development of this traditional party system was the result of specific cleavages. Austrian society at the end of the nineteenth and the beginning of the twentieth century was influenced by the adherence to one of three dichotomies:

1. *Class*: Society was seen as divided into two segments—the working class and the bourgeoisie. According to the socialist camp, all the other divisive factors were considered secondary to this predominant cleavage,
2. *Religion*: This perspective interpreted the society as fragmented into two groups, those who followed the Catholic doctrine and all others. This Christian conservative view logically evolved into political Catholicism.
3. *Ethnicity*: The crucial conflict, according to the third camp, was between the Germans and all others. The pan-Germanic camp rallied all who considered themselves German and pitted them against the others.

This background of the Austrian party system correlated with a marked absence of national loyalty towards the existing state, Habsburg Austria. Incapable of inspiring the degree of patriotism felt in other countries, pre-1918 Austria suffered from a deficit of emotional support by its citizens. These specifically Austrian conditions became responsible for two of the unique characteristics of the Austrian party system.

First, the three camps and the parties at the camps' centers aroused much more emotion than parties usually do under different conditions. For many Austrians, their party affiliation became their real fatherland. This was part of the political radicalism described by John Boyer in late imperial Vienna.[3] It was the beginning of the "subcultures" which were so important for the developments that led to civil wars at the end of the First Republic. But it was also the beginning of an elitist structure which made Austrian-style consociational democracy possible after 1945. The Austrian masses had no great inclination to follow national leaders: the moderate Habsburg-oriented patriotism which existed was a far cry from nationalistic fever sweeping other countries, which were defined as "nation-states". Even the Christian Socials, the party most inclined to represent this moderate Habsburg-oriented Austrian patriotism, sometimes used pan-Germanic rhetoric to appeal to an electorate which was not so much Austrian as it was German-oriented.[4] The masses' greater willingness to follow their party leaders resulted in political mobilization and political control by party elites. The idiosyncratic Austrian party state was born out of this kind of fragmentation.

The pan-Germanic camp and its parties distinguished Austria from other European countries. The Social Democratic Workers' Party and the Christian Social Party reflected a degree of normality: all across Europe, social democratic parties were being established at the same time, and in most Catholic countries, parties like the Austrian Christian Socials were founded. But the pan-Germanic camp and its parties were a deviant case. This camp included a national party which claimed to speak for the national interests not of an underprivileged minority, but of the dominant ethnic group of a neighboring country it considered its own. The very existence of the pan-Germanic camp was proof of the lack of Austrian patriotism. Nationalism in Austria was not Austrian, but German. The official goal of the national party was the Anschluß; the ultimate perspective of nationalism in Austria was the *liquidation* of Austria. That was the most striking of all the Austrian peculiarities.

John Boyer emphasizes the links between the Catholic Church and the radicalism which was so typical for pre-1914 Austria. It was a kind of internal opposition. The younger clergy and the younger politicians founded the Christian Social Party out of a twofold opposition—both against the traditionalists among the bishops and against the traditional conservatives. The ones did not trust the approach the new party used for the mobilization of the masses. The others did not accept the agenda of social reforms that the founders of the Christian Social Party preached: Karl Vogelsang, Alois Liechtenstein, and Franz Schindler, among others. In opposing the conservative forces, the new party used the message Pope Leo XIII offered in his social doctrine.

In the late nineteenth century, this message was clear. The Church tried to reconcile its social existence with the democratic tendencies reaching Austria. After the constitution of 1867, a parliament had to be elected and political parties came into existence. The Church, especially under Pope Leo XIII, wanted to become more involved in democratic politics, so it started to accept politics according to the rules of parliamentarism. But the Catholic Church was still influenced by its opposition to most of the values, bourgeois revolutions—and especially the French—had championed. The Church opposed the separation of state and church, of politics and religion. The Church wanted to influence society by means of the ethical, social doctrine Leo XIII formulated in his 1891 papal encyclical *"Rerum novarum."* In this letter, the Pope encouraged the participation of Catholics in modern politics, but demanded that this participation be organized and controlled by Catholic institutions such as Catholic parties, labor unions, and other groups, in order to distinguish the special Catholic agenda from the others.

At the end of the nineteenth century, the Catholic Church in Europe recognized that it faced two hostile political concepts: liberalism (in the sense of capitalism) and socialism (in the sense of Marxism). In an effort to compete with these concepts, the Church tried to establish Catholic parties such as the Center Party (*Zentrum*) in Germany. The situation in Austria was different from Germany, Italy, and France. In Austria, the government was considered sensitive to Catholic interests. The Habsburgs represented the strongest Catholic tradition among all the ruling families. In Austria, there was no structural conflict between church and state like there was in Italy, where the Pope could not forget that modern Italy was built upon the ruins of the papal state. In Austria, there was no Protestant (or any other non-Catholic) majority like there was in Germany, where it was difficult to successfully represent Catholic interests. Moreover, in Austria, there was no republican, laicist, anti-clerical mood, which dominated politics like it did in France, where the Church had lost its control of sensitive areas such as schools and marriage.

In Austria, the Church had to overcome another problem— Catholics were not used to participating in politics. The delay of the constitution had a particular effect on the Catholic mainstream, traditionally linked to the Habsburgs and therefore not used to organizing themselves into political parties and interest groups. Recognizing that Catholic interests were not being represented because there were too few Catholic laymen in politics, the clergy stepped in. It was especially the young generation of Catholic priests, the low-ranking clergy, who in the 1880s started to organize political groups in order to give Catholics a voice in politics. Together with Catholic intellectuals like Karl von Vogelsang and aristocrats like Prince Alois Liechtenstein, clergymen like Franz M. Schindler became the midwives of political Catholicism in Austria.[5]

This was the case in the Vienna area, where this new breed of Catholic politicians, accepting the rules of the parliamentary game, had to rely heavily on the small bourgeoisie as their constituents. Laborers were already more or less lost to the socialists. For the agricultural areas, the situation was not so different. Farmers, especially in the alpine regions, were politically organized by priests like Aemilian Schöpfer in alliance with reform-minded aristocrats and active farmers like Jodok Fink.[6]

In both urban and rural areas, the fledgling Christian Social Party had to deal with the hostility of some bishops and old conservatives toward a movement that was willing and able to overcome the deep gap separating the Catholic tradition from modern politics. The young movement, thanks to the involvement of the clergy, was able to win the approval of its supreme authority, Pope Leo XIII. The Pope, realizing that the Austrian Christian Socials were exactly the type of party he had in mind, backed their movement and quieted their more conservative critics within the Church by publicly giving the Christian Socials his blessing.[7]

The Pope backed a party that was both clerical and progressive. Clerical by virtue of accepting priests in leading functions and by defining its agenda as the implementation of the Pope's social doctrine; progressive by virtue of opposing rather than defending the existing social order. The Pope's backing was decisive for the structures developed by the party, structures characterized by the alliance between the Church and the party. The rectory became the local party headquarters; Catholic organizations became identical with party organizations. The Christian Social Party was not distinguishable from the Catholic

Church, neither in its social outlook, nor in its political programs. This party represented the Church in politics.

This was the birth of the Christian conservative camp. A closed milieu consisting of various clerical organizations used for political purposes among others, it was also a set of beliefs rationalized as the indisputable consequences of Catholicism and a clear-cut combination of autostereo- as well as heterostereotypes. The latter consisted of the others, the enemies who were also in the process of organizing their parties and organizations in approximately the same style: camps with respective closed milieus, such as the socialist camp and the pan-Germanic camp.

Karl Lueger was the person who most successfully represented the Christian Socials in the first years of their existence, and who became the integrative, heroic figure of political Catholicism. Lueger, a lawyer and a politician who had already tried his luck with some less organized "liberal" bourgeois groups, was the charismatic figure Christian Socials were identified with—and with whom they themselves eagerly identified.

Lueger operated as the mayor of Vienna from 1897 until his death in 1910. He was important for his political techniques and his political programs. He developed extra-parliamentary instruments, "the politics of the rowdy and the mob," and "transformed an ideology of the Old Right—Austrian political Catholicism—into an ideology of a New Left, Christian Socialism."[8] Lueger transformed traditional, political Catholicism into its present-day form by giving Christian Socials their "leftist," interventionist, (comparatively) egalitarian profile, a profile that theory-minded thinkers like Vogelsang had already prepared. But it took the pragmatic Lueger to popularize this new image of political Catholicism. And it took Lueger's "radicalism"—a radicalism of style and less of substance.[9]

Lueger had many admirers, most prominent among them was Adolf Hitler. The Nazi leaders claimed to have been influenced above all by two Austrians. The first was Georg von Schönerer, the passionate leader of racist anti-Semitism and representative of the anti-Catholic, anti-Habsburg wing of pan-Germanism.[10] The second was Karl Lueger, who may have been less consistent in his racist justification of anti-Semitism, but whose populistic techniques and ability to inflame the emotions of the masses impressed Hitler.

Lueger was a democrat in the sense that his style was populistic and anti-elitist and he adapted his policies to suit the moods of those electoral segments he needed to win in the next election. Lueger was a pragmatist, and this pragmatism foreshadowed the pragmatism his successors in the Christian conservative camp would later demonstrate. One such pragmatist was Ignaz Seipel, who was a monarchist until 1918, but mutated into a republican beginning with the fall of the monarchy in that year. Seipel managed to strike a bargain with the Social Democrat Otto Bauer regarding the constitution of 1920, but became more and more of a radical anti-socialist, going so far as to adopt some elements of pro-fascist thinking.[11] This pragmatism was also typical of Engelbert Dollfuss, the founder of the authoritarian regime and its first dictator in 1934, who mixed Catholic traditions, Austrian patriotism, pan-Germanic sentiments and Italian fascism to create a very inconsistent political system.[12] This pragmatism was also responsible for the very successful catch-all party concept of the ÖVP after 1945.

Lueger was a pragmatist even in his anti-Semitism.[13] He used existing anti-Semitic prejudices to stir up emotions for his constant campaigning. Although he used "the Jews" as scapegoats, as whipping boys, he did not invent Catholic, Christian anti-Semitism. Of course, anti-Semitism had been in existence as a Christian, European phenomenon for centuries. Perhaps, Lueger may be called the first democratic anti-Semite in the sense that he proved the usefulness of anti-Semitic rhetoric in election strategies. But his most prominent admirer proved to be superior to him in that respect.

Lueger stands at the beginning of the political movement which led to the Austrian People's Party, one of the two pillars the Second Republic was built upon. But Lueger represents also the links between *fin-de-siècle* Viennese political radicalism and the young Austrian Catholic Adolf Hitler.

John Boyer's books are an important tool for understanding the time when the future was still open; when the political parties were still in their first stages of development, when a former liberal, Karl Lueger, could compete with another former liberal, Georg von Schönerer, for the votes of radical anti-Semites. At the same time, Lueger was able to compete with the third former liberal, Victor Adler, for the votes of the lower classes. This was the incubation of the political culture which would dominate the First and the Second Republic of Austria. This was

the period when the political lava was still fluid—and populist
politicians like Lueger shaped it according to their strategic interests.

NOTES

1. Arend Lijphart, *Democracy in Plural Societies: A Comparative Exploration*
(New Haven: Yale University Press, 1977).

2. Anton Pelinka and Fritz Plasser, eds., *The Austrian Party System* (Boulder,
CO: Westview Press, 1989).

3. John Boyer, *Political Radicalism in Late Imperial Vienna: Origins of the
Christian Social Movement* (Chicago: University of Chicago Press, 1981);
idem, *Culture and Political Crisis in Vienna: Christian Socialism in Power,
1897-1918* (Chicago: University of Chicago Press, 1995).

4. Boyer, *Culture and Political Crisis*, 164-235.

5. Boyer, *Culture Radicalism*, 70-72, 223.

6. Boyer, *Culture and Political Crisis*, 78, 94f.

7. Boyer, *Political Radicalism*, 345.

8. Carl E. Schorske, *Fin-de-Siècle Vienna: Politics and Culture* (New York:
Vintage Books, 1980), 133.

9. Boyer, *Political Radicalism*, 184-246.

10. Schorske, *Fin-de-Siècle Vienna*, 120-33.

11. See Charles A. Gulick, *Austria from Habsburg to Hitler*, vol. 2 (Berkeley:
University of California Press, 1948), 775-819; Klemens von Klemperer, *Ignaz
Seipel: Christian Statesman in a Time of Crisis* (Princeton: Princeton Univer-
sity Press, 1972).

12. Ernst Hanisch, *Der lange Schatten des Staates: Österreichische Gesellschaftsgeschichte im 20 Jahrhundert* (Vienna: Ueberreuther, 1994), 310-23.

13. Peter Pulzer, *The Rise of Political Anti-Semitism in Germany and Austria*,
2nd ed. (Cambridge, MA: Harvard University Press, 1988), 198-201.

REVIEW ESSAYS

Business History in Austria

Herman Freudenberger

In 1971, Alois Brusatti, professor of economic and social history at the Hochschule für Welthandel (Vienna), founded the *Verein der wissentschaftlichen Forschung auf dem Gebiete der Unternehmerbiographie und Firmengeschichte*. Composed of members of the academic and business community, its purpose was (1) to provide scientific criteria for the writing of the history of a particular firm, whether sponsored by a firm to celebrate its own accomplishments or whether for purely academic reasons; (2) to correct the often distorted picture of the entrepreneur as a person; and (3) to offer analytical case studies as part of the training of students and scholars in business administration.[1] As academic godfather to this association, Brusatti pointed specifically to the late Fritz Redlich, who at that time was still active, though long retired from formal duties, at Harvard University. He did not, however, have any direct relationship with the Austrian association.

Redlich, whose influence is also quite apparent in German business history, had for many years been a leading personality in the Center for Entrepreneurial History at Harvard University, a group led by Arthur H. Cole, professor and librarian of the Baker Library of the Harvard Graduate School of Business Administration. Interestingly, N.S.B. Gras, the first holder of the chair of Business History there, based himself in his approach on Richard Ehrenberg, a professor at the University of Rostock early in the twentieth century and, like Gras, himself frequently embroiled in controversy. Clearly, the Harvard Business School introduced the subject into its curriculum in order to study "specific situations as they came to business men...in the past so that we may compare understandingly these situations with our present conditions."[2] While Gras completely agreed with this formulation of the purpose of business history, his colleague in Harvard's Economics Department, Edwin F. Gay, with whom Gras had for a few years published the *Journal of Economic and Business History*, insisted on a more rigorously scholarly approach. The differences between these two approaches typifies at the same time the problems that practitioners of business history experienced for many years and that seemed finally to have been solved by Alfred D. Chandler, Jr., holder of the chair in Business History at Harvard's Business School from the 1960s to the 1990s. Chandler's more analytical approach has appealed to both the predominately scholarly approach of academics as well as the more pragmatic approach of persons whose focus is to train business leaders.

This broader introduction seems appropriate not only because some of the works to be reviewed here specifically used the Harvard model, whether the Redlich or the Chandler examples were used. It also highlights the continuing problems with which business history, no matter where it is practiced, is confronted. Who was right, the Harvard Business School dean with his highly pragmatic approach, or the Harvard economist, who preferred a more scholarly approach? Two small anecdotes may throw some light on this question. Many years ago the leader of the business history group in the German Democratic Republic condemned the careful and objective line that I tried to explain to him and his colleagues as being the way that U.S. business historians thought of their subject. Since I could not control how my type of business history could be used and misused, he found little to recommend it. In East Germany, he assured me, there was no ambiguity on the purpose of business history: it was first to separate the worker from his old loyalties to his capitalistic enterprise and, once that was accomplished, to provide him with pride in his new socialistic enterprise. Strangely, I heard a similar story from the chief executive officer (CEO) of one of America's largest airlines that had financed what on the whole was a very good business history. When asked if management could learn anything from this exercise, his negative answer was coupled with the statement that the 36,000 employees of his firm each received a copy in order to increase their loyalty to the company.

Despite these clearly self-serving reasons, business history does have a scholarly purpose. Whereas Gras takes a position familiar to followers of historical economics as practiced by Gustav Schmoller,

Chandler and Redlich favor a more analytical approach. The Gras-Schmoller type of academic research can be characterized as collecting as many examples that seem vaguely valid to understanding the business and the economic background of a society and then constructing a reasonable edifice with the bricks thus made available. Chandler and Redlich begin with a clearer model that serves as the flashlight, as Redlich at times said, to search for the constituent elements of a coherent whole. Less descriptive than the older type of business history, it comes face to face at its margins with other subdisciplines such as industrial organization, typified in the more recent literature by the work of Oliver Williamson and Ronald Coase, on the side of economics, and Chester Barnard, who was more associated with business administration as a discipline. In these ways both learning from and contributing to sister disciplines, business history also confronts more direct problems such as whether it should primarily describe the role of business in society, certainly an important function in modern economic societies, or whether it should accentuate the role of the entrepreneur as a more or less heroic figure in the way that famous Austrian economist Joseph Schumpeter saw him.

Modifications of Schumpeter's approach have brought us to the theoretical construct of an entrepreneurial function according to which the long-run, strategic decisions are made not only by an owner-operator or a CEO independently but also by various agencies within a firm as well as governments outside of it. In short, business history seen in this way increasingly claims for itself the title of micro-economic history that can inform on the broad role that business enterprises in general are responsible for in our modern industrial or even post-industrial societies.

This somewhat elaborate introduction of the field of business history is meant as a background by which Austrian business history in particular can be judged. It is not meant to rate how faithfully the histories reviewed herein follow any of the models described in the introduction. Above all, it should be emphasized that what follows is a selection of work on business in Austria (to include prominently the old Habsburg Monarchy) that makes no pretence of completeness. Moreover, not unlike Molière's Monsieur Jordain who was surprised to discover that he had spoken prose all of his life, many of the authors referred to herein seemed to have had little feeling that they were in fact contributing to the field of business history. As part of the task that I have set for myself, I also wish to indicate briefly some of the sources that are available at the present time for the use of anyone who wishes seriously to investigate this field.

As catalyst for this essay, several works that have been published over the last decade and a half will serve. Two of them are histories of enterprises and were sponsored by the firms themselves. Two others are contributions to the academic disciplines. Herbert Matis and Dieter Stiefel collaborated on two studies of the first type, in this case of enterprises not well known outside of Austria and not making the list of 189 "big business" firms that Franz Mathis in another study, of the second type, to be examined, compiled. In accordance with Franz Mathis's criteria, these firms would probably have to be characterized as of medium size, but they are nonetheless large and interesting enough so that the rendition of their business existence can still prove to be very rewarding.

One of the works from the pens of Herbert Matis and Dieter Stiefel, *Mit der vereinigten Kraft des Capitals, des Credits und der Technik*, is a very hefty, two-volume set detailing the history of a major Viennese construction company, eventually known as the *Allgemeine Baugesellschaft-A. Porr Aktiengesellschaft*. Incorporated in 1868 to take advantage of the opportunities for new construction associated with the destruction of the wall around the inner city of Vienna and the formation of its famous *Ringstrasse*, this firm was responsible for the construction of many imposing buildings that still grace that avenue. Its history,with its loving details and pictures of many of the edifices built by the company, is obviously meant especially for the enjoyment of Viennese people, for it is an exercise in reading that can be somewhat numbing to an outsider. Equally disconcerting is the long list of all the members of the board of directors from the beginning to very recent times. Since the authors spend so much time on the board, they should have discussed the role of this group, especially how far it influenced strategic entrepreneurial and the day-to-day managerial decisions.

One is not surprised to find that as a construction company the *Allgemeine* did not have a particularly stable history, that among other things, its workforce could change violently from season to season and, moreover, be subject to strong cyclical variations. It was a firm that built not only apartment and office buildings but also harbors and railroads. Aside from the construction for second parties, it also built edifices on its own land and was thus a real-estate owner as well. Of special interest is the fact that among its founders were Jewish businessmen and a bank. Its leading spirit was a Jewish innovative manager, Ottokar Stern, who, after decades of service, was finally forced out of the firm by the Nazi takeover of Austria.

There are a number of questions that arise out of this firm's history, that have, however, more general applicability. For one thing, the reasoning behind the formation of a corporation (*Aktiengesellschaft*) would be highly interesting. A simple answer such as that it was an efficient device for the accumulation of large investment capital derived from many sources would not suffice. The income of corporations was subject to a substantially higher tax rate than enterprises with a sole owner or a few owners. This at least must have been a disincentive for a corporate structure of business. Second, one would wish to be better acquainted with the functions of the construction firm itself. How much of the work was contracted out, for example? Third, the role of the banks in the operation and ownership of Austrian firms is of con-siderable importance. Did they in fact impose a more conservative operation of the firm than a risk-taking single entrepreneur or a small partnership would be willing to undertake? There is evidence that that is exactly what happened with this firm, its major owner, the *Bodencreditanstalt* specifically preventing the construction firm to invest directly in an innovation of A. Porr dealing with reinforced concrete (p. 66 and following).

Over all, the history of this firm makes interesting reading for a business historian, once all the non-essential detail is pushed aside. Moreover, its second volume, taking up the post World War II period, includes more analysis and therefore makes it more pertinent for micro-economic history.

Matis and Stiefel's second collaborative effort deals with a large freight forwarding company, Schenker & Co. The study bears the somewhat peculiar title of the *Schenker Dynasty*, peculiar since Schenker's only son and sole presumptive heir committed suicide while his father was still alive. Schenker, a poor Swiss immigrant, began this firm in 1872 with the help of two Hungarian Jewish businessmen, who were able to contribute not much else than several thousand *Gulden* of capital. As international freight forwarders this company had, of course, numerous associations with foreign firms and consequently failed to have the more parochial outlook of the construction firm that I discussed above. After the First World War that resulted in the breakup of the Austro-Hungarian Monarchy, the focus of Schenker & Co. took a decidedly German direction. A flamboyant "partner" in Berlin essentially tried to make the firm into a German enterprise with the Viennese part at best an important outpost. Playing fast and loose with the firm's assets and faced with a rather weak and unimaginative leader in Vienna, he created major problems so that in the end the German operation had to be sold to the *Reichsbahn*, which at that made a bad bargain in the acquisition.

With this book even more than with that of the Viennese construction company, one gets the feeling that the authors allowed themselves to be led overwhelmingly by the availability of the original-source material. There is, of course, no question that the historian can only report what he actually finds. But a more theoretic or model approach would have at least shown what general and specific evidence would be called for so as to produce a more complete business history. At the same time, one should not lose sight of the customer. While the student of business will certainly find evidence for insights into the way Austrian business firms operated and for the role that they played in the larger society, these two studies are mainly descriptive in nature and appeal to a more general reader.

More analytically-oriented and clearly meant as a scholarly exercise is Alois Mosser's thorough but rather forbidding study of the activities of a select seventy corporations.[3] It concerns itself above all with the reported data and analyzes these data on the basis of clearly enunciated criteria. Unquestionably a pioneer work, as its dust jacket proclaims, it provides raw material that any study of business history for that period cannot ignore. It is a ponderous tome, however, that the more general student of Austria's economic history may consult somewhat rarely. Mosser is obviously an accomplished economic and business historian as some of his other studies, such as the one on spatial concentration of industry and on industrial combines will testify.[4]

A study that from the outset proclaims its interest in analysis and that consciously follows a model enunciated by Alfred D. Chandler, Jr., Franz Mathis's *Big Business in Österreich*, is more ambitious than the business history studies discussed above and possibly for that reason raises more unanswered questions.[5] Mathis deserves much credit for going through the tortuous and tedious procedure of amassing relevant material on the 189 firms that fit into his definition. His norm for inclusion is that a firm at some time or another had at least 1,000 employees on its payroll.[6] This is fine and good, but it violates a basic element of Chandler's model that the definition of big business is directly associated with multi-unit firms.[7] It is, of course, not at all necessary for the student to follow the master slavishly, and, as a matter of fact, Mathis quotes Chandler as encouraging extensions of his model.

Mathis divides his chore into two parts, volume one being comprised of 189 stories of as many firms, and volume two being analysis and commentary. The author clearly faces a most daunting set of problems. For example, many of the firms were partly or wholly owned by foreign investors or by Austrian banks. From his citations, one gets the impression that he did not use the archives of the foreign owners or of the banks. Another problem concerns the all-consuming emphases on the number of the workforce and the designation of the firm as managerial, owner-operator, etc. I have no quarrel with this categorization of business firms, but the absence of any mention of assets, sales, or profits is rather disconcerting. To indicate the source of my problem, a listing of the largest firms outside of the United States in 1974 will serve. Based on annual sales, this list shows Royal Dutch/Shell group as the largest with a workforce of 168,000, Unilever next with 359,000, Nippon Steel, fifth in line, with 98,000, British Steel in the twenty-first spot with 225,000 employees.[8] This sample is meant to show that the number of workers and other employees is not necessarily the most important element in a firm's success.

While Mathis must be commended for taking a very necessary first step in understanding Austria's business environment, in his volume on analysis there is, in my opinion, a considerable void on a number of rather important issues. First, on the entrepreneurial side, I wish that he would have discussed the structural forms more intensively. What, for example, is the benefit that the owners of the firm expected from a corporative structure or its several variations or from individual or partnership ownership?[9]

Second, Chandler places major emphasis on technological innovation when it comes to big business. Mathis, however, concerns himself only rarely with this question. He has much to say on concentration, but he uses the term apparently to mean spatial concentration and not, as is generally accepted in the Anglo-American economic literature, the domination of few firms in a market. He undoubtedly follows the same approach as Alois Mosser in a perceptive article on the subject some years earlier.[10] In that context questions of transportation costs and economies of scale would have to be considered and consequently deserve extensive comment.

Third, he as well as Herbert Matis and Dieter Stiefel are forced to deal with several unique historical events, the most important of which was the breakup of an empire comprising 50 million people and the creation of a country of 6 million. Unquestionably, this was a very traumatic experience and may have led to a feeling of despondency in this new "country against its will." Even though Herbert Matis in a very convincing article asserts that the break with the old environment was far from abrupt and that institutional arrangements were found to successfully meet the new conditions,[11] Franz Mathis should also have addressed this problem more forcefully. War, its preparation and its aftermath as well as its direct effect, cannot be simply shoved aside by declaring that it is abnormal.[12] For example, over a decade after the end of that war, Stiefel found, that the crisis with the *Credit-Anstalt*, Austria's largest bank was an outgrowth of that debacle.[13]

Another problem that Mathis and other Austrian business and economic historians must tackle head on is the effect of the Anschluβ and the Second World War on Austria.[14] These factors, driven by political changes remain open for discussion in Franz Mathis's ambitious effort to understand Austria's big business—and thereby much of its economic development and growth—since before the First World War.

Several other points in my wish list for Mathis's two-volume work include the role of the government as regulator, purchaser, and seller, as well as investor. For a country where the heavy hand of the bureaucracy is well known and in which cartels, as in Germany, were a fact of life, the problems of the political economy should be thoroughly examined. An additional point concerns the railroads, which in Chandler's writings hold such a defining place in the rise of modern, hierarchical management. Since none of the 189 stories dealt with railroads, one must assume that they employed fewer than 1,000 persons.

Last, I wonder why one of the largest businesses, the postal service, is excluded. Even today this governmentally owned business provides some of the greatest managerial problems in many countries.

The discussion of Franz Mathis's work is meant less to suggest any failings in his effort than it is to underline the problems of a formerly large country that then finds itself sharply constricted to a small geographical space. Mathis thus faces a formidable constraint in tracing big business in the severely reduced Austrian republic to its foundation in the old monarchy. This was, in a way, symbolized by the obvious pride with which the industrialists of the old Austro-Hungarian Empire presented the ruler, Francis Joseph with two multi-volume sets fittingly entitled *Die Gross-Industrie Oesterreichs.*[15] Written by representatives of industry to celebrate first the occasion of the emperor's fiftieth anniversary of his reign and subsequently of his sixtieth anniversary, these massive volumes contain brief descriptions of numerous industrial firms as written by functionaries of the respective firms. While one should not hold them to the requirements of rigorous scholarship, they do provide substantial evidence of industrial prowess, although often they also showed a retardation of technological processes when compared with other European economies. Many of these firms were located in Bohemia and Moravia and thus became part of the economy of the Czechoslovak Republic after the First World War, reducing considerably the potential candidates for inclusion in a list of big businesses.

About the same time as these volumes were being published, that is, 1898 and 1908, the *Verein für Geschichte der Deutschen in Böhmen* brought up a number of firm histories that demonstrated some of the vigor of the Bohemian crown lands. Among these Hermann Hallwich's *Firma Franz Leitenberger 1793*1893* presented a very useful portrayal of this multi-unit cotton firm from even before its inception through the nineteenth century.[16] Responsible for the founding of this enterprise was a craftsman who bought out the industrial enterprise of a nobleman. Thus, one of the largest enterprises in the Habsburg Monarchy in the nineteenth century was brought forth through the interplay of an aristocrat's interest in industrial production with that of a middle-class commoner, a phenomenon that, despite the skepticism of some scholars, was fairly common and stamped the Habsburg Monarchy as unusual in the annals of industrial development.[17] In a similar vein, this organization produced two other studies, one on the porcelain and earthenware industry in Bohemia[18] and the other on a linen and cotton firm of note.[19]

Unquestionably, the most important book from this era for our purposes is Johann Slokar's masterful and still unsurpassed history of Austrian industrial history to the middle of the nineteenth century.[20] While it is not a business history in the narrow sense of the term, it is indispensable for the understanding of Austrian industrial firms in the nineteenth century. A companion work that describes the period preceding Slokar's is Přibram's tour-de-force, a rendition of the largely successful efforts of Maria Theresa and Joseph II to lay a sound groundwork for Austrian economic development until the First World War.[21] It, too, should be used primarily as a valuable, highly reliable source for business history.

The broader histories on eighteenth century business and industry include those by three authors who produced highly commendable studies during the Communist period of one of the successor states to the old Habsburg Monarchy. Arnošt Klíma's excellent piece on what he calls the manufactory period in Bohemia deserves pride of place for providing evidence of business enterprises in the eighteenth century.[22] In addition, Anton Špiesz's book on Slovakia's industry at roughly the same period of time[23] and František Mainuš's studies of Moravia's woolen, cotton, and linen industries are required reading.[24] This is no less true for several important studies by Viktor Hofmann on the woolen, cotton, and sugar industries.[25] Among these there is a fine study of the Linz Woolen Fabrics Company that was founded in the 1670s and lasted until the 1840s. At one time, this company employed 48,000 persons, including those that worked outside the factory. While I deplore it that Franz Mathis did not go back to the eighteenth century for examples of big business in Austria, I find it even more puzzling that the sizable managerial problems that were associated with such a large enterprise seemed unworthy of attention.

Leaving a number of other valuable studies aside for the sake of brevity, I would now like to briefly survey several books and articles that deal with individual enterprises or with industries in which particular enterprises have played a major role. A classic example of this is the Brno fine woolen cloth factory in Brno (Brünn), Moravia's capital. Founded in 1764 and entering bankruptcy in 1789, this firm was directly responsible for the subsequent industrial development of that city and its region by virtue of the entrepreneurial talent that it had attracted.[26] With the expansion of this industry came machine manufacturing. Not unlike Manchester in England, to which some nineteenth-century journalists compared it, it became a major textile and machinery center. Unfortunately, the neat model that seems to suggest itself by this industrial regional development cannot be easily reproduced for other regional developments.

Three business histories, financed by Brno firms that became prominent during the nineteenth century, deserve to be mentioned. One of these describes the woolen cloth factory of Johann Heinrich Offermann, a person from the west German textile town of Monschau (Montjoie), whose progeny brought the enterprise that he founded in 1786, before the first woolen factory's demise, to great renown.[27] Directly connected with the textile industry in Brno was what eventually became known as *Die Erste Brünner Maschinen-Fabriks-Gesellschaft*, led like the Offermann enterprise by specialists from Germany proper.[28] More recently a more academic study of the firm, expanding its time horizon considerably, was published in the former Czechoslovakia.[29] The third company history to celebrate an anniversary was the volume detailing the fate of a quite well-known publishing house, Rudolf M. Rohrer.[30] At some remove from Brno but still directly connected to it was the fate of another textile manufacturing family, one of whose progeny set himself up as a wholesaler and private banker in Vienna in 1833. In a fine biography financed by the firm itself, Heinrich Benedikt described the life and activities of Alexander Schoeller, a nephew of three brothers who left Düren near Aachen in 1818 to open up a woolen cloth factory in Brno.[31] Their stated purpose for opening this factory in Brno was to surmount the tariff barriers that the Habsburg Monarchy had raised after the Napoleonic Wars. In this they succeeded, and their nephew became responsible for promoting Austrian industry in a most forceful manner.

The textile and the machine industries in Brno, were not the only examples of manufacturing enterprises that grew to considerable size because of technological innovations. One of the most interesting of these firms was the Vitkovice (Witkowitz) iron works in northern Moravia. Founded by the archbishop of Olomouc, a brother of the reigning monarch, it went finally into the hands of the Rothschild banking house in Vienna in 1843. After a trip to England supported by Salomon Rothschild in Vienna and strongly aided by his brother Nathan in England, Professor F.X. Riepl of the Polytechnical Institute of Vienna learned about the latest methods of smelting iron. With the acquisition of this knowledge, Riepl was able to introduce the puddling method in the Vitkovice iron works, which subsequently became a supplier of rails for the *Kaiser-Ferdinand-Nordbahn*, which the Viennese Rothschild was responsible for building. Milan Myška's various studies provide excellent material for the history of this enterprise and, for that matter, for the rest of the iron industry of the Bohemian crown lands.[32]

The contribution that the Rothschild bank made to the iron and the railroad industries suggests the whole topic of the involvement of banks in the Austrian economy. Salomon Rothschild was not the only private banker who invested in industry and had a strong hand in the management of various firms. Several names are well-known. They include Fries, Geymüller, Sina—all of them houses whose founders came from abroad, as did Rothschild. One of the best known to historians is Johann Fries, a Swiss Protestant who began as intermediary between England and the Habsburg Monarchy under Maria Theresa in the transmission of an English subsidy amounting to £100,000.[33] The house of Fries was subsequently engaged in numerous industrial endeavors, from silk and cotton textiles to sugar refining.

Banks that operated as joint stock companies with limited liability appeared quite early in Austria's drive for industrialization. As far back as 1751 such an institution was opened in Brno and its leader, a government official by the name of Kehrnhofer, was instrumental in bringing the above-mentioned woolen factory to Brno.[34] It was among the first to follow the recommendations of the well-known seventeenth-century Cameralist Wilhelm von Schröder, who had already suggested a development bank in 1686. Another joint stock bank opened its doors in 1787. With a capital of one million *gulden* it proved to be a little known predecessor to the much more famous *Credit-Anstalt* in 1854. Before it fell victim to the state bankruptcy of 1811, it had been engaged in financing among other firms the Pottendorf cotton yarn factory, among the largest in continental Europe in the first half of the nineteenth century.[35] These financial structures testify to the early interest in economic growth in the Habsburg Monarchy. Their histories deserve considerably more attention than they have received in the past.

The *Credit-Anstalt* has, of course, had as its distinguished historian the late Eduard März.[36] Two further studies contribute significantly to Austria's financial history. At the end of the seventeenth century and the beginning of the eighteenth, no banking house was more important for the Habsburg state than the house of Samuel Oppenheimer, a court Jew who served as financier for the government and supplier of war materiel.[37] No less informative of the various financial problems of eighteenth-century Austria is Bidermann's study of the *Wiener Stadtbank*, an institution that was founded to take the place of the Oppenheimer public lending operation after its principal's death and its resultant bankruptcy.[38]

The business histories of the banks and of industrial enterprises, some of which were founded or operated under their strong influence, lead also to other entrepreneurial factors that must be considered. Oppenheimer was a Jew as were Rothschild, Stern of the construction company, and Karpeles, for many years the head of the Schenker company. Fries, Geymüller, Offermann, Schoeller, and the founders of the first machine factory of Brno were originally Protestants from abroad.[39] These distinct groups, as well as the Habsburg aristocracy contributed significantly to the empire's economic growth.

In an interesting way, the role of the aristocracy is highlighted by the Schwarzenberg family, one of whose members was the largest investor and headed the board of directors at the bank bearing his name. His son became an investor in the *Credit-Anstalt* some forty years after the earlier bank had become inoperative due to the state bankruptcy of 1811.

The aristocracy played probably a greater role in the industrialization of the Austrian empire than did aristocracies elsewhere in Europe. This hypothesis deserves more attention than it has received in the past. Without question, even though some of its members were constantly in debt, owing to their lifestyle, they were in fact rich and could call on financial support from their peers as well as from the banking community in general. In terms of business history, one of the oldest works of this genre is the small book containing the speech made in 1815 by the Cistercian monk D. Joachim Cron in commemoration of the 100th anniversary of the founding of the Waldstein woolen factory in Horní Litvínov (Oberleutensdorf).[40] The pride with which its founder, Count John Joseph Waldstein, viewed the enterprise has also been responsible for the creation of twenty copper engravings that show the technological details of the manufacturing process in his factory. The engravings also serve as an excellent source for the state of the art around the year 1730. These and business records of the firm provide the basis of a business history.[41] The history of this firm is instructive, beyond what has been published on it, since in the nineteenth century it was leased out to Ferdinand Römheld, a bourgeois entrepreneur. The combination of noble and bourgeois entrepreneurship proved to be an effective method by which Austrian economic growth was aided.

Unfortunately, the study of the contribution that the Habsburg aristocracy, led by the imperial family itself, made to economic development has not yet been very far advanced. Yet the opportunities for the exposition of the part its members played are available by virtue of the numerous family archives that can be found in the Czech Republic. For example, the records of the Schwarzenberg Bank, referred to above, are located in Česky Krumlov in seeming totality, demonstrating not only how a wealthy landowner operated but also providing a rare look into a private bank's procedures.

A few other interesting attempts of aristocratic entrepreneurship have been recorded. One of the great entrepreneurial personalities was the seventeenth generalissimo Albrecht von Wallenstein.[42] Even before his advancement to power over great armies, when he still was a more or less insignificant colonel, he acted the part of a "military enterpriser," as Fritz Redlich called him.[43] His role is difficult to isolate since he considered himself almost like a head of state. He essentially ran his properties in northern Bohemia like one gigantic enterprise to provide him with the means of running his war. In his attention to detail and his insistence on efficiency in the production of agricultural and industrial goods, he showed himself to be a sharp manager. It matters little whether he did all this "nicht des Nutzens, sondern der Reputation wegen;" the basic point is that he wanted to maximize his production within whatever constraints he wished to set up.[44]

Not long after the publication of that particular study the Czech historian Jindřich Šebánek wrote a most interesting piece on the textile enterprises of the Kaunitz family early in the eighteenth century.[45] A further noteworthy example of aristocratic entrepreneurship concerns the stocking factory that Count Christoph von Salburg erected on his estate Poneggen (Upper Austria) in 1763.[46] Lastly, there are several instructive pieces relating to the entrepreneurial activities of iron works operated by aristocrats. One of these is part of a book on the princely Fürstenberg family in Bohemia.[47] Two others relate to the Salm-Reifferscheidt family, one of whose members, Francis Hugo, at the end of the eighteenth and the first three decades of the nineteenth century, was one of the most devoted persons in the entire monarchy in his efforts to promote industrial technology and economic growth in general.[48] I would like to add here that microfilms on a number of aristocratic, Bohemian enterprises, including the Fürstenberg iron works in the nineteenth century, are available at the Baker Library of the Harvard Graduate School of Business Administration.[49]

Finally, the state as industrial entrepreneur must be considered. One of the most striking personalities in this respect is the consort of Maria Theresa. Disparagingly called the greatest industrialist by the Prussian king Frederick II, Francis Stephan, formerly Duke of Lorraine, created several fairly large business organizations. Best known for his cotton factory in Šaštin (Sassin) and the earthen ware factory in nearby Holič (Hollitsch), he also operated with much less success a woolen cloth factory on the estate Pardibuce (Pardibutz), an estate that he ran until a loan that he had made from his private resources to the Habsburg state and that was mortgaged with this estate could be paid off.[50] The woolen works was subsequently transferred to Brno and became the catalyst for that city's efflorescence in the nineteenth century.

It is not totally clear whether this emperor's industrial efforts should be classified under personal or state entrepreneurship. There is no question, however, regarding the classification of the state tobacco monopoly for which a very commendable study was published some twenty years ago.[51] This study, in particular its focus on internal work organization contains much highly pertinent material that should contribute to the understanding of nineteenth-century factory organization.

Before closing this rather brief survey of business history in Austria and the Habsburg Monarchy, a book that defies strict categorization as a business history but that is nevertheless very important in the understanding of the business environment of the nineteenth century must be mentioned. Franz Baltzarek's portrayal of the Viennese stock exchange is of critical importance concerning the Viennese business climate.[52]

This rather brief survey has omitted numerous business histories and much extremely pertinent material. Nevertheless, this survey is rooted in the conviction that the history of business in Austria is important and deserves much more in-depth examination. Moreover, it lies at the base of a belief that the history of business in Austria can prove to be very instructive for business and economic historians anywhere else in the world. As in all scholarly endeavors, the investigation of business, in Austria as elsewhere, should be informed by methods that benefit from the thinking of the entire world-wide scholarly community, above all because the problems inherent in such an exercise are ubiquitous. The great Austrian Empire may be gone, but its effects on the small Austria of today are still felt. Moreover, the transformation that this fact represents provides valuable lessons for all political economies and demonstrates that institutional arrangements can find ways to create conditions favorable to a benevolent society.

NOTES

1. Alois Brusatti, "Ein neuer Verein für Unternehmerbiographie und Firmengeschichte," *Tradition*, 16 (1971): 105-8.

2. Fritz Redlich, "Approaches of Business History," *Business History Review* 36 (1962): 62.

3. Alois Mosser, *Die Industrieaktiengesellschaft in Österreich 1880-1913* (Vienna: Verlag der österreichischen Akademie der Wissenschaften, 1980).

4. Alois Mosser, "Concentration and the Finance of Austrian Industrial Combines, 1880-1914," in *International Business and Central Europe, 1918-1939*, ed. Alice Teichova and P.L. Cottrell (New York, Leicester University Press-St. Martin's Press, 1983), 57-71.

5. Franz Mathis, *Big Business in Österreich* (Vienna: Verlag für Geschichte und Politik, volume 1, 1987, volume 2, 1990).

6. Franz Mathis, "Erfolg und Mißerfolg der österreichischen Großunternhemen im 20. Jahrhundert," *Zeitschrift für Unternehmergeschichte* 37 (1992): 1.

7. Alfred D. Chandler, Jr., "The Place of Modern Industrial Enterprise in Three Economies," in *International Business in Central Europe, 1918-1939* ed. Alice Teichova and P.L. Cottrell (New York, Leicester University Press- St. Martin's Press, 1983), 3: "By any definition the large modern industrial enterprise is multi-unit."

8. *Fortune Magazine*, August 1974, 176.

9. Dieter Stiefel, "The Reconstruction of the Credit-Anstalt," in *International Business and Central Europe, 1918-1939*, ed. Alice Teichova and P.L. Cottrell (New York, Leicester Univeristy Press-St. Martin's Press, 1983), 415-30.

10. Alois Mosser, "Raumabhänigkeit und Konzentrationsinteresse in der industriellen Entwicklung Österreichs bis 1914," *Bohemia* 17 (1976): 136-92.

11. Herbert Matis, "Disintegration and Multi-national Enterprises in Central Europe during the Post-war Years (1918-23)," in *International Business and Central Europe, 1918-1939*, ed. Alice Teichova and P.L. Cottrell (New York, Leicester University Press, St. Martin's Press, 1983), 73-96.

12. Mathis, "Erfolg," 1.

13. Stiefel, "The Reconstruction of the Credit-Anstalt," 415-30.

14. Stefan Karner, Österreichs Rüstungsindustrie 1944," *Zeitschrift für Unternehmergeschichte* 25 (1980): 179-206.

15. Anon., *Die Gross-Industrie Oesterreichs.* (Vienna, Verlag Leopold Weiss, 1898,1908-1910).

16. Hermann Hallwich, *Firma Franz Leitenberger 1793-1893* (Prague: Verlag des Vereines für Geschichte der Deutschen in Böhmen, 1893)

17. Ralph Melville, "Zu den Anfängen der Industrialisierung in den böhmischen Ländern im Zeitalter des Merkantilismus," in *Die Anfänge der Industrialisierung Niederösterreichs*, ed. Helmuth Feigl and Andreas Kusternig (Vienna: Niederösterreichische Institut für Landeskunde, 1982), 319-41.

18. Ottocar Weber, *Die Entstehung der Porcelain- und Steingutindustrie in Böhmen* (Prague: Verlag des Vereines für Geschichte der Deutschen in Böhmen, 1894).

19. Eduard Langer, *Firma Benedict Schroll's Sohn* (Prague: Verlag des Vereines für Geschichte der Deutschen in Böhmen, 1895).

20. Johann Slokar, *Geschichte der österreichischen Industrie und ihrer Förderung unter Kaiser Franz I* (Vienna: Tempsky Verlag, 1914).

21. Karl Přibram, *Geschichte der österreichischen Gewerbepolitik von 1740 bis 1860* (Leipzig: Duncker & Humblot, 1907).

22. Arnošt Klíma, *Manufakturní období v Čechach* (Prague: Československa akademie věd, 1955); see also idem, "Industrial Growth and Entrepreneurship in the Early Stages of Industrialization in the Czech Lands," *Journal of European Economic History* 6 (1977): 549-74; idem, "The Beginning of the Machine-Building Industry in the Czech Lands in the First Half of the Nineteenth Century," *Journal of European Economic History* 4 (1975): 49-78.

23. Anton Špiesz, *Manufaktúrne obdobie na Slovensku 1725-1825* (Bratislava: Vydavatel'stvo Slovenskej akademie vied, 1961); idem, *Die Manufaktur im östlichen Europa. Kölner Vorträge zur Sozial-und Wirtschaftsgeschichte* (Cologne: Forschungsinstitut für Sozial-und Wirtschaftsgeschichte, 1969).

24. František Mainuš, *Vlnařství a bavlnářství na Moravě a ve Slezsku v XVIII. soletí* (Prague: Statní pedagogické nakladtelství, 1960); idem, *Plátenictví na Moravě a ve Slezsku v XVII. a XVIII. století* (Ostrava: Krajskě nakladeslstvě, 1959).

25. Viktor Hofmann, "Beiträge zur neueren österreichischen Wirtschafts-geschichte," *Archiv für österreichische Geschichte* 110 (1919): 417-741; 112 (1932): 1-210; (1934): 1-165.

26. Herman Freudenberger, *The Industrialization of a Central Eruopean City* (Edington: Pasold Research Fund, 1977); Herman Freudenberger and Gerhard Mensch, *Von der Provinzstadt zur Industrieregion (Brünn-Studie)* (Göttingen: Vandenhoek & Ruprecht, 1977).

27. Anon., *K.K. Priv. Militär-Feintuch-Fabrik Joh. Heinr. Offermann 1786-1911* (Brno: Verlag der Firma Joh. Heinr. Offermann, 1912).

28. Anon., *Die Hundertjährige Geschichte der Ersten Brünner Maschinen-Fabriks-Gesellschaft in Brünn von 1821 bis 1921* (Leipzig: Eckert & Pflug, 1921).

29. Bedřich Steiner, *První Brněnská* (Brno: Krajské nakladelství, 1958).

30. Anon., *Anderthalb Jahrhunderte Rudolf M. Rohrer 1786-1936* (Brno and Baden bei Vienna: Rudolf M. Rohrer, 1937).

31. Heinrich Benedikt, *Alexander von Schoeller 1805-1886* (Vienna: Spies, 1958).

32. Milan Myška, *Počátky vytváření dělnické třídy v železárnárnach na Ostravsku* (Ostrava: Krajské Nakladatelství, 1962); idem, *Založení a počátky vítkovickych železáren* (Ostrava: Krajské Nakladatelství, 1960); idem, "Das Unternehmertum im Eisenhüttenwesen in den böhmischen Ländern während der industriellen Revolution," *Zeitschrift für Unternehmensgeschichte* 28 (1983), 98-119.

33. Herbert Matis, "Die Grafen von Fries," *Tradition* 5 (1967): 484-96; August Graf von Fries, *Die Grafen von Fries* (Dresden-Neustadt: C. Heinrich, 1903).

34. Jindřich Chylík, "První obchodní bank u nas," *Časopis Matice Moravské* 69 (1950): 261-82; see also, Freudenberger, *Industrialization*, 55ff.

35. Herman Freudenberger, "The Schwarzenberg Bank: A Forgotten Contributor to Austrian Economic Development, 1788-1830," *Austrian History Yearbook* 27 (1996): 41-64; Fritz Rager, *Die Wiener Commerzial-, Leih- und Wechselbank (1787-1830)* (Vienna: A. Hölder, 1918).

36. Eduard März, *Österreichische Industrie-und Bankpolitik in der Zeit Franz Josephs I* (Munich: Oldenburg, 1968).

37. Max Grunwald, *Samuel Oppenheimer und sein Kreis* (Vienna and Leipzig: Wilhelm Braumüller, 1913).

38. H.J. Bidermann, "Die Wiener Stadtbank," *Archiv für österreichische Geschichte* 20 (1859): 343-445.

39. Hanns Leo Mikoletzky, "Schweizer Händler und Bankiers in Österreich (vom 17. bis zur Mitte des 19. Jahrhunderts), in *Österreich und Europa. Festgabe für Hugo Hantsch* (Graz-Vienna-Cologne: Styria, 1965), 149-81.

40. D. Joachim Cron, *Lobrede der Arbeitsamkeit und ihrer Beförderer, als in Oberleutensdorf das hundertjährige Jubelfest der, durch Waldsteinische Weisheit errichteten Tuchfabrike gefeiert wurde, am 25ten September 1815* (n.p., no publisher, n.d.)

41. Herman Freudenberger, *The Waldstein Woolen Mill: Noble Entrepreneur-ship in Eighteenth Century Bohemia* (Boston: Harvard Graduate School of Business Adminstration, 1963),

42. Anton Ernstberger, *Wallenstein als Volkswirt im Herzogtum Friedland* (Liberec: Sudetendeutscher Verlag Franz Kraus, 1929).

43. Fritz Redlich, *The German Military Enterpriser and his Work Force*, 2 vols. (Wiesbaden: Franz Steiner, 1964), I, 160.

44. Ernstberger, *Wallenstein*, 17.

45. Jindřich Šebánek, "Textilní podniky moravskych Kouniců," *Časopis Matice Moravské* 55 (1931), 95-168, 418-68; 56 (1932), 101-80.

46. Georg Grüll, "Die Strumpfabrik Poneggen 1763-1818," *Mitteilungen des Oberösterreichischen Landesarchivs* 6 (1959): 5-135. For a translation see, idem, "The Poneggen Hosiery Enterprise, 1730-1818, ed. and translated N.B. and Eva Harte, *Textile History* 5 (1974): 38-79.

47. Erwein H. Eltz and Arno Strohmeyer, eds., *Die Fürstenberger: 800 Jahre Herrschaft und Kultur in Mitteleuropa* (Korneuburg Ueberreuter: 1994), 329-64. (I wish to thank Lothar Höbelt for making this information available to me).

48. Miloš Kreps, *Dějiny blanenskych žezláren* (Brno: Blok Nakladelství, 1978); Josef Pilnáček, *250 let blanenskych železáren 1698-1948* (Blansko: Českomoravská-Kolben-Daněk, 1948).

49. Herman Freudenberger, "Records of the Bohemian Iron Industry, 1694-1875: The Basis for a Study of Modern Factories," *Business History Review* 43 (1969): 381-4.

50. Hanns Leo Mikoletzky, "Holics und Sassin, die beiden Mustergüter des Kaisers Franz I. Stephan," *Mitteilungen des österreichischen Staatsarchivs* 14 (1961): 190-212; idem, "Franz Stephan von Lothringen als Wirtschafts-politiker," *Mitteilungen des österreichischen Staatsarchivs* 13 (1960): 231-57.

51. Harald Hitz and Hugo Huber, *Geschichte der österreichischen Tabakregie 1784-1835* (Vienna: Ôsterreichische Akademie der Wissenschaften, 1975).

52. Franz Baltzarek, *Die Geschichte der Wiener Börse* (Vienna: Österreichische Akademie der Wissenschaften, 1973).

Ernst Hanisch, *Der lange Schatten des Staates.*
Österreichische Gesellschaftsgeschichte im 20.
Jahrhundert, ed. Herwig Wolfram, vol. 9 of
Österreichische Geschichte
(Wien: Ueberreuter, 1994)

Roman Sandgruber, *Ökonomie und Politik.*
Österreichische Wirtschaftsgeschichte vom
Mittelalter bis zur Gegenwart,
ed. Herwig Wolfram, vol. 10 of
Österreichische Geschichte
(Wien: Ueberreuter, 1995)

Peter Berger[*]

It does not happen often that books written by historians provoke a heated debate in Austria. The two volumes of the ten volume history of Austria edited by Herwig Wolfram are an exception to this.[1] The attention they attracted after their publication is understandable. Due to scarce research funds and the limitations of the domestic book market, the project of a comprehensive "national history" will not be repeated so soon. Hanisch's and Sandgruber's books will be considered standard works for some time to come. Both studies represent a kind of synoptic history-writing which is very controversial amongst historians, some of whom think it is condemned to become extinct. This is one more

* I should like to thank Liselotte Pope-Hofmann and Giles Pope for the translation of this review essay.

reason for the curious reader to have a close look at such "dinosaurs." Both Ernst Hanisch, Professor of Modern Austrian History at the University of Salzburg, and Roman Sandgruber, holder of the chair of Economic History at the University of Linz, have set their sights very high. Hanisch, in his introduction, formulates the guidelines of a modern social history as it is to be presented in *Der lange Schatten des Staates* in an extremely self-confident way. So it is only logical to judge the book by the criteria which the author has himself established. In the expectation of precisely this, the author has dedicated the book with a lofty gesture to "all his present and future critics."

A work like Hanisch's social history cannot stand without a methodological and theoretical framework, and is thus naturally indebted to other works. As far as methodology is concerned, the intellectual affinity with the studies of the Annales-School is obvious, the more so, as Hanisch explicitly cites Marc Bloch and Lucien Fèbvre several times. Like the two famous Frenchmen, he intends to create an organic fusion of structural and personal history. The long-term structures based on statistical data or analytical approaches are supposed to be the skeleton of his work, while the testimonies of living people of all social strata form the flesh. The technique of systematic change of perspective between quantitative data and oral history, which Hanisch consciously uses as a stylistic device, gives his text a special flavor. In any case, his particular style prevents the book from being a rigorous work of scholarship. This must have been the intention of both publisher and author. Nevertheless, the fact that some tables (if only a few) are inadequately explained, is annoying. For example, it is nowhere explicitly stated, what we are to understand by upper classes, middle classes, and lower classes, which are supposed to make up the Austrian population (Table 11, p. 67). The method of calculating an "index of economic development" remains similarly unexplained (Table 33, p. 295).

Beside the *Annaliens*, Ralf Dahrendorf is treated as another prominent authority. It is from the latter that Hanisch derives the category of "life opportunities."[2] This offspring that modernization debate of the late 1970s arose as part of an attempt to take the wind out of the sails of those who criticized modernization theory as being vague. Of course Hanisch is also aware of the ambivalence regarding the concept of modernity that still persists today. He explicitly draws our attention to the fact that Austria not only witnessed a rising life expectancy and improving standards of education and material welfare for decades, but, in the same period of time, has also brought forth the concentration camp of Mauthausen, the "radical destruction of all life opportunities for thousands." Nevertheless, like Hans-Ulrich Wehler before him, he does not succeed in finding an alternative to a critical modernization theory. Even the "despoliation of nature" by the production and consumption patterns of the last decade is, for Hanisch—who does not shun the comparison between destruction of the environment and abortion—a factor which can only be analyzed through scientific rationalism. After such a profession of faith in scientific rationalism, one is disappointed to see the history of science treated so sparingly in his book. All the more so, as the Austria of the fin-de-siècle and the 1920s brought forth splendid examples of a superbly rational philosophy, natural science, jurisprudence, and economics.

Hanisch willingly acknowledges his debt to some thinkers, for example the economist Rudolf Hilferding (why he is presented as "the son of a Galician cashier" remains unclear), the political scientists Stein Rokkan and Arend Lijphart, and others. However, he is less inclined to acknowledge his debt to the Austrian historian Friedrich Heer, who died in 1984 and who is only mentioned three times in 500 pages. Like Hanisch, Heer was a Catholic who struggled with the authoritarian tendencies of the Church. It is not only the language of *Der lange Schatten des Staates* which is inspired by Heer. The idea that the Austrian identity goes back to the age of the Baroque, which according to Hanisch is one of the two formative phases of the Austrian national character, certainly comes from Heer.[3] The second formative phase is Josephinism. Hanisch discerns the dichotomy of the Counter-Reformation Baroque and enlightened Josephinism in Austrian society, down to the present day. Even today Austrians cultivate their titles, their love of formal ceremony and the theater, a deliberately florid way of speaking, political opportunism and the sentimentality of the *"Heurigen"*—so much for the baroque element. The Josephinist tradition has, according to Hanisch, survived in the tendency to initiate reforms from above, in the welfare state, which is decreed by the authorities, but also in latent civil disobedience and attempts to establish a living democracy. The practical value of such theses probably consists in opening up the possibility of interpreting Austrian social history as an alternating pattern of authoritarian and democratic phases. Hanisch does not pursue this idea, and contents himself with the assertion that the Austrian in the twentieth century has essentially remained a good underling. According to surveys conducted in 1990, which Hanisch cites, the political absenteeism of the population is a fact: about 70 percent would not take part in a demonstration, and more than 50 percent would not participate in a citizens' initiative (p. 24).

After all, the structure and style of narration of *Der lange Schatten des Staates* are more conventional than the introduction would have one think. After about 200 pages dedicated to sketching major trends of demographic and economic development, social stratification, the formation of political camps and national identity, not to forget the transformation from an elitist to a mass culture, Hanisch falls into the well-worn groove of political chronology. His next four main chapters are called Monarchy, First Republic, National Socialist Regime, and Second Republic. Each of these sections contains statements about the business cycle and economic policy, about those who rule and the legitimacy of their power, about social conformism and resistance on the part of the ruled, and about contemporaneous art which, according to Hanisch, provides a kind of key to understanding the mental state of society in its different stages. Conspicuously, the only period where art does not receive any special attention is the era of the *Ostmark*. While Hanisch concedes that National Socialism at least produced a political culture, Austria's writers, painters, sculptors, and musicians in the Nazi period are simply nonexistent. That may be well-intentioned, but, bearing in mind what Hanisch said about the power of art to explain reality, it is a missed opportunity for his critical method.

Hanisch makes up for the loss by writing all the more extensively about the Austrian *fin-de-siècle* culture and its echoes in the interwar period. His theoretical framework consists of juxtaposing an "aesthetic culture of the emotions" and a "rational culture of words." In literature, where he feels most at home, Hanisch puts Hofmannsthal, Werfel, and Doderer in the aesthetic category and Karl Kraus in the rational one, without bothering to go into Kraus' work in detail. (All he does is take over the clear "diagram of creative interaction in Vienna around 1910" contained in Timms' portrait of the "apocalyptical satirist".[4]) By contrast, he does explore the works of Gustav Mahler, Sigmund Freud,

Robert Musil, and Adolph Loos in a style he calls exemplary analysis, which is clearly inspired by Carl E. Schorske, William M. Johnston, and Allan Janik and Stephen Toulmin.[5] However, so little space is devoted to the enterprise, that it can hardly do justice to its subjects. Mahler's Third Symphony gets no more than thirty-six lines, Freud's *The Interpretation of Dreams* all of two pages, and Musil's *Young Torless* about as much. Loos' unadorned building on Vienna's Michaelerplatz, which was a massive piece of provocation for his contemporaries, is granted just twenty-five lines. It is thus representative of what Hanisch has to say about modern Austrian architecture in general, that is to say, hardly anything. Only Hans Hollein is mentioned, who "triumphantly" placed a "temple of consumerism" (Hanisch means the *Haas-Haus* shopping center) opposite Saint Stephen's Cathedral in Vienna, thus "destroying the sacred aura of the square." Another brief remark in connection with Hanisch's discussion of Gustav Mahler would be in place here. The same historian, who once quoted Marc Bloch's dictum that a bad historian can be recognized by a moralizing tone, refers to the composer's spouse, Alma Mahler-Werfel, as a "loquacious wife." That is far below the level at which Elias Canetti, for example, expressed his contempt for "Alma"—and Canetti had a good reason for feeling like that. He admired Anna Mahler, her daughter, who was not taken seriously by the mother.

This leads us to a point which various critics of Ernst Hanisch's social history have stressed emphatically: the author's supposed lack of sensibility, or perhaps even lack of understanding, with regard to women. Some passages in connection with the history of the Jews in Austria were also received badly. The criticism is probably at its most serious when it is said that Hanisch has composed a manifesto of the village against the town, rural culture against the culture of workers and grande bourgeoisie, of provincialism brimming with resentment against urban cosmopolitanism.[6] Such attacks are made easier by Hanisch's frank admission, given in his introduction, that he has an emotional attachment to his rural and Catholic background. This is unmistakably present in his language, too, when he describes Bruno Kreisky's press conferences, held after the Tuesday cabinet meetings, as a "high mass for the media," or when he describes Austrian youths' reaction to Beatles' songs as "levitation." Apart from that, there are, admittedly, worse gaffes, which one notes with astonishment. When the industrialist Karl Wittgenstein and the Austro-Marxist Otto Bauer, with one voice, attack the backwardness of alpine farming as well as the servility of the peasants, then for Hanisch this is "urban, liberal and social democratic arrogance." Bertha von Suttner, the winner of the Nobel Peace Prize, is not only "liberal, anti-clerical and a friend of Jews," she only receives her high award with the help of "intrigues and sulks." When Sudeten-German refugees from Czechoslovakia travel through Austria, they are "staggering in their misery," while Jewish displaced persons want to emigrate "covertly" via Austria to Palestine, and, while in transit, occasionally break the laws of their host country. The list of such *faux pas* is even longer, and it is difficult to say whether one should be grateful to the lectors for leaving them in or whether a few touch-ups by the author would be desirable for the next edition of *Der lange Schatten des Staates*. Probably the latter. For, on the whole, Hanisch is a scholar who aims at balance and objectivity, and it is not only his chapter on Austria in the Nazi period which attests to this. He has taken on a difficult task and produced respectable results. It would be a pity to let a valuable contribution to Austrian social history remain tarnished with occasional poor judgment. The more so, as this would be in contradiction with the author's belief, stated explicitly in his introduction, in the enlightening effects of scholarship.

In some respects, the task which Roman Sandgruber set himself was even more difficult than that of his Salzburg colleague. Sandgruber is the only one amongst the contributors to the ten volume history of Austria who had to cover a period reaching from the Middle Ages to the present day. This is a consequence of the prominent position allotted to economic history by the editor of the series. The attempt to grasp a whole millennium of a country's economic development at one go is easier to succeed in if there are clear theoretical and method-ological criteria to guide the work of the author. In the nearly twenty-five years which have passed since the publication of the last overview of Austrian economic history by Anton Tautscher,[7] a great deal has changed in this field. Various theories have arisen beside the old descriptive approaches of regional economic history and the history of economic thought, beside the growth-oriented paradigms of the 1960s and the various theories of developmental stages from Maurice Dobb to Walt W. Rostow and Alexander Gerschenkron. One only has to think of Immanuel Wallerstein's model of central and peripheral development or the ideas of neoliberal authors like Eric Jones and Rondo Cameron, who are convinced opponents of any type of stage theory.[8] A wealth of new insights and methodological approaches has to be incorporated into the economic historian's work: women's history, "history from below," environmental history, oral history, anthropometrics, and econometrics. This *embarras de richesse* teaches the scholar to be modest, as Sandgruber notes in his introduction, and certainly justifies viewing his attempts to achieve a synthesis with respect, despite criticism of individual points.

Sandgruber's theoretical starting point was the logistical growth curve, a concept which has already been presented by Rondo Cameron in his *Concise Economic History of the World.* Globally speaking, Cameron thought he discerned four major growth phases: the first from 900 to the crisis of Feudalism around 1350, the second between 1450 and the middle of the "short" seventeenth century, the third from 1750 to the outbreak of the First World War, and the last in the era of the economic miracle after 1945. Sandgruber more or less takes over this periodization, but applies a more finely differentiated grid to the way he structures his work. He dedicates a complete chapter to the Baroque age, in other words the epoch from 1600 to 1750, in which the Habsburg princes from Ferdinand II to Karl VI laid and/or secured the foundations of the Austrian central state. Cameron's long period of growth from 1750 to 1914 is divided by Sandgruber into two parts, with the 1848 revolution as a watershed. The era between the two World Wars is upgraded to a period in its own right. The same is true for the "seven long years" of the German occupation of Austria, which are treated separately in their own section of *Ökonomie und Politik.* It is worth mentioning that the title of the book is programmatic. It indicates that events in the political sphere, such as the institutional reforms of Maria Theresa and Joseph II, the Napoleonic Wars, the collapse of the Habsburg Monarchy, and the rule of National Socialism can influence the economic development of a country or region just as much as climatic, demographic or technological factors. Sandgruber of course writes about the latter, sometimes in considerable detail. Nevertheless his book is an account of human living, laboring, investing, and consuming under the influence of political power.

In contrast to Hanisch, who explicitly aims at breaking "historicising journalism's" interpretation monopoly of the most recent history of Austria (a dig at the extremely successful series of books about the First and Second Republics by the television and newspaper commentator Hugo Portisch), Sandgruber has in this respect no missionary appeal. An occasional columnist in the *feuilleton* part of the newspaper *Die Presse*, Sandgruber knows how to combine scholarly standards with a pleasing style of writing for readers who are educated but are not trained as historians. *Ökonomie und Politik*, by and large very well written, only makes one concession to the practices of modern journalese (in a negative sense): its racy chapter titles. They give few hints about what can be expected in the following pages, and sometimes they are downright platitudinous ("Money is the World," "The Strength of Sport"). Apart from this point, Sandgruber tells his story well, a story which stands up to comparison with Fernand Braudel's great Social History of the fifteenth to eighteenth centuries.[9] Unfortunately, he fails to do two things which would have increased the value of the work.

First, he fails to include researchers' discourses upon which *Ökonomie und Politik* is built, as a parallel to the historical narrative. To keep up the comparison with Braudel, the latter's recipe for success consists in his deliberate strategy of letting the reader look inside the workshops of the historians' guild, to lay bare the theoretical controversies which make history as a scholarly discipline—above and beyond merely supplying factual information—so delightful. Sandgruber either wholly omits such excursions into the theoretical dimension, or undertakes them in a highly abbreviated form. Only occasionally do we get a glimpse of the fundamental issues of researchers, such as: "Alexander Gerschenkron attributed a leading role to the Central European crédit mobilier banks in founding new industries, where there was an intermediate degree of backwardness, where private initiative was inadequate and banks took the lead." (p. 296). Apart from the problems which the educated layman has in comprehending such cursory statements, there is not a word about the way in which Gerschenkron's theory[10] is embedded in contemporary debates, no word about its merits or weaknesses. In other instances Sandgruber is more reticent than is necessary. For example, he conceals from the reader the highly thought-provoking controversy between U.S. and Austrian scholars about the significance

to be attached to the process of industrialization in Austria, a controversy which involved such names as Nachum Gross, Richard Rudolph,
Eduard März, John Komlos, and David Good.[11]

The second regrettable omission in Sandgruber's book concerns
comparisons in the field of international economics, not counting a few
summary comments and a table in the last chapter. It is a well-known
fact that the economy of the territories which today make up the
Austrian Republic had to adapt to drastically changed conditions
several times. The industrialization of the western part of the Habsburg
Monarchy took place in an "autocentered way," to use a phrase taken
from recent research into modernization. What is meant here is a process which depended on resources existing inside the borders of a state
and which was geared to a large domestic market protected by tariff
barriers, making export drives superfluous. As far as the conditions for
economic growth are concerned, it is true to say that, until 1914,
Austria-Hungary played in the same league as France or the Germany
which was unified in 1871. Attempts to compare Austria-Hungary's
performance with such countries are worthwhile. After the caesura of
1918, the new Austria was suddenly a small open economy, depending
on access to foreign markets, raw materials, food, and investment. In
many respects it now had to act like other small European national
economies (Switzerland, Belgium, the Netherlands, the Scandinavian
states), which once again is an interesting and inviting field for
comparisons. One misses them in Sandgruber's book, although the
author justifiably remarks in his introduction that there exists "no
Austrian model of economic development."

The danger for the historian who fixates his gaze on one single
country is that the events and processes observed in it may appear
unique or more important than they actually are. This is what often
happens to Sandgruber when he discusses the period from 1945 to the
present. To take just one example, he discusses in considerable detail
the economic policy of the so-called "Raab-Kamitz course" in the
1950s, a kind of supply-side policy to stimulate growth with public investment as the Keynesian element, which bore similarities to the German social market economy. Sandgruber's book lacks any trace of parallels between Austria and other European countries. Instead, Chancellor Julius Raab, introduced as a brilliant autodidact in the field of
economics, is built up as the person mainly responsible for the Alpine

Republic's economic miracle, a great organizer without whom finance minister Reinhard Kamitz would not have been able to steer "his" course. Such a myopic perspective can lead to explaining the undeniable problems of the Austrian economy in the past two decades—Sandgruber is above all concerned about the national debt and the rising cost of servicing it—in terms of a decline in statecraft since Raab's time, and to seeing the situation divorced from its global framework. It seems that precisely this is the case when one reads that such high levels of debt as that in Austria in 1994 (65 percent of GNP) used to be brought down in the past by hyperinflation. From a global perspective, nothing seems less likely today than a return to inflationary policies.

The question of the political correctness of an economic history of Austria may not be so central as may be the case with works of social history. Nevertheless, a word is in order here. One might say that, concerning the gender aspect, *Ökonomie und Politik* falls well short of reasonable expectations of emancipated history-writing. It is not that women are dealt with in a derisive manner, but that the briefness of the references to women in the economy make this aspect of the book appear little less than an alibi. Not so with minorities. Sandgruber does not forget to point out that the forced confiscation of Jewish property after the Anschluß was not made good after 1945, even in the cases when it could have been. Neither does he shrink from giving a clear picture of the fate of National Socialism's victims. The balance of Nazi rule in Austria is drawn up in detail, including the murders in the concentration camps. It is most likely only a slip of the pen, when Sandgruber writes, "Of the Jews who were driven out of the country or fled in 1938, only 6 percent returned. Lingering anti-Semitism, acute supply problems and the unresolved question of compensation deterred most of them." In truth, many had been caught by Hitler's executioners in Czechoslovakia, Holland, and France. Otherwise, they might perhaps have ventured a return to their former homeland—which, in turn, might have been encouraged by a clear and friendly invitation from the politicians of the Second Republic. As is well known, this invitation to return was never given.

Any discussion of *Ökonomie und Politik* would be incomplete if it did not mention the approximately seventy-page list of sources, which follows the chronological structure of the book and sums up nearly everything of importance written by economic and social historians in Austria since the turn of the century. Sandgruber has built upon this foundation and has produced a genuinely pioneering work. It will hold its own, even when, as is to be hoped, future researchers take up the challenge of writing a great history of the Austrian economy.

NOTES

1. Hanisch's work received particular attention from the editors of the journal *Österreichische Zeitschrift für Geschichtswissenschaften* (ÖZG-Redaktion, "Der lange Schatten der Historiographie oder: Barocke Aufklärung": 58-118). An extensive discussion of Sandgruber's book has appeared in the same journal, 7/1996/4: 535-553.

2. Ralf Dahrendorf, *Lebenschancen: Anläufe zur sozialen und politischen Theorie* (Frankfurt/Main: Suhrkamp, 1979).

3. Friedrich Heer, *Der Kampf um die österreichische Identität* (Vienna: Böhlau, 1981).

4. Edward Timms, *Karl Kraus. Apocalyptic Satirist. Culture and Catastrophe in Habsburg Vienna* (New Haven: Yale University Press, 1986).

5. Carl E. Schorske, *Fin de Siècle Vienna, Politics and Culture* (New York: Knopf, 1980); William M. Johnston, *The Austrian Mind: An Intellectual and Social History, 1848-1938* (Berkeley: University of California Press, 1972); Allan Janik and Stephen Toulmin, *Wittgenstein's Vienna* (New York: Simon & Schuster, 1973).

6. This line of argument is adopted by Ruth Beckermann and Wolfgang Reiter in their review article: "Heimatfibel. Der Lange Schatten der Provinz, Österreichische Zeitschrift für Geschichtswissenschaften" 7 (1996): 135-143.

7. Anton Tautscher, *Wirtschaftsgeschichte Österreichs: auf der Grundlage abendländischer Kulturgeschichte* (Berlin: Duncker & Humblot, 1974).

8. Eric Jones, *The European Miracle: Environments, Economies and Geopolitics in the History of Europe and Asia* (Cambridge: Cambridge University Press, 1992); Rondo Cameron, *A Concise Economic History of the World from Paleolithic Times to the Present* (New York: Oxford University Press, 1989).

9. Fernand Braudel, *Civilization and Capitalism, Fifteenth-Eighteenth Century* (London: Collins, 1985).

10. Alexander Gerschenkron, *Economic Backwardness in Historical Perspective: A Book of Essays* (Cambridge: Belknap Press, 1962).

11. For a short résumé of this debate see the review article by David F. Good, "Issues in the Study of Habsburg Economic Development," reprinted in Herbert Matis, ed., *The Economic Development of Austria since 1870* (Cambridge: Elgar Press, 1994), 3-18.

New Literature on Women in Austria

Erika Thurner

Johanna Gehmacher, *Jugend ohne Zukunft: Hitler-Jugend und
Bund Deutscher Mädel in Österreich vor 1938*
(Vienna: Picus-Verlag, 1994)

Maria Mesner, *Frauensache? Zur Auseinandersetzung um den
Schwangerschaftsabbruch* in *Österreich Veröffentlichung
des Ludwig-Boltzmann-Institutes für Geschichte de
Gesellschaftswissenschaften*, vol. 23 (Vienna:
J&V, Edition Wien, 1994)

Charlotte Kohn-Ley and Ilse Korotin, eds., *Der
feministische Sündenfall? Antisemitische Vorurteile in
der Frauenbewegung* (Vienna: Picus-Verlag, 1994)

It has only been within the last decade that Women's Studies and
Gender Studies have gained significant ground in Austrian academia.
This shift has gradually begun to assume a tangible form with the
appearance of published works. Three recent publications, in which,
among other factors, gender is accorded decisive significance as a
highly complex category of scholarly investigation, redress key research deficiencies and/or offer a fresh look both into areas of study
which have been neglected as well as into the current state of research
and discussion in Austria.

To distill a common denominator applicable to all of these highly
varied works (monographs and essays), it can be stated that "being
favored by having been born a woman" is no favor at all. Although
membership in the other—the female—gender also brings with it
"positive forms of discrimination" whereby women, as a result of

exclusion and relegation to specific roles and spaces, have been barred from assuming leadership positions and thus spared the perpetration of wrongdoing such leadership may entail, membership in the "women's group" has nevertheless not prevented female involvement and complicity in such wrongdoing.

From this perceptual background, the authors address and analyze the fact that women took part in National Socialism; that being a woman has by no means hindered the formation of anti-Semitic prejudices and attitudes; and that whenever and wherever women have been subject to discrimination on account of their gender, when their autonomy has been denied, and when the will of others has been imposed upon them, a segment of the female population has been involved in safeguarding and sustaining the corresponding patriarchal structures and ideologies.

Whereas German scholars began turning their attention to the complex of topics related to Nazi youth organizations as early as the 1950s, this issue has long been neglected by historical research in Austria. It was dealt with in a cursory manner at best. The history of the organization's dual structure as politics by, as well as politics directed toward, young people was omitted from consideration. However, our German colleagues have also neglected gender as a category of investigation for much too long. From the perspective of "National Socialism as a masculine political project," the organizations for young men and boys were accorded the main focus of attention; the *Bund Deutscher Mädel* was treated as an "insignificant matter" of secondary importance, an incidental "appendage." The name *Hitler Jugend* (HJ) stood for the entire organization of youth groups separated according to gender, as well as for the component organization for male youths. This "classic" division undertaken by the National Socialists—into general (masculine) and special (feminine) categories—was long left intact by scholarly research.

With the publication of *Jugend ohne Aukunft*, the Viennese historian Johanna Gehmacher has redressed this, as well as other, deficiencies. She examines the male and female HJ organizations, including the way in which they functioned together, and sheds light upon the hierarchical gender relationships which constituted them and according to which they were structured. Even if (bourgeois) girls and young women were only tangentially and conditionally integrated into the HJ, a "bleak future" and generational conflicts nevertheless mobilized women and girls from all walks of life in support of the movement. Here, it was precisely the aggressive anti-Semitism developed in youth groups that played a decisive role for middle-class young people. Furthermore, Gehmacher depicts the *Ostmark* organizations (beginning in 1923) not just as extensions of German Nazi associations, rather she filters out their unique developments and peculiarities. A decisive change and thus an important break was brought about by the "illegal period" in Austria and the seizure of power by the National Socialists in Germany. Between 1933 and 1938, the centralization of the Austrian agenda was carried out in the German HJ.

This rich and impressive work by Johanna Gehmacher fills a significant gap in research and constitutes an additional building block in the body of scholarship dealing with the "Austrian Nazi movement." Nevertheless, certain questions posed by the author remain open, and certain expectations had to be diminished in the face of the "incomplete" source materials available. On the other hand, a gender-specific factor must be kept in mind, particularly for the illegal period, in that internal party literature, such as brochures and flyers, were primarily directed toward boys and rarely toward girls. Furthermore, illegal activities by women were held in much lower esteem by the bureaucratic machinery, so that these incidents were documented to a much lesser extent. Johanna Gehmacher's book has established an extremely solid foundation for potential follow-up studies featuring supplementary oral history interviews.

The controversy surrounding the legally established ban on abortion constitutes the focal point of Maria Mesner's *Frauensache*. According to the author's introduction, the object of investigation is the social realm of political policymaking, that is to say, the sphere in which "consistent and goal-oriented action, including every form of involvement with and every kind of influence exerted upon the formation and regulation of the polity" takes place, as well as the individuals, groups, and institutions whose activities make up the centerpiece of this sphere.

This confrontation with the Austrian State of the Second Republic, including the political policies and institutions which constitute the framework in which this body of criminal law was produced, means the confrontation with a "male state." Maria Mesner follows the findings and definitions of Eva Kreisky, whereby the state in its provenance is to be regarded purely "as sedimented male interests and male life experiences."

In Austria immediately following the end of the Third Reich—without any public discussion—the legal regulations governing the termination of pregnancy which had been on the books up to 1934 were again put in force. On one hand, legislators thereby aligned their action with the process of "denazification." On the other, a seamless linkage to the democratic First Republic was suggested, in that the even more severe anti-abortion measures implemented by the Austro-Fascists were not revived within the Austrian legal system. The judicial elite which carried out this legal revision was a homogeneous group of men.

The discourse surrounding female reproduction and its regulation—by politicians, physicians, jurists, and the clergy—was conducted, until late in the 1960s, almost exclusively by men. The legally recognized authority to decide questions of pregnancy and abortion—and thus, what is regarded from the perspective of everyday life as "the quintessential matter pertaining to women"—was denied those most immediately affected. The reform proposals introduced by the Social Democrats as early as the 1920s calling for the abolishment of the legal prohibition of abortion were simply passed over and ignored.

From the point of view of the controversy surrounding the termination of pregnancy and trimester regulations, the author recounts events during the decades following World War II, providing an enriching and highly comprehensive contribution to the historical scenario. It once again becomes clear that a scholarly analysis which acknowledges and takes into account gender as a structuring characteristic and as a category of investigation delineates historical breaks and watersheds far differently than studies which presume to be gender-neutral. Thus, the phase of stable democratic development which began to emerge in the 1950s proved to be very much resistant to a democracy of the genders. Viewed from this perspective, "laws left over from the days of the horse and buggy," such as Paragraph 144 in the Penal Code and the patriarchal marriage and family rights provisions, have delayed the dismantling of gender hierarchies.

Mesner amply documents the intense bitterness with which this "symbolic crusade" was conducted: pitting proponents of liberalization (Social Democratic and autonomous women's groups) against opponents of liberalization (the Catholic Church and its lay organizations) and continuing until the amendment of Paragraph 144. However, the hopes for wide-ranging emancipation which emerged thereafter as an upshot of the elimination of the "abortion issue as a symbol of repression" in 1975 have not been fulfilled. The work summarizes this with a sense of resignation: "As far as the political, economic and social asymmetries of gender relationships are concerned, there have been no qualitative changes since the removal of the ban on abortion." An additional, more positive outcome has been that, as a result of the struggle for and with the taking effect of the trimester regulations, abortion has at least partially been made into a "women's matter."

If this is to remain so, or to even further speed up the process of change, additional works like Maria Mesner's will be necessary. This is an important addition to the arsenal of argumentation against repression and countercurrents. A rollback in Austria is by no means out of the question. This threat constantly reappears when advocates of economic interests, accompanied by—and in the guise of—(ecclesiastical) ideological elements, would once again presume to take "women's matters" out of women's hands and thus deny them the right to a life of self-determination.

Kohn-Ley and Korotin's *Der feministische Sündenfall* is the first feminist book dealing with the anti-Judaism debate in Austria. An important new political and interpretational direction has thus been opened up, which is underscored by the interdisciplinary concept of the work. The nine articles making up this volume, written by female scholars specialized in closely related fields of theology, philosophy, sociology, and history, diverge sharply in their areas of concentration, as well as in the quality of their scholarship. The work as a whole suffers from the fact that the terms anti-Judaism and anti-Semitism are neither employed in a consistent manner, distinguished from one another, nor clearly defined.

The Protestant theologians Susanne Heine (Zurich) and Anita Natmeßnig (Vienna) take as their subject characteristics of feminist theology which are conducive to anti-Jewish attitudes, the former concentrating more strongly on mental structures and mutual traditions of thought; the latter focusing upon common mental and linguistic stereotypes. Whereas Heine goes into a detailed analysis of two lines of thinking with respect to "modern" concepts of femininity, Natmeßnig offers what is essentially a collage of quotations taken from works of Protestant theologians. We learn nothing of the reception accorded by the feminist scene in Austria to these texts which have appeared in Germany.

An article has also been contributed by Susannah Heschel (Cleveland, Ohio), the American-Jewish feminist who was one of the earliest and most vehement critics "of the long, unthinking anti-Jewish tradition." During her time spent in Germany, most recently as Martin Buber Guest Professor in Frankfurt am Main in 1992-93, she was "confronted by German feminist thinking which still largely precluded coming to terms with anti-Semitism." Heschel analyzes this as stemming from failed policies of denazification in Germany.

The deafening silence accorded to topics such as this in "German feminist thinking" is a matter which is also taken up by Johanna Gehmacher in her highly detailed overview of "Feminist Historical Research and the Question of Anti-Semitism on the Part of Women." In the new aspects she offers on the subject of gender-specificity in historiographic research into anti-Semitism, she limits her approach "to the geographical area in which the German language is spoken and to the time frame encompassing what can be referred to as modern anti-Semitism." In Gehmacher's estimation, a more intensive confrontation with "Women and Anti-Semitism" is most likely to occur in conjunction with the numerous research efforts dealing with women in the Nazi movement and in the National Socialist state. Perhaps this will even proceed in Austria or from Austrian scholars, who have contributed little to this field until now.

The philosopher Hannelore Schröder (Amsterdam) describes the highly emotionally-charged reception given to the work of Otto Weininger, both immediately following publication and once again during the last two decades. She works out a structural analogy between Weininger's anti-feminism and anti-Semitism. Schröder's summary and conclusions are highly problematic, ultimately pleading for a ban on Weininger's writings. In her overwrought critique of Weininger, her equating of Jews and women as well as anti-feminism and anti-Semitism, she overlooks one important aspect. The problematic issue of Jewish anti-Semitism and Jewish self-hate should not be omitted from consideration in the case of Weininger, who converted from Judaism.

The Viennese philosopher and sociologist Ilse Korotin provides an overview of matriarchy myths. She shows how ideas of Johann Jakob Bachofen, a forerunner of feminist criticism as well as feminist concepts of utopia, were dubiously interpreted by leading advocates of the "myth of the primal mother" such as Alfred Baeumler, Ludwig Klages, Ernst Bergmann, Sophie Rogge-Börner, and Mathilde von Ludendorf, and placed into the intellectual proximity of "fascist ideologies."

Charlotte Kohn-Ley, an architect and teacher in adult continuing education programs in Vienna, focuses upon anti-Zionist political involvement within the feminist movement after 1968. According to Kohn-Ley, women who believed that a leftist political orientation was the way to escape from the (Nazi) traditions of their mothers and grandmothers have become entangled in old and new forms of anti-Semitism, with which they make it impossible for Jewish feminists "to join feminist groups in Germany and Austria without disavowing their very identities." From this perspective, Charlotte Kohn-Ley takes up the conflict which broke out within the "German left" surrounding the Gulf War, whereby her attention is centered upon the women's movement—a significant undertaking, since a frank discussion of this kind has been lacking in Austria until now. However, many of Kohn-Ley's assessments and theses are unsupported by references to source materials as well as being modeled on stereotypes. For example, she discovers "a close relationship of many feminists to the Church" and describes "anti-Zionism as a factor essential to the identity of the women's movement." In many instances, circumstances prevailing in Germany, as well as the analysis of them, are applied indiscriminately to Austria, such as the failure to differentiate between the Nazi victim and perpetrator positions of the two states, or the corresponding definitions and subsequent ramifications.

Maria Wölflingseder (Salzburg) gives an account of the depoliticized approaches of the "new age" movement and attempts to demonstrate "biological deterministic and racist tendencies" on the part of spiritual eco-feminism. Her critique, though, deals almost exclusively with biological determinism and conceptions of a feminine, naturally superior mode of thought which have been developed from it. Racism is given scant attention and is by no means treated in a manner related specifically to women.

In spite of the points of criticism raised above, the significance and strengths of this book deserve special emphasis. They lie in the breaking of taboos, in the initiation and furtherance of the scholarly discourse, and in the stimulus provided for further research. Here, the impetus has come—as in so many other cases—from Germany. The heated discussions which have been carried on there since the end of the 1980s, on issues such as involvement by women in National Socialism and anti-Semitism, acted as a catalyst in 1993 for a corresponding lecture series at the Jewish Institute for Adult Education in Vienna. This collection of essays is the result. The confrontation by scholars with this issue, one which—above all in Austria—had previously been completely absent or only of limited extent, has demanded truly groundbreaking work from the speakers and authors involved.

BOOK REVIEWS

Michael Gehler and Hubert Sickinger, eds.,
Politische Affären und Skandale in Österreich.
Von Mayerling bis Waldheim
(Thaur: Kulturverlag, 1995)

Andrei S. Markovits

It is always a thankless job to review anthologies. With very few exceptions, the whole is invariably less than the sum of its parts, the quality of the contributions uneven to say the least, and the overall theme never compellingly developed. In short, edited volumes more often than not convey the characteristics of telephone books: they are useful documents, to be sure, they contain fascinating information if one knows how and where to look for it, but one most certainly would not want to rely on them for a systematic exposé and insightful analysis of a problem. These ills are most definitely compounded by any anthology's sheer length and weight which, in the case of the present volume's 776 pages and miscellany of topics, is beyond excessive.

The phone book quality of edited volumes hails most often from the laxness, maybe even negligence, of the respective anthology's editors who typically "underedit" the collection by offering insufficient guidelines to the contributors and by including contributions in the volume whose relation to the overall theme is tangential at best. Curiously, the exact opposite is the main shortfall of the anthology under review. Michael Gehler and Hubert Sickinger impose a framework on their contributors which is in and of itself commendable. However, by doing so in an overambitious context which includes far too many cases to be of even minimal analytic use, the editors' imposition of this framework appears like a Procrustean bed in which the contributors are compelled to fit their cases conceptually even if they simply do not by dint of their empirical reality. This then leads to contortions and distortions of the otherwise commendable task at hand which need not have been the case had the editors been less ambitious yet more disciplined in their endeavor. For few books that I have recently read would the old adage of less being more apply with greater validity than the volume under review.

Michael Gehler and Hubert Sickinger pursue two valuable theoretical propositions. First, they offer to test the apparently widely-held perception that Austria, especially in the course of the last two decades of its existence, had developed into a *Skandalrepublik*. In order to ascertain this proposition, the editors resort to an historical approach which looks at scandals in Austria roughly throughout the past century. By invoking history, the editors presume themselves able to conclude that the current accumulation of scandals seems to have had its parallels in earlier epochs of Austrian politics, thus falsifying the commonly held view that present-day Austria is more scandal prone than its various predecessors. Second, the editors propose to test certain key conceptual writings on political scandals by applying them to the empirical case of Austria.[1] Both of these endeavors represent scholarship at its best. But in their attempt to be historically and empirically all-inclusive, as well as conceptually innovative, the editors render the book into a potpourri of interesting—even major—events in Austrian politics, many of which, however, should never have been classified as scandals because they were—in most cases—of much greater social and political significance than scandals could ever be. In the editors' legitimate, indeed useful, attempt to amend the major tenets of the leading theoretical frameworks in the study of scandals, most of which err on the side of constriction and stringency *precisely* to differentiate scandals from much more weighty political conflicts such as class and ethnic tensions, problems in governance and governability, deficits of regime legitimation and elite rule, shortcomings in managerial performance and management style, and ugly manifestations of hatred and prejudice to name but a few, Gehler and Sickinger arrive at an all-encompassing—*thus meaningless*—conceptualization of political scandal. They basically see scandals as any event that certain people perceive as "scandalous," that represents a salacious story, or—analytically much more troublesome—that embodies some kind of *conflict*, usually of the spectacular sort. Add to this the completely uncritical assemblage of such diverse regimes as the Dual Monarchy (in peace and during the exacting years of the Great War), the First Republic, the Austrofascist years of the *Vaterländische Front*, and the Second Republic, and one arrives at a conceptually jumbled book whose redeeming feature lies solely in the excellence of some of its individual contributions. Given the editors' penchant for inclusiveness, it is puzzling why they suddenly resort to the stringency of the conventional scandal literature in excluding from consideration in their volume "cultural" scandals such as the ones surrounding Arthur Schnitzler's play *Der Reigen*, or various recent dramaturgical controversies with major political overtones in the world of Austrian theater, or scandals during the Nazi period. At 776 pages, it obviously could not have been the editors' concern regarding the book's excessive length or verbiage.

The volume is divided into two segments. The first features an introductory chapter authored by Michael Gehler, followed by eleven scandals of the final years of the Monarchy and the First Republic; the second comprises sixteen scandals of the Second Republic bracketed by two interpretive chapters written by Hubert Sickinger. In the former segment, Angelika Mayr offers a fine account of the Mayerling affair which—congruent with the prurient attraction which all scandals evoke in us—fits the bill perfectly: a clear challenge to existing morality by surreptitious events that remained partly hidden at the time, and remain so today. The next three chapters are all fine accounts of events that might have appeared "scandalous" to many participants at the time, and may in fact appear so to us, but they represent political conflicts that reach far beyond scandals and are thus erroneously placed. Hannelore Burger and Helmut Wohnout present an excellent account of the language clashes which beset the monarchy in the late 1890s, leading to the Badeni government's ill-fated language decree of 1897. The whole event, and the ensuing disturbances in parliament and society, were manifestations of a deep linguistic and social conflict that represented irreconcilable cleavages rather than a scandal. The same pertains to the so-called Wahrmund affair in which, as nicely recounted by Hermann J.W. Kuprian, we encounter, in the battle surrounding the University of Innsbruck theologian Ludwig Wahrmund, major clashes among the three political *Lager* of the late Monarchy over the issue of curricular content at universities, public discourse in politics, and the contestation of power in state and society. No scandal this, but a grave political conflict. Nor is the next chapter on the assassination of Count Stürgkh at the hands of Friedrich Adler a scandal. As brilliantly presented by Wolfgang Maderthaner, this was an act of personal defiance in the context of a deep political conflict which had come to characterize the final years of the Empire. The clash between radical elements of social democracy and authoritarian tendencies of a fading aristocratic regime exhibits elements more akin to revolution than scandal.

Only the so-called "Sixtus" affair, also known as the "Czernin-Clemenceau" affair of 1917/18 qualifies as a *bona fide* scandal among the remaining chapters in this segment of the book. This scandal concerns a letter in French which Emperor Karl allegedly wrote (but most certainly signed) and sent to his relative Prince Sixtus of Bourbon-Parma offering the French government terms under which Austria and the Entente powers might come to some agreements that could have potentially ended hostilities between these warring states. Written behind the backs of the Germans and in clear violation of Austria's pact with Imperial Germany, as well described by Manfried Rauchensteiner, the letter caused immense controversy and fury all over Europe once the French published it. Karl's vehement denials were never accepted by the Germans who used this letter to strengthen their already substantial control over a weakening Austria. Thus ended any hopes of an Austrian exit from the Dual Alliance and with it any possibilities, however remote in 1917, of saving the Habsburg Monarchy. Here we have all the ingredients of a scandal and *not* of a social or political conflict: the entire event was circumscribed and limited, there was a clear clash between public and private, existing mores were violated, conventional process was circumvented, power was abused.

None of these pertain to the terrible Halsmann affair of 1928 - 1930, for example, in which the young Latvian student Philipp Halsmann stood accused of patricide following his father's death in a hiking accident in the Tyrolian Alps. To be sure, the horrible expressions of xenophobia and anti-Semitism were nothing short of scandalous as well described by Niko Hofinger, as was the clear miscarriage of justice and the constant abuse which Halsmann—and vicariously Austria's Jewish community—had to endure throughout the two trials. But the acerbity of prejudice and the manifestation of anti-Semitism were part of Austria's political landscape at the time; they were the norm of political discourse and were thus part of public reality in the political cleavage structure of the First Austrian Republic. Anti-

Semitism in Austria was (and is) a societal problem which many perceive as scandalous; as such, it was something far too constant, far too serious to be classified as a scandal.

Most telling of the editors' conceptual problems is the explicit "revolt" on the part of Jürgen Nautz who all but refuses to call his contribution on the *Creditanstalt's* crisis of 1931 a "political scandal." When one reads Nautz's fine empirical study, it is obvious that his "revolt" against the editors is justified because, though problematic and full of conflict and trouble, the story simply fails to reveal a scandal. We encounter lots of incompetence, management errors, faulty decisions, structural difficulties, economic problems, all of which lead to a major crisis in one of Austria's (and Central Europe's) most influential banks that in turn was to have devastating consequences for the economic stability of the region. But mismanagement and economic crises, though scandalous to those most seriously afflicted by their ills, are not scandals.

Turning to the Second Republic, the cases remain as inconsistent and problematic as those presented for the First. Just as in the first segment of the book, here, too, one encounters fascinating stories and fine presentations of events that have been crucial in the history of the Second Republic but which I most certainly would not see as scandals. I will mention a few of the contributions which fall into this category.

Most prominent among them is Michael Gehler's excellent discussion of the Waldheim affair. In his nuanced account it becomes amply evident that the Waldheim event represented one of the most essential turning points in the political development of the Second Republic. Waldheim's victory, his term as president, his ostracism by the international community, his burdened past, his symbolism for many Austrians on both sides of the divide, in short the whole event galvanized Austrian politics to a degree that rendered the matter a watershed in the country's recent past. While passions ran high and many Austrians found any number of developments in the course of the event "scandalous," there were simply no procedural or contextual dimensions to the affair which would justify calling it a "scandal." Conflict, yes; altercation, yes; crisis, yes; scandal, no!

The same pertains to the ugly "Bruno Kreisky-Friedrich Peter-Simon Wiesenthal" affair ably presented by Ingrid Böhler. Appropriately entitled with that most tasteless and blatantly anti-Semitic of

Kreisky quotes *"Wenn die Juden ein Volk sind, so ist es ein mieses Volk"* (if the Jews are a people, then they are a wretched people), which the chapter's author as well as this reviewer find "scandalous," the essay makes clear that the affair as such reflected various tensions in Austrian politics, mirrored Kreisky's political genius in using the Austrian people's anti-Semitism for his strategic purposes, highlighted even Kreisky's undeniably eminent tendencies of being a self-hating Jew, and assumed a number of other factors prevalent in the politics of Austria at the time, but it did not embody a political scandal.

To be sure, this segment of the book offers a number of studies that depict events that *do* qualify as scandals even according to my much more stringent delineations of this political animal than those offered by Gehler and Sickinger. Among them are Anton Pelinka's fine presentation of the AKH affair (centering on kickbacks, bribes and other "irregularities" in the process of constructing Central Europe's largest hospital in Vienna); Gerald Freihofer's detailed account of the "Lucona" affair, a classic scandal involving money (an insurance fraud), murder (the drowned crew of a sunken freighter), and the cabals of political leaders (high-level social democrats who met regularly above one of Austria's most venerable institutions, the pastry shop "Demel" in the center of Vienna); and Doris Schmidauer's description of the Noricum scandal involving the illegal and clandestine sale of weapons by one of Austria's leading state-owned companies—and thus by proxy parts of the Austrian political class—to countries such as Chile, Iran, Iraq and Lybia among others, in direct violation of Austria's neutrality and other tenets of law.

So no reader of this review needs to worry that Austria is such an "island of the blessed" that it has not produced juicy scandals. Far from it. While the sobriquet *Skandalrepublik* may not be fully deserved, there have been plenty of scandals in the Second Republic to enliven its quotidian political life, and they are well represented in this volume. While I believe that this book's analytic framework adds little to a better understanding of political scandals as ubiquitous phenomena in modern societies, I am convinced that its case studies offer a fine mirror of Austrian conflicts, crises, and altercations over more than one hundred years. Unwittingly, the book thus provides a useful overview of Austrian political history which, though not its primary intention, is no mean feat.

NOTE

1. The editors rely almost exclusively on the German-language literature on scandals. The sole English-language publication that receives ample consideration is Andrei S. Markovits and Mark Silverstein, eds., *The Politics of Scandal: Power and Process in Liberal Democracies* (New York: Holmes and Meier, 1988). As will be clear in my review, Markovits and Silverstein have a much more confined interpretation of political scandal than do Gehler and Sickinger.

Daniel Jonah Goldhagen. *Hitler's Willing Executioners: Ordinary Germans and the Holocaust.* (New York: A. Knopf, 1996)

Christopher R. Jackson

Goldhagen's Willing Executioners

It is quite rare for academic books to receive much attention in the United States. Most university teachers publish with university presses, which run off only about two thousand copies. They rarely sell out, almost never make the author any money, and only occasionally attract the attention of colleagues. The public generally ignores them, even if they attract respect and praise from within the academic community.

Only occasionally will an academic write something that makes a splash. If the author is lucky, that book will be reviewed widely (hopefully in a positive manner, and hopefully in a popular venue as well as in academic journals), and if the author is *very* lucky, that book will be placed on the book-of-the-month club regular selection list, in which case he or she can begin to start talking with colleagues about investment funds, instead of lamenting their library fines.

One such fortunate academic is Daniel Goldhagen, a thirty-eight-year-old Harvard political scientist whose book, *Hitler's Willing Executioners: Ordinary Germans and the Holocaust* was recently published by a commercial press, Alfred A. Knopf. His book has been a best-seller, with more than 130,000 hard-cover copies sold in the United States thus far. Sales of the German translation have been even more brisk, a paperback edition has recently been published, and plans are underway to have it translated into almost a dozen different languages. Professor Goldhagen has traveled extensively in Germany and Britain on promotional tours, with Holland, France, and Italy coming up. He has made many appearances on television, radio, and an entire symposium, held at the United States Holocaust Memorial Museum, was dedicated to the book. Recently, an unrelated exhibition in Munich of photographic evidence of the *Wehrmacht's* contribution to the slaughter of civilians on the eastern front has given birth to the theory that the German nation is itself the victim of a genocidal campaign—with Daniel Goldhagen's name and book never far from this allegation sponsored by the Bavarian Christian Social Union Party.[1] The Internet has been buzzing for months.

What is curious, is the contrast between the reaction of the general public and the reaction of the experts in the field to his book. Based upon the sales of his book and newspaper coverage, the public, both in the United States and Germany, seems to have embraced his book wholeheartedly; based on the reviews by academics, it has been largely dismissed as misconceived, unhistorical, and arrogant. Why would there be such a bifurcation of the reaction to this book?

The simple answer is its thesis. Goldhagen claims to have found *the* answer to the monumental question "how": How was it possible for a modern state to carry out the systematic murder of a whole people for no reason other than that they were Jews? Having examined the myriad explanations for the Holocaust, a Harvard assistant professor in his mid-thirties has pronounced them all wrong. Goldhagen's answer is that the "how" can be answered quite simply: they were all *Germans*. Their culture was imbued with anti-Semitism. But not just ordinary, run-of-the-mill anti-Semitism, but virulent, racist, eliminationist anti-Semitism—the sort of anti-Semitism that would want to be rid of Jews by any means possible. Indeed, to Goldhagen's mind, it was not at all surprising that the Holocaust occurred: "When the Nazis...assume[d] power, they found themselves the masters of a society already imbued with notions about Jews that were ready to be mobilized for the most extreme form of 'elimination' imaginable."

Goldhagen's focus is on the Germans, and the focus is not incorrect. After all, it was from the government of Germany that the policies of anti-Semitism were produced, and it was Germans who were in charge of carrying out these policies—from confiscating pets to confiscating property, and finally to confiscating lives. Goldhagen shifts the focus onto the perpetrators of the Holocaust, and he does not conceal his fury at those people who did such a thing: "Death is a master from Germany."

The sharp difference between the public reaction to Goldhagen's book and the scholarly reaction was most dramatically highlighted at a public symposium held in April 1996 at the United States Holocaust Memorial Museum in Washington D.C. An overflow capacity crowd of more than 600 jammed into an auditorium, while late-comers watched outside the hall on television monitors. After a brief introduction, Goldhagen explained the book and how it has changed our understanding of the Holocaust. The public's applause was warm and loud.

The panel of experts, including such prominent scholars as Yehuda Bauer, Konrad Kwiet, and Christopher R. Browning, was not quite as warm. Kwiet attacked the publisher's promotional claims that the book would forever change Holocaust studies, noting that neither the material nor the thesis were new—the book sounds like it was written in 1944, albeit with some early 1980s anthropological windowdressing. Bauer plainly implied that Goldhagen's Harvard advisors had committed an error in even awarding him a doctorate, and concluded (to the stunned silence of the audience) that "you shouldn't have written this book." Browning, whose book *Ordinary Men* is the explicit target of Goldhagen's polemical footnotes, accused him of writing "keyhole history," looking only at evidence that supported his preformulated thesis, and ignoring all other evidence that would give a more nuanced version of the behavior of the executioners.[2] When he noted that Goldhagen's thesis is by no means new, the audience audibly groaned its disapproval. This scene was repeated many times in Germany during his promotional tour.

There are a number of reasons for the hostile academic reaction to *Hitler's Willing Executioners*, and a number of reasons for its public success. Goldhagen's tone of self-confident certainty—every assertion is "self-evident," "incontrovertible," and "undeniable"—constitutes "dazzling arrogance," according to Fritz Stern of Columbia University.[3] Henry Friedlander of the City University of New York has noted that Goldhagen has a marked tendency to substitute argument for evidence.[4] His claim to have forced a complete revision of Holocaust studies and to have found *the* reason for one of the most momentous (and most studied) crimes in history likewise can be seen as more than somewhat presumptuous. Other authors have dealt with anti-Semitism, the killing squads, and the death marches, making Goldhagen's claim to originality suspect (he does not even acknowledge some of these authors).[5] The enormous attention and lavish publicity campaign probably also evoke a certain amount of resentment among professional historians in the United States where their status and income are not particularly noteworthy.

Hitler's Willing Executioners does indeed have a number of problems. Goldhagen's portrayal of anti-Semitism in nineteenth century Germany is superficial at best, and, lacking as it does a thorough account of anti-Semitism in other European countries, it is logically impossible to define *German* anti-Semitism as unique. (Even Goldhagen's Harvard advisor, Stanley Hoffmann, noted the lack of a comparative approach in what was otherwise a predictably favorable review in the prestigious journal *Foreign Affairs*.)[6] As Günter Bischof of the University of New Orleans has correctly noted, the "German" perpetrators seemed disproportionately Austrian.[7] Likewise, the Ukrainians, Lithuanians, Estonians, and various other national groups directly involved in the killing do not seem to be an issue for Goldhagen, since they were often merely pulling the triggers (sometimes to the relief of the Germans who were ordered to shoot, as Browning has noted).[8]

Nor does Goldhagen sufficiently address the murder of other groups of people by the Nazi regime. Millions of Russians, Poles, Gypsies, mentally ill, and various other unlucky groups were murdered by the Nazi death machine (whether by bullets or Zyklon-B), but historians have normally distinguished these slaughters from the Holocaust based on the intentions of the Nazi leadership, that is, to wipe out all Jews, but merely enslave and oppress Slavs. Goldhagen, the political scientist, goes the historians one better and inserts the intentions of the top Nazis into the minds of the men actually shooting, and claims that this is proof of the entire culture's attitude toward Jews; indeed, one of the central flaws of the book is to shift the perspective of late twentieth century historians into the minds of the killers, and thereby gain access to the *meaning* of the Holocaust *for the killers*, and deduce that it not only was a *unique* hatred that led the killers to enjoy their killing, but also that the object of their hatred *could only be Jews*. (All this is based, of course, on anthropological "thick description" of events that occurred before Goldhagen was born, and derived from records of trials that he did not attend.) That many—probably most— Germans disliked Jews (often intensely) is not news. But the same could be said of other European cultures. Proof that German anti-Semitism was *uniquely* virulent is the fact that the Holocaust occurred. Thus as Robert Gellately[9] and others have noted, Goldhagen's argument is ultimately tautological: a culture of eliminationist anti-Semitism caused the Holocaust to occur. How do we know that particular culture was uniquely anti-Semitic? Because the Holocaust occurred.

Given all these seeming flaws, why then has the public embraced the book so warmly? Why has it sold so well, and made him such a star (if only in the public's eye, not the academy's)? That is indeed the interesting question, and to answer it one must turn to the different audiences he is addressing. In the case of the Germans, the response might be labeled as truly remarkable. The book was quickly and prominently reviewed in the German press even before the translation was published, and the reaction was quite harsh. The book was initially attacked as a "collective guilt thesis;" prominent German historians such as Volker Ulrich[10] and Eberhard Jäckel[11] ripped into it in much the same way U.S. and Israeli historians did when it first appeared in the United States, and even Rudolf Augstein managed to find time to write a critical review in *Der Spiegel*.[12] When Goldhagen traveled to Germany on his first publicity tour, he must have wondered only half-jokingly how expensive bullet-proof vests run these days.

A funny thing happened on the way to Goldhagen's German execution, however. He quite simply charmed the pants off the Germans.[13] Crowds in Germany were large and enthusiastic, media coverage was extensive, and his friendly photogenic nature was played up. He deftly parried the charge of a "collective guilt thesis" by arguing that he thinks that the Germans are now "just like us," and that guilt only applies to someone who actually committed a crime—he had merely portrayed pre-1945 German *culture* as so anti-Semitic that it led to the Holocaust. His rejoinders to questions regarding the role of the state in the process of destruction put more emphasis on the nature of a totalitarian dictatorship than his book did (though it must be said that most authors would probably relish such a privilege of retrospectively sharpening their arguments). Instead of headhunters, Goldhagen stood before an audience of veritable groupies.

Goldhagen's German audience is an interesting phenomenon: given the initial labeling of the book as purporting a "collective guilt," one would have thought that Germans would have reacted with hostility, rejecting the book and its thesis. Surprisingly, the opposite is true: the audiences at his German tours, often of the generation of 1968 and sometimes even younger, seem determined to prove just how guilty their parents' and grandparents' generation truly was. In doing so, they seem to experience a form of absolution, as if, by taking sides with Goldhagen, they wash themselves of the stain of guilt that seems to adhere to being German. Not long ago, the *Journal for German and International Politics* awarded Goldhagen the "Democracy Prize," an act that Jürgen Habermas, Germany's most prominent living philosopher, has hailed in *Die Zeit* as furthering the democratic development of Germany's new "Berlin Republic," because the book demonstrates that a nation that was once evil can change fundamentally (a point actually emphasized by Goldhagen more in interviews than in the book).[14] Goldhagen has emerged as a sort of loyalty-test of political correctness in Germany: in praising the book, the German liberal public performs an act of expiation not dissimilar from the repeated telephone calls made to the Israeli embassy in Bonn during the Gulf War offering to adopt any children orphaned by Scud missile attacks.[15] The Nazi past will not fade away in Germany—it is too important to the Germans.

The reason for the book's popularity in the United States, on the other hand, is rather simple: the book is simple. Goldhagen's book merely tells its U.S. audience what it already believes. Many Americans still believe quite firmly that the Germans are an inherently twisted nation—warlike and hateful—and Goldhagen just as firmly confirms to them that they were. (Indeed, Omer Bartov of Rutgers University has asked whether Goldhagen has created a bizarre inversion of the Nazi view of the Jews as an inherently evil nation.)[16] In any case, it is the simplicity of the argument that makes the book easy to understand—one does not have to plow through complex chronologies, deal with confusing happenstance, or wade through cautious qualifications. An entire nation was filled with a blood lust for the Jews, and happily murdered as many as they could as cruelly as they could. The simplicity of the formula—"no Germans, no Holocaust"—seems to have a powerful appeal. It also makes for good "sound bites."

An enormous crime must bespeak an enormous hatred, and Goldhagen, in insisting on speaking the unspeakable cruelty of mass murder, relies on our sense of proportion to prove his thesis. No one could be so bestial, so sadistic, without containing in their heart some enormous hatred. Ordinary Germans must have hated the Jews to have acted in such a monstrous manner. This sense of proportionality has similarly driven any number of biographers to try to find the origins of Adolf Hitler's hatred of Jews—was he secretly afraid that he was part Jewish? Was he infected with syphilis by a Jewish prostitute? These and other theories abound, but no one has found any clear evidence for an *event* that caused Hitler to hate the Jews. But what if no such event occurred?

What might be even more frightening than the existence of a "societal cognitive model" (read "hatred") calling for the elimination of Jews, is the possibility that no such degree of hatred was in fact required to murder the Jews. Goldhagen's insistence on the uniqueness of the murder of the Jews (in contrast to the millions of other non-Jewish victims) demands a *specific* murderous mentality, and that mentality is easy to understand—hatred makes for murder. But one could ask Goldhagen, and his superintentionalist colleagues in political science, what if hatred is not a necessary element of murder and cruelty? Cruelty and murder were displayed toward other victims of the Nazi death machine; were the Germans also filled with an "elimina-tionist anti-Gypsy-ism"? Goldhagen does not appreciate how easily people can be turned into monsters, and that their victims might not even be the object of a unique culture of hate. Tamerlane's fourteenth century hordes built mountains of skulls from peoples they did not even know existed before they murdered them. Murder does not require hatred, and cruelty can be thoughtlessly easy.

Yet Goldhagen's book continues to sell, and he continues to defend his thesis at conferences and in the media (or more exactly, he con-tinues to reassert it, since its circular nature admits no further proof). In person, he is quite charming and modest about his book; in print, he is obstreperous and certain. The contrast has been noticed by many reviewers, as if there were two Goldhagens. In any case, reviews are now beginning to pour in from academic journals, most of which now proclaim that the book is simply bad. Is this a case of spite, envy, or normal academic discourse?

It should be noted from the outset that anti-Semitism does not play a role in the condemnation of his book, as Goldhagen's harshest critics are often Jewish scholars themselves. Nor does it seem likely that envy plays a large role in the attacks on his book: other bad books on impor-tant subjects have been roundly criticized before, even if they did not make their authors a lot of money. The claims made in the lavish publicity campaign, on the other hand, might be the source of the academy's animosity to the book: time after time Goldhagen has gone on television and radio to attack the "historical theory" that the perpetrators of the Holocaust were forced to do what they did; no reputable historian of the Holocaust argues that they were, and thus his claim to ground-breaking originality ("The Holocaust finally explained!" is the breathless headline on the dustjacket of the German edition) is rather hollow. Perhaps where Goldhagen has erred, is in dressing up a cliché about an entire nation in academic garb, demanding special attention be paid to it as "new," and expecting the academy to salute him for it.

What exactly is the contribution of *Hitler's Willing Executioners* to Holocaust scholarship? The book has forced a re-examination of the relative importance of anti-Semitism in explaining the Holocaust, though that subject has hardly been ignored by past scholarship. People have been forced to discuss the Holocaust and its causes anew, though the subject had not been neglected by historians. Perhaps the greatest impact of the book on the academy has been to divert attention from other, more important books on the Nazi past and the origins of the Holocaust—Henry Friedlander's book on euthanasia immediately comes to mind.[17] The hype surrounding Goldhagen's book has certainly kept academics busy, but unfortunately they have spent their time with a poor book.

The impact of *Hitler's Willing Executioners* might say more about the U.S. publishing market than the Holocaust. Expensive hardcover non-fiction books will not sell unless they contain something *sensational*—even if the experts say it is illogical, repetitive, and jejune. Simple generalities about entire nations are simple to understand (even if they substitute the word "culture" for "people"), and make the public feel smart by confirming what they already believe. They are especially welcome if they are hyped in the popular press as "ground-breaking" (and even more so when they carry the Harvard imprimatur). Perhaps Professor Goldhagen's experience is one of the finest example of the transposition of the old Hollywood adage into academia: "There is no such thing as bad publicity."

Ironically, however, the unintended effect of Goldhagen's book is to seal off the Holocaust's dark warnings and lessons from us. A unique German culture produced the Holocaust; that culture is now gone forever. Parallels to other instances of genocide and lessons for the human condition as a whole are thus curiously defeated by Goldhagen's logic. We need not fear becoming something akin to Nazi murderers, and we need not ask ourselves what we would have done. Goldhagen has comfortingly constructed a German "Other" whose opacity does not threaten to reflect our own image. And that is ultimately why the book is both so popular, and so reviled.

NOTES

1. Alan Cowell, "In Munich, Past Erupts as War-Guilt is Put on Display," *New York Times*, 3 March, 1997.

2. Christopher R. Browning, *Ordinary Men: Reserve Police Battalion 101 and the Final Solution* (New York: Harper Collins, 1982); for an account of the Washington D.C. symposium see Adam Shatz, "Browning's Version," *Lingua Franca*, February 1997, 48-57.

3. Fritz Stern, "The Goldhagen Controversy," *Foreign Affairs* (November/December 1996): 128-137.

4. Henry Friedlander, "Hitler's Willing Executioners," *German Studies Review* 19 (1996): 578-580.

5. Martin Gilbert's *The Holocaust: A History of the Jews of Europe during the Second World War* (New York: Holt, Rinehart & Winston, 1986) covered the death marches extensively, and the role of anti-Semitism in German society and its connection with the Holocaust was emphasized by Lucy Dawidowicz's *The War Against the Jews, 1939-1945* (New York: Holt, Rinehart & Winston, 1975).

6. Stanley Hoffmann, "Hitler's Willing Executioners," *Foreign Affairs* (May/June 1996): 144-5.

7. Günter Bischof, "Die normalen Deutschen als Täter," *Die Furche*, 2 May 1996.

8. See Browning, *Ordinary Men*, 85.

9. Robert Gellately, "Hitler's Willing Executioners," *Journal of Modern History*, 69 (1997): 187-191.

10. Volker Ulrich, "Die Deutschen—Hitlers willige Mordgesellen," *Die Zeit*, 12 April 1996.

11. Eberhard Jäckel, "Einfach ein schlechtes Buch," *Die Zeit*, 17 May 1996.

12. Rudolf Augstein, "Der Soziolog als Scharfrichter," *Der Spiegel*, 15 April 1996.

13. Josef Joffe, "Goldhagen in Germany," *New York Review of Books*, 28 November 1996, 18-21.

14. Jürgen Habermas, "Warum ein "Demokratiepreis" für Daniel J. Goldhagen? Eine Laudatio," *Die Zeit*, 13 March 1997.

15. See Ian Buruma, *The Wages of Guilt: Memories of War in Germany and Japan* (Harmondsworth: Penguin, 1994).

16. Omer Bartov, "Hitler's Willing Executioners," *New Republic*, 29 April 1996.

17. Henry Friedlander, *The Origins of Nazi Genocide: From Euthanasia to the Final Solution* (Chapel Hill: University of North Carolina Press, 1995).

Hermann Hagspiel, *Die Ostmark: Österreich im Großdeutschen Reich 1938 bis 1945* (Vienna: Braumüller, 1995)

Evan Burr Bukey

This book is the best comprehensive history of Nazi Austria to appear since Radomir Luza's pioneering *Austro-German Relations in the Anschluß Era*. Based on a mastery of the sources, it both synthesizes the secondary literature—including important local studies—and provides telling new documentation from repositories in Vienna, Klagenfurt, Graz, and Innsbruck. Aside from a gratuitous swipe at Gerhard Botz for "monopolizing" the study of Austrian Nazism, Hagspiel's account is exceptionally fair, straightforward, and non-ideological. It is also clear and to the point, providing both a chronological account of the period 1938-1945 and an analysis of important structures and institutions. The approach occasionally borders on the encyclopedic, but the prose is sufficiently vigorous to propel the reader forward.

As both a professional diplomat and a trained historian, Hagspiel seeks to explain the experience of Nazi rule in Austria from the viewpoint of an outsider. This is both a welcome and commendable procedure, but the author falls short of the mark in a number of ways.

First, he completely overlooks the contributions of Anglo-American scholars whose studies offer the sort of "outsider's" perspective he seeks to emulate. While such a comment may appear self-serving here, even Austrian historians may be baffled by the omission of critical works by Robert Keyserlingk, Fred Parkinson, and Gordon Horwitz.[1] Second, Hagspiel pays no attention to the pathbreaking research of Marlis Steinert and Ian Kershaw on the German scene, studies absolutely essential to any understanding of the *Ostmark* as an integral part of Hitler's Reich.[2] Third, the author tends to make extrapolations about wartime conditions that are sometimes unsubstantiated, fuzzy, or wrong. Finally, the author addresses a purely Austrian audience, making only a half-hearted attempt to explain his country's past within the larger context of the Second World War or European history. While there is nothing inherently wrong with this approach, it does narrow the book's appeal, rendering it unduly solipsistic.

Nevertheless, Hagspiel succeeds brilliantly in tackling a sensitive subject with admirable detachment and objectivity—a rare achievement in an age of ideological advocacy and political correctness. He devotes the first third of his study to a neo-Rankean survey of events; in it he analyzes the Anschluß and April plebiscite, the consolidation of Nazi rule under Hitler's palladin Josef Bürckel, and various Austrian reactions to critical issues such as the German revival of the economy, the persecution of the Jews, and the Second World War.

In contrast to other historians, Hagspiel spends little time examining the Anschluß movement or castigating the Christian Corporative regime for its many failures. Given Hitler's aggressive aims, Hagspiel sees German annexation as virtually inevitable. But he also condemns Chancellor Kurt Schuschnigg for diplomatic ineptitude, conjecturing that greater patience might have kept the Führer at bay until a favorable change occurred in the international climate. While the author concedes the futility of counterfactual speculation, he exploits the opportunity to make two important points:

1. The Social Democrats, far from strengthening Austrian independence, unwittingly undermined it by demanding concessions as the price for their support of Schuschnigg's proposed plebiscite.

2. Those individuals who gave the most serious thought to resisting a German invasion were primarily reactionaries—the dyed-in-the-wool supporters of the Dollfuss-Schuschnigg regime.

In discussing the Anschluß the author adds little new to the traditional story. He assigns primary blame to the Germans, but makes no excuses for the enthusiastic reception of most Austrians, taking pains in fact to stress both the spontaneity and authenticity of their approval. His treatment of the April plebiscite is another matter. Here he harshly condemns Theodor Cardinal Innitzer as the "driving force" behind the Catholic hierarchy's declaration of support for the regime;

Nazi pressure, he demonstrates, exerted only minimal influence on the primate's deliberations and behavior. As for Karl Renner's endorsement, the author is slightly more forgiving but only to a marginal degree.

What Hagspiel writes about Bürckel's consolidation of Nazi control in annexed Austria—the *Ostmark*—is exceptionally illuminating. He portrays the Reich Commissioner as an astute politician, a man much more attuned to Austrian Nazi demands than the figure depicted in earlier accounts. Since none of Hitler's homeland retainers possessed power sufficient to challenge Bürckel, they sought to strengthen their own position by ingratiating themselves with him, a ploy that proved successful, but one that also enhanced the Reich Commissioner's personal power and provoked widespread resentment. Well aware of the contradictions confronting him, Bürckel nonetheless demonstrated great skill in liquidating Austria as an entity and devolving power to the provinces. He also played a key role in reviving the economy, in winning working-class support, and even in outlining the sort of cultural policies that brought his successor, Baldur von Schirch, some success in mollifying the feelings of the self-pitying Viennese Nazis. What both men failed to achieve was the oxymoronic conflation of Viennese culture and Prusso-German values demanded by Hitler.

In surveying Austria's role in World War II, Hagspiel offers little new or original. It is hardly a secret, for example, that most Austrians showed little enthusiasm for the conflict, that the country remained immune to Allied bombing until late 1943, and that both industrialization and economic modernization continued right up the collapse of Hitler's Reich. On the other hand, it is startling to read that the Moscow Declaration of 1943 constituted a *firm* Allied commitment to restore Austrian independence. As Robert Keyserlingk has demonstrated in innumerable publications, the document "represented only a propaganda ploy designed to speed the end of Nazi Germany," nothing more.[3] There are also several errors about the war itself: the Germans did not rely on the Schlieffen plan to conquer France in 1940, the outcome of the war was by no means certain in 1943, and the Russians never possessed the unlimited supplies of manpower imagined by their foes.[4]

Once he returns to purely Austrian affairs, Hagspiel regains his touch, writing with clarity, precision, and acuity. He is particularly astute in his analysis of the Austrian National Socialist Party (NSDAP), pointing out that while few party officials rose to paramount positions in Berlin, they did call the shots in the Ostmark. They also wielded a kind of veto power over bureaucratic and judicial agencies and kept the population under cooperative surveillance. For those Nazis with greater aspirations, of course, the real path to power lay in the SS and the killing fields of Eastern Europe. This is not to say that opportunities declined at home; indeed, economic growth accelerated in both the industrial and service sectors. That the top managerial positions tended to be dominated by Reich Germans appears to have provoked little discontent, primarily because so many Austrians profited from the experience.

Given the anti-Prussian resentment that eventually did develop in the *Ostmark*, the author seeks to explore the attitudes of a wide spectrum of social groups, among them civil servants, industrialists, tradesmen, professional people, artists, writers, musicians, the clergy, blue-collar workers, and peasants. The account is inevitably repetitious, but it leaves little doubt that most Austrians were deeply infected by Nazi values, arguably more so than their German cousins. The pages detailing the strong grassroots support for the regime's persecution of minorities, especially the Jews and Gypsies, are especially chilling.[5] Exactly why so many Austrians subsequently became disenchanted with the Anschluß thus remains a bit of a mystery. Hagspiel suggests a number of reasons, but the most compelling one seems to combine cultural arrogance with a desperate desire to escape the consequences of Hitler's war.

In examining the record of those few individuals who actively opposed Nazism, the author provides a masterful survey of existing knowledge. He emphasizes that no other aspect of the Anschluß period has been so exhaustively studied or yielded such meager results. The much vaunted Austrian Resistance he dismisses as a "marginal phe-nomenon," important primarily to postwar politicians of the Second Republic. Without denigrating the heroism of those 100,000 men and women who actually risked their lives against the regime—primarily Monarchists or Communists—he stresses that their activities never represented a threat to the Anschluß system. With regard to the so-called church struggle, he castigates the Roman Catholic hierarchy for a pathetic record of collaboration. At the same time, he pays tribute to the "reckless courage" of Communist fighters and to innumerable parish priests who denounced Hitlerism from the pulpit or "immunized" remote communities from the Nazi virus.

The final pages of this study combine a thoughtful commentary on Hitler's legacy in Austria with useful suggestions at squaring confusing historical memories with a painful past. One particularly useful insight is to remind readers that Nazi rule varied sharply from province to province; in Tyrol it led to a bitter *Kulturkampf*, in Upper Austria to breathtaking industrialization, in Vienna to political degradation, in Styria and Carinthia to partisan warfare. That this comparative perspective does not extend to other regions of Greater Germany or Nazi-occupied Europe (for example, Vichy France) leaves a stimulating conclusion a bit wanting. For all that, the overall effort constitutes a superb introduction to the *Ostmark* and will surely stand as one of a half-dozen authoritative works on the subject for decades to come.

NOTES

1. Robert H. Keyserlingk, *Austria in World War II: An Anglo-American Dilemma* (Kingston, Ont.: McGill-Queens University Press, 1988); Fred Parkinson, ed., *Conquering the Past: Austrian Nazism Yesterday and Today* (Detroit: Wayne State University Press, 1989); Gordon Horwitz, *In the Shadow of Death: Living Outside the Gates of Mauthausen* (New York: Free Press, 1990). Also neglected are important essays by Robert Knight, John Bernbaum, Harry Ritter, Maurice Williams, and Günter Bischof, most of which have appeared in the *Times Literary Supplement*, the *Austrian History Yearbook, Central European History*, and *Zeitgeschichte*.

2. Marlis Steinert, *Hitlers Krieg und die Deutschen: Stimmung und Haltung der deutschen Bevölkerung im Zweiten Weltkrieg* (Düsseldorf: Econ Verlag. 1970); Ian Kershaw, *Der Hitler-Mythos: Volksmeinung und Propaganda im Dritten Reich* (Düsseldorf: Deutsche Verlags-Anstalt, 1980); idem, *Popular Opinion and Political Dissent in the Third Reich: Bavaria 1933-1945* (Oxford: Claredon Press, 1983).

3. Keyserlingk, *Austria in World War II*, 144. On the postwar instru-mentalization of the Moscow Declaration see Günter Bischof, "Die Instrumentalisierung der Moskauer Erklärung nach dem 2. Weltkrieg," *Zeitgeschichte* 20 (November/December 1993): 345-66.

4. Gerhard Weinberg, *A World at Arms: A Global History of World War II* (Cambridge: Cambridge University Press, 1994); Richard Overy, *Why the Aliies Won* (New York: W.W. Norton, 1995); David M. Glantz and Jonathan House, *When Titans Clashed: How the Red Army Stopped Hitler* (Lawrence, Kan.: University Press of Kansas, 1995).

5. At the same time, the account suffers from the omission of Horwitz, *In the Shadow of Death*, the most detailed and terrifying study of the Holocaust in Austria.

Neal H. Petersen, ed., *From Hitler's Doorstep: The Wartime Intelligence Reports of Allen Dulles 1942-1945* (University Park, PA: Penn State University Press, 1995)

Gerald Schwab, *OSS Agents in Hitler's Heartland: Destination Innsbruck* (Westport, CT: Praeger, 1996)

Siegfried Beer

The last ten to fifteen years have seen a veritable blossoming of historical scholarship in the field of intelligence, espionage, and sabotage, especially in the English speaking world. This phenomenon has even been called an intelligence revolution.[1] While it is commonly known that quadripartitely divided post-war Austria and particularly the city of Vienna, itself divided into sectoral parts, had served as one of the spy centers of the early Cold War, very little scientific research has hitherto been applied to describe and analyze the conditions and mechanisms under which these activities took place or the consequences thereof for Austria and the larger intelligence confrontation of the Cold War.[2]

Understandably, most of the archivally-based research has been concentrated on the international crisis period of the Second World War, particularly on the period between Pearl Harbor and VJ-Day in August 1945.

Both volumes under review deal with U.S. intelligence directed at the center of Europe by men and women working for the first U.S. central intelligence agency which was created by President Roosevelt in July of 1941 under the name of Coordinator of Information (COI).

It was continued from June 1942 to September 1945 under the designation of Office of Strategic Services (OSS), both headed by a Republican lawyer-politician and World War I hero by the name of William J. Donovan. COI had to be started from scratch, but the trauma of Pearl Harbor accelerated both the growth and scope of this largely civilian intelligence organization which by 1942/43 had become active on most continents.

Neal Petersen's documentary volume covers the wartime reporting from just one major OSS observation post, Allen W. Dulles' station in Bern, Switzerland, at which the future and first civilian Central Intelligence Agency (CIA) director had arrived in November of 1942 to remain until the European war was won. Dulles, by training and experience, was well equipped to handle sensitive tasks; he had been diplomatically stationed in Bern and Vienna during World War I and had been actively involved in intelligence work both at the Paris Peace Conference and occasionally also during the interwar years when he had returned to the private practice of law.

Switzerland and Bern proved to be an ideal spot to report on Axis military matters and to develop contacts to resistance groups in France, Italy, and Germany, which, of course, became the natural focal point of most of the reporting and penetrating efforts.[3] OSS Bern also managed to develop contacts to representatives of Balkan countries, Hungary, and Austria, through emigrants and exiles as well as through occasional business travelers.

The outline of Dulles' role and accomplishments, notably his work with the German resistance (represented mainly by *Abwehr* men Bernd Gisevius and Eduard Waetjen), his contacts to the German Foreign Office (mainly Fritz Kolbe, whom Petersen characterizes as "among the most important agents-in-place of the war") and his efforts to negotiate the surrender of German forces in Italy (Operation "Sunrise") have been known for some time.[4] What has not been known, except by OSS research specialists, was the sheer volume of what Dulles was able to report to Washington practically on a daily basis.

Petersen, a retired State Department historian who is now with the CIA history office, has selected 708 dispatches and reports which show the variety of the information gathered through nets of informers mainly from France, Italy, and Germany. The editor provides a succinct introduction and several appendices of highly useful references to understand these texts: a list of persons residing in and visiting Switzerland, many of them informants for OSS, and a list of code and cover names as well as of code number identifications and a general index of names, locations and topics. Practically every document receives commentary and further elucidation through endnotes fraught with references to other available sources or secondary literature.

In our context, the question arises as to what extent the editor has included intelligence on Austrian matters. Here the reviewer can be precise: of 708 documents altogether, merely thirty-eight deal with Austria. This translates to approximately 5 percent of the material included. This figure roughly coincides with the quantitative coverage of Austria in the context of the entire OSS activities as reflected in its archives, a body of nearly 12,000 boxes of documents containing nearly 10 million pages. This reinforces the realization that Austria figured as a side show (as remembered by veterans in diaries, memoirs, and oral history interviews) both during the war and even during the occupation period.

It may also be interesting to note which Austrian topics are included: there are only two reports dating from the year 1943, the earliest dealing with defense construction and one inevitable reference to the Moscow Declaration of 1 November 1943. We can find fourteen documents of the year 1944 dealing with subjects like Austrian sources (e.g. Anton Linder, Josef Joham, Franz-Josef Messner) and active contacts (especially "K-28," that is, Fritz Molden, and agent "Hofer," that is, Ernst Lemberger) on conditions and activities within Austria, on several Austrian resistance groups, and on the so-called Alpine Redoubt.

Twenty-one documents cover Austrian topics from January to May 1945, among them questions of the Redoubt, but mainly of the K-28 chain in Austria (POEN and O5) and of the approaches of a group of Austrians within the German intelligence apparatus (for example, Ernst Kaltenbrunner, Wilhelm Höttl, Edmund von Glaise-Horstenau, and others) in the spring of 1945, which Dulles acknowledged without much response. The last two documents deal with the almost enthusiastic reaction of the Austrians in Switzerland towards the Provisional Renner Government which the Soviets installed at the end of April 1945. Dulles' main Austrian adviser and informer from 1942 through to 1945 was Dr. Kurt Grimm, an émigré Viennese lawyer and banking expert. There were other important Austrian contacts to Otto of Habsburg, Robert Blum-Jungk, Hans Weigel, Hans Thalberg, Prinz Alois von Auersperg, Ludwig Klein and Johannes Schwarzenberg.

Petersen's documentary treatment of the intelligence efforts of OSS Switzerland, run almost single-handedly by Allen Dulles, constitutes a milestone in the quest of intelligence historians to provide information and insight into the world of allied espionage during a bitter struggle against fascist regimes. This unfortunately very pricy ($ 85.00) edition of reports and messages between Bern and Washington as well as other centers of American intelligence activities is not without its drawbacks and mistakes. It all but ignored the operational side of the efforts originating from Bern or otherwise involving OSS Switzerland. Also, upon closer inspection one detects a number of small mistakes and misconceptions, for example concerning Austrian resistance and exile politics. A few examples will have to suffice. It was the émigré social democrat Ludwig (not Hans) Klein who provided OSS with information on Austrian labor matters (p. 545); it was Josef Joham (not Johan) who may well have been the important Austrian contact K-6 (p. 548); it was Ernst (not Robert) Fischer who spent the war in Moscow (p. 633 and 642) and the writer Hans (not Karl) Weigel who acted as informant 835 (p. 218 and 549). Unfortunately, Petersen fails to identify one of the most important Austrian resistance personalities liaisoned with OSS and code-named "Hofer." It was not Dr. Josef Hofer, "a resistance figure in Upper Austria," (p. 633) or a Robert Lambert (p. 642) but Dr. Ernst Lemberger, code-named Jean Lambert, who served as Fritz Molden's most important Austrian partner in western intelligence circles. Nevertheless, these mistakes are only small blemishes on an otherwise painstaking editorial effort.

Gerald Schwab, a German emigrant who served in the U.S. Army in Italy during the war, then with a military intelligence unit, and finally in the diplomatic service in post-war Austria, has concentrated his book mainly on one of the more successful OSS missions into Austria undertaken during the last weeks of the war. GREENUP was one of close to fifty planned secret operations behind enemy lines in Austria which the OSS undertook mostly by parachuting from southern Italy (Bari/Caserta), central Italy (Siena), England (mainly via Dijon), and overland through partisan Yugoslavia. About thirty of these penetration missions were actually undertaken, most of them during the last three months of the war in Europe. Of the seventy-six OSS agents thus infiltrated into Austrian "enemy territory," about a third were so-called deserter volunteers (DVs), that is, Austrian patriots volunteering their services to the allied cause. GREENUP, which parachuted into the mountainous regions of Tyrol on 25 February 1945, consisted of two naturalized U.S. citizens and one Austrian deserter volunteer and has probably become the best- researched of all Austrian OSS missions.[5] It also turned out to be the most successful of all operations in Austria, and its three agents, who are all still alive today, have been asked to tell their tales again and again.[6]

The author has looked at all the available records in the National Archives and has even added most of the cable communication between the GREENUP group and its controlling station in Bari from 13 March to 1 May 1945. GREENUP managed to establish friendly contacts in several villages outside of Innsbruck and, through these, gained intelligence on the rail traffic across the Brenner Pass and on last-ditch defense preparations in the Redoubt. It was also able to connect to indigenous resistance groups working for a smooth transition of power from the Nazis to democratic forces. When one of the U.S. agents was caught, mistreated, and brought in front of Gauleiter Hofer, the immanent arrival of U.S. forces persuaded the latter to use the OSS lieutenant to meet officers of the 103rd Division and assure them that Innsbruck was an open city.

A useful epilogue providing the *dramatis personae* as well as a traditional index provide easy access to the particulars of this spectacular intelligence operation in western Austria. As with Petersen's edition of documents, this book suffers somewhat from negligence of available secondary literature in German, though there are fewer mistakes due also to the much narrower focus of its topic.

Both these books represent major contributions to the understanding of allied intelligence efforts in World War II and deserve a wide and general audience. They attest to the fact that U.S. central intelligence had already come of age and maturity in the last year of the war.

NOTES

1. Walter T. Hitchcock, ed., *The Intelligence Revolution. A Historical Perspective* (Washington, D.C.: U.S. Air Force Academy, 1988).

2. For a recent attempt at dealing with espionage in Austria, see Siegfried Beer, "Von Alfred Redl zum 'Dritten Mann'. Österreich und ÖsterreicherInnen im internationalen Geheimdienstgeschehen 1918-1947," *Geschichte und Gegenwart* 16 (1997): 3-25.

3. See Jürgen Heideking and Christof Mauch, eds., *American Intelligence and the German Resistance to Hitler: A Documentary History* (Boulder, CO: Westview Press, 1996).

4. These are most recently Peter Grose, *Gentleman Spy: The Life of Allen Dulles* (Boston: Houghton Mifflin, 1994).

5. See Joseph E. Persico, *Piercing the Reich: The Penetration of Nazi Germany by American Secret Agents During World War II* (New York: Ballantine, 1979).

6. E.g. in *Das Fenster* Nr. 46 (1989).

Helga Embacher, *Neubeginn ohne Illusionen: Juden in Österreich nach 1945* (Vienna: Picus Verlag, 1995).

Bruce F. Pauley

The last two decades have seen a growing literature on the history of Austrian Jews between about 1867 and 1945. General studies of the post-World War II era, however, have been comparatively neglected. Helga Embacher, an adjunct professor (*Vertragsassistentin*) at the Historical Institute of the University of Salzburg, has done much to rectify this omission.

Neubeginn ohne Illusionen is somewhat narrower in scope than its title implies. The book is primarily a political history of Vienna's Jews, especially between 1945 and 1952, although some references are made to later developments including the Waldheim affair in 1986. In many ways it is a continuation of Harriet Pass Freidenreich's *Jewish Politics in Vienna, 1918-1938.*

Nevertheless, this well-researched book does provide a plethora of details; some are already reasonably well known, but others are new and rather surprising. In the former category, readers will not be amazed to learn that Jewish refugees were not welcomed back into Austria after the war. Not only was anti-Semitism still prevalent in Austria, but the country was also suffering from a shortage of jobs and housing, especially in the immediate postwar era. Viennese physicians were especially adamant in their opposition to the return of Jewish doctors who had fled to Shanghai after the Anschluß. Thomas Albrich has already pointed out the anti-Semitism which resulted from the passage of over 100,000 Eastern European Jews through Austria between 1945 and 1948, even though these refugees were not supported by the Austrian government. It is also a reasonably well-known fact that those Jews who returned to Austria on a permanent basis, were often old and sick and had been incapable of learning a new language abroad or could not accustom themselves to Israel's relatively hot and dry climate.

However, there is much in Embacher's book that is new and fascinating. For example, of those who returned to Austria few showed much interest in religion or Zionism. The one Jewish school in Vienna had to close its doors in 1967 because of a shortage of students. On the other hand, newcomers to Austria from Eastern Europe were often enthusiastic Zionists. However, in an almost bizarre repetition of interwar Zionist politics in Vienna, postwar Zionists remained divided into numerous hostile groups. Also reminiscent of the interwar period was the enmity between Zionists and non-Zionists. The latter thought that Zionists were obligated to emigrate to Palestine, especially after the establishment of the independent state of Israel in 1948, and feared that extreme Zionism could lead to the Jews losing their civil equality and to being treated as a mere majority. Zionists thought that any Jew who remained in Austria lacked Jewish consciousness. Oddly enough, however, there were more Jews who fled from Austria to Palestine after 1938 and eventually returned to Austria than there were postwar Austrian Jews (excluding Displaced Persons in transit through Austria) who emigrated to Israel.

The most interesting aspect of *Neubeginn ohne Illusionen*, at least for Americans, is Embacher's account of the impact of the Cold War, the World Jewish Congress, and the Joint Distribution Committee in the United States on the politics of the *Israelitische Kultusgemeinde* (IKG, or Jewish Communal Organization) of Vienna. From 1945 to 1948, the IKG was dominated by Communists, much to the chagrin of U.S. Jewish organizations upon which the Viennese Jews were financially dependent. Austrian Jews had voted for Communists out of gratitude for the Soviet Union having rescued so many victims of National Socialism. However, the growing anti-Zionism of the Austrian Communist Party and the Soviet Union helped undermine support for the Communists in the IKG. This process was aided by threats from the Joint in the early 1950s that it would withdraw its critical financial support to Austrian Jews if the Communists continued to hold power in the IKG. Moreover, the otherwise divided parties in the IKG saw the Communists as a common enemy. By 1955, the Jewish Socialists had gained an absolute majority in the IKG. Soviet opposition to Israel's Six-Day War in 1967 and its invasion of Czechoslovakia the following year cost the Communists their last seat in the Kultusgemeinde in 1968.

In her final chapter, Embacher maintains that relations between Jews and non-Jewish Austrians actually improved—at least in the long run—as a result of the Waldheim affair. In contrast to postwar Germany, there had never been a real dialogue on the national level in Austria between Jews and gentiles, only between individuals. However, in 1986, leaders of the Jewish and Christian communities got together. Cardinal Franz König publicly acknowledged the co-responsibility of the Catholic Church for National Socialism. Since 1991, several high Austrian officials including Chancellor Franz Vranitzky, President Thomas Klestil, and Viennese mayor Helmut Zilk have paid official visits to Israel and have apologized for Austria's role in the Holocaust.

Neubeginn ohne Illusionen contains numerous useful aids. There are several interesting photographs, forty-two pages of endnotes, two pages of IKG election results between 1946 and 1984, a list of abbreviations, and a fourteen-page bibliography. The latter is especially impressive because it includes twenty Jewish and twenty-six non-Jewish newspapers and the archives of numerous Jewish organizations on three continents. Embacher also conducted sixty interviews with Austrian and former Austrian Jews who lived in Israel, Great Britain, and the United States, although she does not list their names. The only serious omission is an article about reparations published by Thomas Albrich in the first issue of *Contemporary Austrian Studies*. Unfortunately, as is the case with so many books published in Austria, the Picus Verlag includes no index of any kind.

Neubeginn ohne Illusionen would have been enriched if Embacher had cited more information about attempts by Austrian Jews to be compensated by the Austrian government for their material losses after the Anschluß. She might also have included material about the recent opening of a Jewish museum in the center of Vienna as well as the older Jewish museums in Eisenstadt and Hohenems, and efforts by the Austrian government to combat anti-Semitism—especially those made during the fiftieth anniversary of the Anschluß—and to restore some of the damaged synagogues such as those in Innsbruck and St. Pölten.

A more serious criticism is the book's lack of context. There is no information on the Jews of Austria before the war and during the

Holocaust beyond a few statistics, and no comparisons with postwar Jewish communities in other European countries. It would be very interesting to know, for example, if the extreme divisiveness of the Austrian Jewish community was replicated in places like Berlin, Paris, London, and Budapest. Most of all, *Neubeginn* suffers from lacking a real concluding chapter which could have tied together the book's many disparate facts. Nevertheless, Helga Embacher deserves to be congratulated for her very substantial scholarly achievement.

Kurt Waldheim, *Die Antwort*
(Vienna: Amalthea, 1996)

Jonathan Petropoulos

As the title suggests, this book represents the long-awaited response to critics by the former United Nations Secretary General and Austrian President. The title, however, is misleading in that the volume provides few answers, but instead repeats Waldheim's earlier claims of innocence and victimization. Yet his defense in itself provides fascinating insight into the author's mentality (and arguably that of many Austrians of his generation). While the American reader might be inclined to compare Waldheim's defense strategy to that of O.J. Simpson in his recent legal proceedings—both advance an array of conspiracy theories and then add a sophisticated public relations initiative in an attempt to explain away any incriminating evidence— the response here is more typically Austrian. According to Waldheim, he is a victim of a great misunderstanding: the postwar generation simply does not understand those who were just doing their duty (*Pflichterfüllung*), and cannot appreciate their predecessors's tragic victimization during and after the Third Reich. Waldheim's answer, then, offers little that is new or persuasive; though in according him a sort of due process, it is instructive to consider his account.

The first chapter of the book, which concerns Kurt Waldheim's ousting as U.N. Secretary General in 1980 because of friction in United States-Chinese relations over Taiwan, establishes the theme of victimization (and also inaugurates his habit of shamelessly name-dropping as he cites as his source Henry Kissinger at a Rockefeller family party). But Waldheim quickly moves on to the core issue: his experiences during the Third Reich. He tells of growing up in Tulln as the son of a regional school inspector, an anti-Nazi Christian Social who lost his position after the Anschluß and moved his family to nearby *Baden bei Wien* in order to start again. This story has been told often, although Waldheim adds here that his father's best friend was later *Bundeskanzler* Leopold Figl. Similarly, he repeats the account of beginning his studies at the Wiener *Konsularakademie* in 1937 and his forced induction into the *National Sozialistische Studentenbund* the following year. Here he also explains how he ended up in the *SA-Reitstandarte* 5/90: all student groups concerned with *Freizeitaktivitäten* (an interesting spin on the SA) were taken over by the Nazi party as part of the *Gleichschaltungs* process. There is no explanation for the well-known photograph of Waldheim in uniform at a 1 May 1938 rally organized by *Reichskommissar* Josef Bürckel, just as he does not address reports that his wife "Cissy" was an enthusiastic National Socialist and party member (the latter is portrayed as a Catholic so devout that there were concerns of appearing too subversive; this in marked contrast to certain critics' claims that she distanced herself from the Church so as to conform better to Nazi ideology). He presents himself as an ambitious student who was doing only what was necessary in order to succeed.

In Waldheim's account of his military experience, he presents himself alternatively as a victim and factotum. His victimization began early because the Austrian army regiment for which he had volunteered in 1936/37 was incorporated into the German *Wehrmacht* and he was forced to rejoin it in autumn 1938. The unfortunate *Pflichterfüller* was suddenly a member of Hitler's army and by December 1941, found himself on the Eastern Front not far from Moscow where he was injured by grenade splinters to the foot. He also had the "bad luck" to serve under commanders like General Helmut von Pannwitz and later General Alexander Löhr—both of whom were eventually executed for war crimes. Waldheim's own war experience had moments of high drama, such as his ordeal on the Eastern Front after sustaining the shrapnel wound. But he prefers to characterize most of his service as unremarkable and undistinguished: he describes his position under Löhr in Heeresgruppe E in Southern Europe from 1942-45 as "*Sekretariatsarbeit ohne jegliche Befehlsgewalt*" (p. 71).

Waldheim dodges accusations that he knew about specific events such as the killings and reprisals at Kozara and the deportation of Salonika's Jews (he claims, for example, to have been on a study break in Vienna and then in Tirana and Athens when the latter occurred).

Waldheim admits knowledge of deportations and internment camps, but in a manner reminiscent of Albert Speer, he maintains that he had only vague suspicions of the killings, and no specific information. Whether it was possible for either a *Reichsminister* or an intelligence officer with combat experience on the Eastern Front to be ignorant of *Einsatz-gruppen* and the like is a matter already taken up by others. But for all Waldheim's shortcomings, incompetence was never one of them. He even takes pride in certain accomplishments of his unit under General Löhr, especially during the final stage of the war when the remaining soldiers evaded the Red Army and surrendered to the Western Allies.

Waldheim's portrayal of defeat and *Stunde Null* in Austria is dramatic and vivid, though again the main theme is one of victimization. He describes his internment by the Americans after being transported to Bad Tölz where he "spent weeks in a notorious outdoor camp on the edge of a swamp without tents and without many provisions" ["*Wochen auf einem der berüchtigten Wiesenlager zubrachten, am Rande eines Sumpfes, ohne Zelte und ohne viel Verpflegung*" (p. 92).] It is interesting that much of this section utilizes the pronoun "*Wir*," which connotes a fate shared by others. Additionally, certain images, such as the Allied prisoner of war camps, elicit specific associations with victimization: even if James Bacque's and others' claims of atrocities have been discredited by careful historical analysis, the subject still resonates in the consciousness of many veterans and members of the public.[1] Much of Waldheim's account here is emotional (one might say sentimental), such as the reunion with his wife, children, and parents and their joy at having survived the war. He does not address reports that he saved his skin by providing the Western Allies with information.

The most disturbing parts of this book stem from the conspiracy theories he advances to explain the controversy about his relationship to the Nazi regime which erupted in the mid-1980s. Waldheim offers a variety of culprits: from the World Jewish Congress who supposedly launched a crusade against him (and went so far as to pressure U.S. Attorney General Edwin Meese to put him on the Watch List) to incompetent journalists who succumbed to herd instincts and relayed sensational reports because they did not know enough to investigate the story properly. The Israelis, Waldheim suggests, bore a special grudge against him because of U.N. Resolution 242 which equated Zionism with racism. But the true source of Waldheim's misery stems from the

United States: the last remaining superpower used its economic clout as a means of pressuring other countries to ostracize the Austrian President. Waldheim's assertions have highly problematic implications, although they do conform to a mindset not unknown to Austrians. One can imagine Jörg Haider nodding his head in agreement to these theories about nefarious "foreigners."

It is evident that Waldheim and Austria have suffered as a result of the Watch List decision and the ensuing controversy. Ironically, this becomes evident as he tries to cast a positive light on his tenure as President. Waldheim points to the many state visits abroad that he made and argues that it represents an impressive record for anyone occupying that office. But with the notable exception of German Chancellor Helmut Kohl and Pope John Paul II, both of whom received him, most of the leaders he visited were from Arab countries. The numerous photographs in the volume that show Waldheim with George Bush, Ronald Reagan, and Jimmy Carter, among other prominent Western leaders, are notable because they pre-date the advent of the scandal in 1985. Contrary to the author's claims, Waldheim's pariah status represented a significant setback for the Austrians in their attempt to play an active role among the community of nations.

Waldheim's history is an especially sad one in part because he actually engineered an extraordinarily accomplished career. This includes his swift rise through the ranks of the Austrian government to the position of Minister of Foreign Affairs from 1968-70; distinguished work at the United Nations, first as Austrian Ambassador from 1958-62, then as Secretary General from 1972 to 1980; and finally his triumphant victory as Austrian President in 1986 when he received 53.9 percent of the popular vote. Waldheim has shown himself a capable diplomat and his efforts to secure the release of hostages in the Middle East (most notably his dealings with Iraq's Saddam Hussein in 1990), are testimony to his considerable abilities. For many years Waldheim was indeed a genuine "player" on the stage of world affairs.

The second half of the book is devoted to his reflections on Austrian domestic politics, international relations, and the United Nations. With respect to the first, he often attempts to appear presidential or *überparteilich*, but his sympathies do not lie far below the surface, and it is not difficult to discern allies from enemies. His reflections regarding international affairs and the U.N. are generally sensible. But perhaps because this book is aimed at a popular audience much of the discussion is fairly pedestrian. Waldheim does not shine as a great thinker or analyst, but he demonstrates impressive familiarity with world leaders and a vision which is global in scope. His concern for still developing nations—one of the legacies of his career at the U.N. one would suspect—appears genuine, and it is in this area that his thoughts on current affairs are most illuminating.

Despite his many accomplishments, one does not get the impression that Kurt Waldheim has grown as a person in the way one would hope. His supporters will no doubt view this book as a convincing account and even take pride in him as a notable Austrian. Indeed, one often gains the impression here that he is "preaching to the choir" by trying to identify with fellow-Austrians on certain points (in particular their victimization at the hands of first the "Germans" and then the Allies). His efforts to portray his successes as Austrian comprise another means of trying to gain sympathy among compatriots. On the other hand, those who are not so enamored with Waldheim will view this book as evidence of his defiance of serious *Vergangenheitsbewältigung*. He still has little sense of Austrian complicity in the crimes of the Third Reich: for example, his remark that *"Hunderttausende von Österreichern und Millionen von Deutschen"* (p. 83) reacted enthusiastically to the outbreak of war in 1939 is one of many cases where he subtly tries to diminish the responsibility of his countrymen. On a more personal level, Waldheim evinces some understanding of the inadequacy of the earlier accounts about his past, but again falls short of true understanding. In typical fashion, he places much of the blame on others, as he attempts to implicate a co-author and then a translator for the glaring inadequacies of a previous autobiography. To repeat, this book reveals a great deal about the author, but it says more about the *Geschichtsbild* of Waldheim and certain contemporary Austrians than it does about *Geschichte*.

NOTE

1. James Bacque, *Der geplante Tod* (Berlin: Ullstein, 1989); Günter Bischof and Stephen E. Ambrose, eds., *Eisenhower and the German POWs: Facts Against Falsehood* (Baton Rouge: Louisiana State University Press, 1992).

ANNUAL REVIEW

Survey of Austrian Politics 1996

Reinhold Gärtner

These were the most conspicuous events in Austria in 1996:
* Changes in the New (Old) Coalition government;
* The Brauneder Affair;
* Burgenland State Diet elections on 2 June;
* European Union Elections on 13 October;
* Vienna State Diet elections on 13 October;
* Bankruptcies;
* The extreme right and letter bombs;
* The desecration of the Jewish Cemetery in Eisenstadt;
* *Wehrmachtsausstellung;*
* The sale of Creditanstalt Bankverein;
* Ten years of Vranitzky and Haider.

The New (Old) Coalition
After the National Council Elections in December 1995, the SPÖ and ÖVP built a new government with very few new faces. Short term Minister of Finance, Andreas Staribacher, was replaced by Viktor Klima (former Minister of Public Economy and Traffic); Johannes Ditz (Minister of Economics) resigned in June (and was replaced by Johann Farnleitner); and Martin Bartenstein—now Minster for Environment, Youth and Family—took the agenda of the Ministry of Youth and Family (formerly led by Minister Sonja Moser). The number of State Secretaries was reduced from four to two (with Karl Schlögl and Benitta Ferrero-Waldner remaining).

The Brauneder Affair
In January, the three presidents of the National Council were elected. As usual, the first president is a member of the largest party,

the second president is a member of the runner-up party, and the third president member of the third largest party. Thus, until January 1996, Herbert Haupt (FPÖ) was third president. Haupt, though, was very reluctant to distance himself from Jörg Haider's comments on the *Waffen-SS* made in Krumpendorf in September 1995 (see CAS, vol. V, p. 394). As a result, the FPÖ, assisted by Andreas Khol of the ÖVP, presented Wilhelm Brauneder as candidate. Brauneder, a professor at the University of Vienna, is well known within right wing groups in Austria. For example, he frequently wrote articles for the extreme right paper *Aula*. Asked about these connections, Brauneder said that these articles had not been written exclusively for the *Aula* but were reprints or articles written for other publications. His explanation was not very convincing. In at least one article, Brauneder quotes another of his *Aula* articles. If the article had not been written exclusively for *Aula*, he would have—as is usual in scientific publishing—quoted the original article.

Anyway, Brauneder joined Heinz Fischer (SPÖ, first president) and Heinrich Neisser (ÖVP, second president) as the new third president of the National Council. For the first time in the era of the new coalition built after the December 1995 elections, the ÖVP—assisted by the FPÖ—outvoted its coalition partner (the SPÖ) in the National Council.

The Burgenland and Vienna State Diet Elections

The State Diet Elections in Burgenland had little effect on domestic politics. Moderate losses for both the SPÖ and ÖVP (-3.6 percent and -1.9 percent respectively) were accompanied by gains for the FPÖ (+4.9 percent). The Greens and Liberals couldn't take the 4 percent hurdle and gain representation in the state diet.

Table 1:   Results of the Burgenland State Diet elections, 1991 and 1996, in percentage of votes gained.

Burgenland	SPÖ	ÖVP	FPÖ	Greens	Liberals Forum
1996	44.5	36.1	14.6	2.5	1.4
1991	48.1	38.2	9.7	3.4	

Source: Compiled from official data

Table 2:   Results of the Vienna Diet elections 1991 and 1996 in
            percentage of votes gained.

Vienna	SPÖ	ÖVP	FPÖ	Greens	Liberals Forum
1996	39.2	15.3	28.0	7.9	7.9
1991	47.8	18.1	22.5	9.1	

Source: Compiled from official data

The Viennese elections, though, were a kind of watershed. For the first time ever, the SPÖ lost its absolute majority of seats and went below the 40 percent margin. The FPÖ once again raised its share to 28 percent, and the ÖVP continued its decline (down 6.4 percent from 1983 to 1987; down 10.3 percent from 1987 to 1991; down 2.8 percent from 1991 to 1996). In 1983, the ÖVP had some 34 percent, but in 1996, it had only 15.3. percent.

In the course of the election campaign, the FPÖ used the slogan "Vienna must not become Chicago." The message behind this slogan was clear to the public. For Haider, "Chicago" signifies the uncontrollable rampaging crime of the modern metropolis; the subtext is Al Capone and the Mafia gone mad. Allowing more foreigners to immigrate to Austria and Vienna implies more crime. Haider caters to the xenophobia of many Austrians for whom foreigners have become the scapegoats for their unsolved problems. Thus, keeping foreigners out presumably would make Vienna a safer city. Together with other lightly veiled hostilities toward foreigners, the FPÖ successfully emotionalized the Vienna election campaign. The FPÖ increased its percentage to 28 percent, up from 22.5 percent in 1991. The SPÖ decreased to a historic low of 39.2 percent, down from 47.8 percent in 1991.

Despite the losses, the SPÖ and ÖVP formed a coalition government with Michael Häupl (SPÖ) remaining major of Vienna.

The European Union Elections
The first European Union elections were held on 13 October and ended with disaster for the SPÖ.

Table 3: Results of the European Union elections 1996, and the National Council elections 1995, in percentage of votes gained.

	SPÖ	ÖVP	FPÖ	Greens	Liberals Forum
EU Elections	29.2	29.6	27.6	6.8	4.2
National Council Elections 1995	38.1	28.3	21.9	4.8	5.5

Source: Compiled from official data

Though EU Elections cannot exactly be compared with National Council elections, the losses for the SPÖ were nevertheless dramatic. For the first time since 1970, the SPÖ lost its relative majority in nationwide elections. More importantly, however, the FPÖ has become a serious challenger for the votes of workers. In 1983, 2 percent of workers voted for the FPÖ, and some 70 percent voted for the SPÖ. In 1996, 40 percent voted for the SPÖ and FPÖ respectively. Thus the FPÖ, according to Fritz Plasser, can be called a *"protestorientierte Arbeiterpartei neuen Typs."*

Bankruptcies

In 1995, Austria suffered enormous economic losses as far as bankruptcies were concerned. The total liabilities amounted to more than ATS 62 billion (approximately $5.6 billion). In 1996, this trend continued. During 1996, the liabilities of 5,500 insolvencies amounted to some ATS 52 billion (approximately $4.7 billion). Hardest hit were private citizens, the tourism industry, and the building and construction trade. The biggest bankruptcy was suffered by Maculan's (ATS 11 billion), a construction company with formerly strong involvement in Eastern European countries. Bearing in mind that in 1995, the bankruptcy of Konsum (ATS 26 billion) was some 40 percent of all liabilities, 1996 seems to be even worse than 1995, because more individuals and businesses are declaring bankruptcy.

Austria's rate of unemployment was about the same as in 1995; in December 1996 there was a very slight decrease in the number of unemployed.

The Extreme Right and Letter Bombs

Though without the serious effects of the 1995 bombings (in February 1995 four gypsies were killed in Oberwart by a bomb), the series of letter bombs continued in 1996. The last one was sent to Caspar Einem's stepmother (Einem was Minister of Interior Affairs) and exploded when police tried to deactivate it. Fortunately, no one was injured by the 1996 series of letter bombs.

The right-wing extremist paper *Aula* has been published in Graz since 1951. In 1994, an anonymous author quoted Austrian Walter Lüftl as having said that, from a national scientific point of view, murders with gas in Auschwitz could not have happened. *Aula* called this a milestone on the path to truth (*Meilenstein auf dem Weg zur Wahrheit*). In May 1996, the editor of *Aula*, Herwig Nachtmann, was sentenced to eight months (conditional) and fined ATS 192,000, (approximately $17,500). The monthly *Aula* is published by *Freiheitlicher Akademikerverband*, a group of academics closely connected to the FPÖ. Many FPÖ politicians are listed as *Aula* contributors, and there is lot of evidence that the FPÖ and *Aula* have close connections, too.

An interesting incident involves Judge Hans Peter Januschke. In May, he was presiding over the case of Richard R. This R. is a teacher and accused of denying the Holocaust in school. Judge Januschke was dismissed because he was found to be biased and too eager in defending Richard R. Finally, R. was acquitted because the witnesses—many of them R.'s pupils—couldn't accurately testify as to what R. said. Three members of the jury found R. guilty, whereas five did not.

Desecration of the Jewish Cemetery in Eisenstadt

In 1992, the Jewish cemetery in Eisenstadt (Burgenland) was defiled. Finally in 1996, two young people, Wilhelm A. and Wolfgang Tomsits, were apprehended and questioned. In the course of this questioning, it became clear that both were members of the FPÖ (in Oberwart) and that they had good connections to FPÖ *Bundesgeschäftsführer* (manager) Karl Schweitzer. Tomsits argued that Schweitzer had recruited him for *Ring Freiheitlicher Jugend* (the FPÖ's youth organization). Though Schweitzer insisted that he had broken these connections by 1992, there were serious indications that these connections were still alive in 1995. For the FPÖ, though, these facts did not constitute a reason for dismissing Schweitzer. In December, Tomsits was sentenced to four years in prison.

Vernichtungskrieg—Verbrechen der Wehrmacht 1941-1944

In 1995, the exhibition *Vernichtungskrieg—Verbrechen der Wehrmacht 1941-1944* was shown in Vienna and Innsbruck. In both cities, the reaction of the public was mixed.

The exhibition tried to uncover the crimes of the *Wehrmacht* and its participation in the extermination of Jews during World War II. On the one hand, some people thought it was time to reveal the crimes of the past and to refute the myth of the clean *Wehrmacht* (in contrast to the "dirty SS"). On the other hand, some people thought this exhibition was unnecessary since it misleadingly represented a whole generation as having been criminal.

In 1996, the exhibition came to Klagenfurt and Linz—and the same arguments were raised once more. Thus, in Carinthia, many prominent politicians issued public statements against the exhibition, and in Linz, no public money could be raised to support its costs.

According to statements by the governor of Salzburg, the same response can be expected there in 1998, when the exhibition will be shown in the fifth Austrian city.

The Sale of Creditanstalt Bankverein

Since the late 1980s, Austria has been trying to sell *Creditanstalt Bankverein* (CA), the country's second largest bank. For various reasons, no buyer could be found.

In 1996, the Minister of Finance tried again to find wealthy buyers. In autumn of 1996, Bank Austria, the country's biggest bank (with strong connections to the city of Vienna), made an interesting offer. After long debate between the SPÖ (which favored the sale of CA to Bank Austria) and the ÖVP (which opposed this sale), the coalition partners found a solution in the beginning of 1997: CA was sold to Bank Austria on 12 January 1997.

Ten Years of Vranitzky and Haider

In 1996, both Franz Vranitzky and Jörg Haider celebrated their tenth anniversary in office: Vranitzky as chancellor and Haider as party chairman and would-be chancellor. During these ten years, Haider's FPÖ increased its share in elections from 5 percent to 22 percent, thus becoming a serious challenger to both the ÖVP and SPÖ. Haider has led the FPÖ onto a stout right-wing path. This made the ÖVP and SPÖ repeatedly state that any kind of governmental cooperation with the FPÖ would be denied. Thus, the rise of the FPÖ, happened at the expense of governmental participation.

Vranitzky became chancellor in 1986 and made sure that the SPÖ remained the strongest political party in Austria. Vranitzky was the first chancellor who, in 1991, publicly emphasized Austria's responsibility for National Socialist crimes. At the beginning of 1997, Vranitzky resigned as chancellor, thus smoothing the way for the new chancellor, Viktor Klima, well before the next elections, due in 1999.

FURTHER LITERATURE

Bundespressedienst des Bundeskanzleramtes, *Der Österreich-Bericht*, vol. 46 (Vienna: 1996).

Wolfgang C. Müller, Fritz Plasser, and Peter A. Ulram, eds., *Wählerverhalten und Parteienwettbewerb* (Vienna: Signum Verlag, 1995).

Rainer Nick and Anton Pelinka, *Österreichs politische Landschaft* (Innsbruck: Haymon-Verlag, 1993).

Fritz Plasser, Peter A. Ulram, and Günther Ogris, eds., *Wahlkampf und Wählerentscheidung* (Vienna: Signum Verlag, 1996)

Der Standard

Die Presse

News

Profil

Salzburger Nachrichten

List of Authors

Erna M. Appelt is an associate professor of political science at the University Innsbruck; in the spring of 1997 she was a visiting professor of European politics at the University of New Orleans.

Brigitte Bailer is a senior research fellow at the *Dokumentationsarchiv des Österreichischen Widerstandes* in Vienna.

Ingrid Bauer is an assistant professor of history at the University of Salzburg.

Siegfried Beer is an assistant professor of history at the University of Graz. In 1996/97 he was the Austrian Schumpeter Fellow at the Minda de Gunzburg Center for European Studies at Harvard University.

Steven Beller is a historian who resides in Washington, D.C.

Peter Berger is an assistant professor of economic history at the Economics University in Vienna.

Evan Burr Bukey is a professor of history at the University of Arkansas in Fayetteville.

Helga Embacher is an assistant professor of history at the University of Salzburg.

Herman Freudenberger is professor emeritus of Economic History at Tulane University in New Orleans.

Reinhold Gärtner is a research fellow with the Institute of Politics at the University of Innsbruck.

Doris Gödl is a psychologist who is affiliated with the *Institut für Alltagskultur* in Salzburg.

Ernst Hanisch is a professor of Modern History at the University of Salzburg.

Gabriella Hauch is an associate professor of history at the University of Linz.

Gabriele Holzer is a diplomat with the Austrian Foreign Service presently at the *Ballhausplatz* in Vienna.

Christopher R. Jackson is an adjunct professor of history at the University of California in Berkeley and at San Francisco State College.

Pieter M. Judson is an associate professor of history at Swarthmore College.

Tony Judt is the Remarque Professor of European Studies at New York University.

Andrei S. Markovits is professor and chair, Board of Studies in Politics, at the University of California in Santa Cruz.

Wolfgang Neugebauer is the director of the *Dokumentationsarchiv des Österreichischen Widerstandes* and is an honorary professor at the University of Vienna.

Thomas Nowotny is a diplomat with the Austrian Foreign Service and presently posted with the OECD in Paris.

Bruce F. Pauley is a professor of history at the University of Central Florida in Orlando.

Jonathan Petropoulos is an associate professor of history at Loyola College in Maryland.

Sieglinde Katharina Rosenberger is an associate professor of political science at the University of Innsbruck and a visiting professor at the University of Vienna.

Erika Thurner is a visiting professor of political science at the University of Innsbruck.